Sextarianism

SEXTARIANISM

Sovereignty, Secularism, and the State in Lebanon

Maya Mikdashi

Dear Saman,

I'm so glad we "met" and I'm excited to work together — can't wait to hear what you think about this book on the place we love, and hurt for, so much.

yours,
Maya

Stanford University Press

Stanford, California

STANFORD UNIVERSITY PRESS
Stanford, California

This book has been partially underwritten by the Stanford Authors Fund. We are grateful to the Fund for its support of scholarship by first-time authors. For more information, please see www.sup.org/authors/authorsfund

Printed in the United States of America on acid-free, archival-quality paper

Library of Congress Cataloging-in-Publication Data

Names: Mikdashi, Maya, author.
Title: Sextarianism : sovereignty, secularism, and the state in Lebanon / Maya Mikdashi.
Description: Stanford, California : Stanford University Press, 2022. | Includes bibliographical references and index.
Identifiers: LCCN 2021049998 (print) | LCCN 2021049999 (ebook) | ISBN 9781503628878 (cloth) | ISBN 9781503631557 (paperback) | ISBN 9781503631564 (epub)
Subjects: LCSH: Power (Social sciences)—Lebanon. | Religion and state—Lebanon. | Secularism—Lebanon. | Sex—Political aspects—Lebanon. | Cultural pluralism—Political aspects—Lebanon. | Lebanon—Politics and government—1990– | Lebanon—Ethnic relations.
Classification: LCC DS87.54 .M54 2022 (print) | LCC DS87.54 (ebook) | DDC 956.9204/5—dc23/eng/20211027
LC record available at https://lccn.loc.gov/2021049998
LC ebook record available at https://lccn.loc.gov/2021049999

Cover art: Untitled, 1973. Huguette Caland.
Reprinted with permission from Caland Family.
Cover design: Rob Ehle

Typeset by Newgen North America in 10/15 Sabon LT Std

Contents

Preface   vii

INTRODUCTION. Sextarianism
1

1   Afterlives of a Census: Rethinking State Power
and Political Difference
24

2   A Fire in the Archive: History, Ethnography, Multiplicity
48

3   Regulating Conversion: Sovereignty, Bureaucracy,
and the Banality of Religion
83

4   Are You Going to Pride? Evangelical Secularism
and the Politics of Law
117

5   The Epidermal State: Violence and the Materiality of Power
153

Epilogue
183

Acknowledgments   193
Notes   197
Bibliography   231
Index   251

Preface

THIS ETHNOGRAPHY OF Lebanon began in Iraq. In 2003 I traveled from Beirut to Baghdad to film a documentary, *About Baghdad*, with a group of collaborators. We arrived in July and stayed for four weeks—a precipitous time in the US occupation of Iraq. While we were there the Iraqi state was actively being dismantled. I was in Baghdad for two coinciding, interrelated events that have not since left me, events that were formative to my sense of the world. The first was an Iraqi Communist Party (ICP) march commemorating the overthrow of the British-appointed Iraqi monarchy in 1958. The second event was the July 2003 announcement of the Iraqi Governing Council, an occupation-appointed council that was supposed to rule Iraq until elections could be organized. It was the first substantive attempt to bring a "Lebanese model"—a modulated form of political sectarianism—of governance to Iraq. Instead of communists, socialists, republicans, liberals, Arab nationalists, or Iraqi nationalists, the council was composed of Shi'is, Sunnis, and Kurds. This was the first time that Iraqi politics and governance had been structurally defined this way. I was disturbed by the assumption that people in Iraq had identities as opposed to politics or ideological affiliations. I was also intrigued by the honesty with which political sectarianism was discussed as a divide and rule model, echoing not only French Mandate rule in Lebanon but legacies of indirect rule in British, French, and Ottoman Empires. I was frightened by what I imagined to be archives of violence that were sure to travel *with* the "Lebanese model" to Iraq. I thought it obvious that the Lebanese model was doomed, or engineered, to fail in Iraq—just as it had and would continue to do so in Lebanon.

At the time, I had never seen a protest as large, joyous, and complex as that of the Iraqi Communist Party in 2003. In graduate school, I had read and debated and written about Iraqi history and politics. But no book could have taught me what I experienced that day. Being in Iraq was a lesson in the political and epistemic limits of academic understanding and writing—the chasm between comprehending and understanding. If anything, comprehension was a sensorial experience that included a knowledge of the limits of understanding. In Iraq, I was liberated by the knowledge that I was, on some level, *never* going to get it. I revisited the frustration and anger I had felt most of my life toward people outside the borders of shared experience: people who had not felt violence and contingency as a structuring force, as sociality, as intimacy. Suddenly, in Iraq, that anger felt like comradery. Like power.

Not everyone at the Iraqi Communist Party protest was a communist or perhaps even a leftist. The ICP was not just a political party in that moment but rather a manifestation of an unbroken political tradition of resistance. The day provided a space for joy and exuberance for people who had at that point lived through wars, sanctions, brutal authoritarian rule, and occupation. I was riding in the back of a pickup truck filming the marchers when a young boy who stood at the front of a large group caught my attention. He was no more than twelve years old. He was dancing as he walked and yelled for kilometers, his body somehow incoherent, uncontained, in movement. He was happy. I have spent some nights imagining the different paths, or dead ends, this boy might have walked in the intervening years.

It is difficult to comprehend, let alone understand or explain, the cycles of hope and despair, inspiration and devastation, and creation and destruction that people in the Middle East and North Africa[1] have lived since that day. Across the region, in Iraq, Yemen, and Syria, tens of millions have been killed or maimed, have experienced mass displacement, and/or have lived as refugees. This is only the history that begins in 2003, with the American invasion and occupation of Iraq. Almost half of the population of Syria, more than twelve million people, are living as displaced people or as refugees. Genocide has been committed against Yazidis, and famine and blockade are regularly used as weapons of war against people in Yemen and Syria. A brutal civil war in Sudan, followed quickly by another in South Sudan. Hundreds of thousands of women, girls, men, and boys have been assaulted and tortured both inside and outside of prisons and detention centers in Iraq, Syria, Libya, Saudi Arabia, and Egypt. A supposedly cold war between Iran and Saudi Arabia[2] has scorched Yemen, Syria, and Iraq. Generations of Palestinians have lived, resisted, created, and died under Israeli military and settler occupation or as refugees in hostile and impoverished circumstances. More than two million people in Gaza, who are for the most part refugees, live under a fifteen-year, illegal Israeli siege. Kurds and Sahrawis continue to fight for sovereignty, and they continue to live under colonization. Since 2010 there have been two cycles of popular uprisings across the region—both of which led to further securitization and authoritarianism in most countries. A carceral horizon stretches from Turkey to Egypt to Iran to Saudi Arabia, where intellectuals, activists, revolutionaries, journalists, and academics have been detained, arrested, exiled, and brutalized. The overwhelming "eventness" of contemporary Middle East history, moreover, papers over and mutes everyday forms of precarity: yawning wealth and income concentration, an erosion of the free press, ecological devastation, broken public health systems, disappearing social safety nets, austerity budgets and rampant corruption, gender inequality, skyrocketing youth unemployment, and hardening racism and xenophobia toward refugees, displaced people, and migrant laborers. But people in the Middle East are not only destroyed and destroying bodies. They are also effervescent.

In October 2019 popular uprisings took to the streets in Lebanon[3] and in Iraq. Both demanded a new, capable government committed to rooting out corruption and promoting the well-being of its people. Protestors were not calling for a new economic, political, or national orders. They were, in many ways, calling for good governance. These were not radical demands. But in both Iraq and in Lebanon, the ruling political-economic regimes could not even stand a demand for accountability, a demand for them to *be better*. In both countries, though at different scales, the uprisings were brutally suppressed.

In the immediate sense, the protests in Lebanon were over a monthly tax on the widely used communications application WhatsApp,[4] financial austerity measures planned by the government, and the spectacle of the government being unable to put out one of the worst wildfires in

Lebanese history. However, this moment had been building for at least a decade,[5] and October 17 was more akin to the cresting of a wave than an earthquake. Hundreds of thousands, and at some points millions, of people took to the streets, went on strike, blocked roads, and effectively paralyzed the country. The protests were regional, expressly cross and anti-sectarian, multigenerational, and, in certain actions, different socio-economic classes worked together.

Two and a half years later, in 2022, people in Lebanon are living through an economic crisis that is the worst in the country's history, brought on by a trifecta of public debt, unmitigated and widespread corruption, and a financial Ponzi scheme that united the banking sector, governments and politicians, and the Central Bank.[6] There is no electricity, no money in the banks, no food in fridges, no water in the faucets—no floor or ceiling to the structure of circumstances that shape life daily and hourly. People have died in desperate scrambles for fuel, medicine, for anything that can and will and has been hoarded or smuggled for profit. In 2018, the UN estimated that about 30 percent of Lebanon were living in poverty. Three years later, in 2021, the UN revised their assessment; more than 82 percent of people in Lebanon were living in multidimensional poverty, and almost 40 percent lived in extreme multidimensional poverty As of this writing, the political class not only has weathered the storm but stands poised to gain strength by consolidating and distributing necessary goods and services through their client networks, networks they nourished by being parasites on the state and public sectors. What and whom they cannot buy, they intimidate and threaten. This trend was only accelerated by the emergency measures and further economic punishment of Covid-19.

Crises is perhaps not the best word to explain Lebanon in 2020–2022. Crisis implies a discrete before and after—a fall through cracks that become craters only in extraordinary times. A quick look at contemporary history teaches us that "crises" is a recursive temporality. In between "crises" there are months, maybe years, but somehow never decades, of status quo.[7] I was eleven years old when the violence of the Lebanese Civil War ended. I was fifteen when Israel launched its "Grapes of Wrath" campaign, twenty when Israel was forced to withdraw from Lebanon and the South was liberated, twenty-five when a series of political assassinations shook the country, twenty-six when the 2006 Lebanon-Israel war broke out, and twenty-eight when in 2008 a "mini" civil war happened, pitting parties and the sects they claimed to represent against each other in armed clashes for days. I was twenty-nine when the Lebanese Army decimated a Palestinian refugee camp in the name of its own war on terror; thirty-one when a political uprising in Syria was deliberately turned into a grinding, brutal, global civil war; thirty-three when ISIS, Nusra and their affiliates began a series of bombings in Lebanon; thirty-four when the country was intentionally paralyzed for two years to enable the presidency of someone whose name adorns an entire chapter of the Lebanese Civil War. I was thirty-eight when the 2019 uprising erupted, and thirty-nine when one of the largest nonnuclear explosions in the world blew up Beirut's port. The explosion ripped through the city, killed and disappeared hundreds, displaced thousands, destroyed any residual crumb of a world that made sense. As I write today, I am forty, and my families' life savings have been swallowed by a government-sanctioned, corruption-greased Ponzi scheme run by Lebanon's central and commercial banks. Family members and friends were killed by COVID-19 and policies of necrocapital that enabled its spread in Lebanon. These are only the headlines. And still, things can always, and often do, get worse. When I called my parents, desperate to hear their voice seconds after I watched and felt the explosion at the Beirut Port from half a world away, my father, surveying damage to our home, a home already damaged by two wars, laughed.

I've heard this laugh many times. From him, from many friends and family members, and welling up from my own body. It is a laugh that can be heard around the world. A laugh of recognition, a laugh of comprehension, of shock, of madness, of humor that hurts, of survival. A laugh that unites the past of memory with the future of anticipation.

This is not a particularly Lebanese story. Any one of my Lebanese, Palestinian, Syrian, or Iraqi friends could have narrated their lives through a series of macabre punctuations. This is not even a particularly Middle Eastern story. Even if the experience of compounding loss feels desperately lonely, we are never alone in that feeling. When I was younger I used to believe that there was something particularly tragic about being from Lebanon, from the Arabic speaking world, or from the Middle East, something few could understand and, even then, that they wouldn't "get it." The older I am, the more I comprehend how wrong I was. To live in expectation of continuity—to experience "crisis" as a bounded event—is something few in the world enjoy. Moreover, that blissful, unthought expectation of continuity is inextricable from the pain of others.

A theory of state power might look different if it were grounded in the histories, experiences, archives, aspirations, transitions, actions, displacements, and violence that people in the Middle East continue to live. Such a theory might be more open to contingency, less soldered to notions of authenticity, and less invested in curating archival truths or origin stories. A theory that does not pretend to produce standards applicable, and thus measurable, replicable and intervenable, across the world. Centered on a lived understanding of contingency, opacity, continuity, and rupture across histories of violence, experience, and resistance. A collective sense, an animating fear, of déjà vu.

By the end of *Sextarianism* I hope to have persuaded you of the need to rethink much of what we take for granted when we think about how and *where*[8] to think about secular power, biopolitical power, sovereignty, citizenship, and expansive understandings of sex and sexuality. What can a state that has been at war, with itself or with others, for more than half of its lifetime teach us about the endurance of the nation-state form in our era? What can a state where at least 25 percent of its residents are refugees displaced from other wars teach us about forms, attachments, practices, and ideologies of citizenship? What can a state that functions through political sectarianism teach us about the ways that secularism is lived and practiced—at a time when secular evangelizing has become a discursive technology of war and an animating force in the reemergence of cultural/civilizational nationalism across the world? Focusing on the multiplying relationships between sexual, secular, and religious difference at the structural, affective, and ideological levels may deepen our understanding of secularism as the condition of possibility for the nation-state and as the structuring force through which religious and sexual difference is managed. Nation-states that structure and manage religious difference as governmental, identitarian, and bureaucratic categories produce practices of religion, such as conversion, that are as banal and opaque as they are contradictory. "Muslim" and "Christian," in all their sectarian modulations, are compulsory biopolitical categories. Moreover, each is already multiple, only able to be articulated at and through their sexed inflection points. That is, they are sextarian, not sectarian, categories of experience and practice. What can we learn about the ways that secular power and one of its manifestations, citizenship, is practiced at this knot of religion, sect, and sex?

In this book I stage a conversation about the relationship between epistemology, methodology, and ideology. I stress the relational, polyvalent, and sometimes surprising nature of archival, ethnographic, and feminist research, knowledge production, and theory.[9] I frame state power as kinetic—the energy created and amplified through governing, managing, and securitizing the intersections of governmental, disciplinary, and biopolitical categories—bureaucratic, hypervisible, and inescapable forms of difference. Power builds as it is practiced. Sovereignty is that which can disentangle, entangle, arrange, and rearrange the components of political and sexual difference relationally. We have much to learn from moving away from the successes and effects of power—whether it be the study of sexualities as discrete, the sex binary as predisciplinary, or sectarian categories as self-explanatory—as our analytic starting points. The staging of state power, secularism, sexual difference, citizenship, and sovereignty is legal, bureaucratic, embodied, ideological, and contradictory. Moreover, this staging is multiply authored by courts, lawyers, archivists and other public sector employees, people and social movements, and, of course, academics.

Sextarianism

Sextarianism

SAMERA DIED IN January 1975. I met her, and the multiple lives she led, through an archived court case related to her estate and her marital status. The case file contained more than a century of evidence and presented a material history of the court system and of Lebanon itself: hundreds of pages, stamps, documents, and references from and to the Ottoman Empire, the French Mandate, and the first and second postcolonial Lebanese Republics. The stamps alone wrote a history of colonialism, war, currency, and inflation. But all of that material history—from Greek Orthodox courts and churches in Lebanon and in Syria, from Lebanese courts and the country's highest court, from imperial, colonial and postcolonial bureaucracy—sharpened into one question: Did Samera have a son? If so, was she married at the time of his birth, or was she an unmarried, single mother? The evidence presented proved that she had been both married and unmarried, and that she had a son who was "legitimate" in some documents, "illegitimate" in others. In yet another set of documents this son, Jean, did not exist at all. Samera contained multitudes.

Three months after Samera died, the Lebanese Civil War began, and Jean presented himself as Samera's son and heir.[1] Other would-be heirs, a group of distant cousins, argued that Jean was lying. Samera had never been married. Even if Jean *was* Samera's son, he was born out of wedlock and was thus barred from inheriting. To "recover his mother's honor," and her estate, Jean turned to the courts. After Jean died, the case was reopened and amended twice by *his* children, in 2005 and in 2008.[2] The intergenerational fight over Samera's estate presented a vantage point to think about the apocryphal origin stories of nation-states and the citational logic of sovereignty—a logic that folded the colonial within the

FIGURE 1. A photograph of the Great Hall at the
Ministry of Justice/Cassation Courthouse.

postcolonial via the mediums of law and bureaucracy.[3] More than anything, however, the case highlighted the intergenerational, financial, and
affective stakes of being an "illegitimate" child. It was fundamentally
about what I term "sextarianism"—how sex, sexuality, and sect structure legal bureaucratic systems, as well as how citizenship and statecraft
are performed at the mutually constitutive intersections and suffusions
between sex and sect. Sextarian-specific inheritance laws—laws that are
central to capital accumulation—determined which courts would hear the
case, and sextarian laws and bureaucracies made children "legitimate" or
"illegitimate" heirs. Decades before her death and the subsequent court
case over her estate, Samera's actions regarding her marital status were
informed by the knowledge of how sextarianism structured gendered,
sectarian, and financial procedures for divorce. In trying to evade one
aspect of a sextarian system, however, she, her son, and her grandchildren
were caught in another: the census bureaucracy and its afterlives.

This book rethinks state power and resilience; elaborates political difference at the site of religious and sexual difference; and traces how secularism is staged nationally and transnationally as both a structural form of power and as a set of values, practices, and aspirations. It introduces sextarianism as a concept and theorizes it across different sites that include law and bureaucracy; the archives of the Plenary Assembly at the Court of Cassation; court decisions related to religious conversion and the experiences of converts themselves; social movements and activists that advocate for a culture of secularism and new laws and bureaucracies; and finally, the regulation of sex and sexuality through the state's courts and interrogation rooms.[4] The book introduces two companion concepts to sextarianism; evangelical secularism and the epidermal state.

Sextarianism emphasizes how state power articulates, disarticulates, and manages sexual difference bureaucratically, ideologically, and legally. Statecraft is fundamentally practiced as the disciplining of sextarianism into its component parts: sex and sect. Sovereignty is performed at the intersections of sexual and sectarian difference. As a theory and method, sextarianism helps us understand how rule through discrete and abstract regulatory categories distributes the spoils and underbellies of liberal democracy along the same logics and exclusions that liberalism was founded through in the first place; property, sex, race, and law.[5] Making visible the intersectional experience and distribution of power and its effects within any given system is key to understanding and dismantling the promises of liberal abstraction and universalization. Lebanon is exemplary, not exceptional, in how it ties sect and sex. It represents an intensification of the foundational relationship between political and sexual difference.

Sextarianism builds on Joan Scott's theorization of the constitutive nature of sexual difference to the history of secularism. It is indebted to Saba Mahmood's argument that sex is a key technology through which secular state power produces and manages religious difference.[6] I follow Scott's understanding of sexual difference, emphasizing the relationship between sexuality, sex, and the secular.[7] *Sextarianism* foregrounds the secular state's role in both structuring political society through sexual difference, and gendering and personalizing the stakes of sexual difference.

Sexual difference is political difference, to repeat Carole Pateman's foundational claim,[8] and it is also a term for power relations. Sexual difference is a process through which sectarian, gendered, and sexual positions are structurally *produced*, in addition to being represented, imagined, desired, and managed.[9] In other words, sexual difference is a vector of state power. Thinking from Lebanon allows us to trace colonial and postcolonial modes of producing and regulating religion, secularism, and political/sexual difference.[10] Colonial French Mandate laws, practices, and administrative rules, building on and in some cases doing away with Ottoman precedents, grounded the legal, bureaucratic, and secular political legitimacy of sectarian groups in the regulation of sexual difference. Criminal and civil laws as well as the state's bureaucratic practices were and are grounded in sexual difference. Ideological, bureaucratic, and legal "crossing," as M Jacqui Alexander puts it, between imperial, colonial, and postcolonial eras, as well as between "religion" and "the secular,"[11] is key to how sextarianism operates. Thus sextarianism draws attention to the relationship between modern forms of secular state power and colonial forms of indirect rule.

A central point in Samera's case concerned differences from three historical iterations of Lebanon: Ottoman-era Mount Lebanon, the colonial French Mandate over Lebanon, and postcolonial, independent Lebanon. Jean's distant cousins showed evidence that Samera first identified herself as "single" in the 1932 French Mandate. She was identified as "single" in state bureaucracy until she died. But Jean had his own set of documents. He presented religious and civil courts with copies of the first French Mandate land census of 1925, his 1940 French Mandate–issued identification card, and a certificate of his 1922 baptism from the Greek Orthodox Church. He also presented evidence that his parents were married in 1917, in the midst of World War I, a devastating famine, and the final year of Ottoman rule over the territory that became Lebanon. All of the documents Jean presented to the court listed him as the legal son of his mother and his father, although no marriage certificate had ever been registered with the colonial or postcolonial state. Jean did not dispute the presence or veracity of his cousins' set of documents. Instead, he offered a narrative explaining how two contradictory sets of state documents could *both* be true.

In 1932 Jean's mother and father were separated and living in different areas of Lebanon. She did not have the money to obtain a divorce from the Greek Orthodox Church. When the census takers came to Samera's home, she saw an opportunity to get out of a bad marriage. Samera told the census takers that she was single, seeing this as a free and efficient way to leave her husband. A bureaucratic do-over instead of a divorce. It was as if she had never been married at all. Jean, in accordance with the patriarchal bureaucratic system organized under colonial rule and still in place today, was listed only under his father's census entry. Samera died as a "single/unmarried" woman rather than as a "single/divorced" or "single/widowed" woman—the only possible bureaucratic categories for unmarried women in Lebanon. Samera used the 1932 census to begin a new life as an officially "single" woman.[12] In doing so, she lost legal and bureaucratic ties, and claims, to Jean. She answered the door and the census takers' questions, but while she danced to the song of the census and of state power, to paraphrase James Scott, she may have been humming a different tune in her head.[13]

The 1932 national census, conducted under French Mandate, is the only census that has ever been published in Lebanon.[14] It performed, and continues to perform, the colonial conditions under which the state was founded and the violence and sovereignty of the postcolonial state.[15] The system of census taking under the French Mandate, based on the legal categories of sex, sect, and kinship, remains largely in place today. The sectarian demography of the area that became the Lebanese nation-state was produced and made legible through it. The 1932 census identified, organized, and enumerated sects and determined the nascent body of citizens, which were recorded, managed, and produced through the national registries also forged at that time. It was a biopolitical technology of securitization, where sexuality—as that which ties the individual to the population—was key. The census staged an origin story: a land where sect, religion, and region were the primary and inherently competing[16] markers of political difference that had to compromise their autonomy by contracting into the newly founded state. The methodology of the census scaffolded both the religious personal status system and political sectarianism, a system of political representation based on religious and sectarian quotas. The claim that the Lebanese state is a zone of compromise for preexisting political communities is central to an ideology and a self-fulfilling prophesy: Political sectarianism was and is a representative system that channels an underlying sectarian reality.

Sovereignty

Throughout the colonized world, imperial powers staged the apocalyptic origin story of social contract theory and liberalism, organizing and defining states as zones of compromise between preexisting and hopelessly warring political communities defined by sect, caste, tribe, ethnicity, race, and religion.[17] This restaging departed from classical social contract theory in that the individual traveled alongside and was sometimes subsumed by the group. A colonial mode of social contract theory can be productively read through Lebanon. At the level of the individual, citizenship was theoretically the medium of universalism and equality, but not, even theoretically, if you were a woman. Women were and continue to be excluded from many of the most basic political and economic rights of citizenship. On the other hand, an always-warring, tribal, religious, and sectarian state of nature was transcended through a social contract that emphasized sectarian power sharing in the state. Every sectarian group was equal in the public sphere. Key to this transcendence and equality under law in the public sphere was the production of a private sphere where sectarian religious authorities enjoyed a limited form of sovereignty.[18] However, to follow feminist revisions of liberalism, the private sphere was also the space where so-called natural, prepolitical, or cultural forms of inequality, such as that between men and women, flourished under the guise of the right to privacy.[19] The itinerary of the private/public distinction was global. Over time, the heteropatriarchal "family" and "the market" were produced, universalized, and understood to mean "the private" and "the public."[20] In Lebanon, the sexual contract within the social contract was consecrated through the personal status system.

The power of social contract theory emerged in part through the compelling and supposedly universal narrative structure of the origin story.[21] Origin stories are ideologically powerful, and they play a key role in maintaining the narrative that the nation-state is a "natural" outcome or unfolding of political, economic, and social difference.[22] Origin stories simultaneously birth nation-states and serve as their historical alibi, helping to secure the notion of the nation-state as destiny and as a container of political imagination.[23] Samera's interaction with the nascent colonial bureaucracy and later, with postcolonial state bureaucracy pointed to moments in history where the nation-state was not destiny,[24] moments in which previous laws and bureaucracies and institutions—an Ottoman-era transnational Greek Orthodox community—determined the fabric of everyday life.

Far from the comforts of origin stories, the nation-state is a historical formation that is continuously consolidating and erupting under shifting patterns of political, economic, and social friction.[25] Feminist political theorists have emphasized three important and critical revisions of liberal political theory. First, the production of the public sphere, civil society, and unitary sovereignty—the social contract—is itself simultaneously a sexual contract, one that produces a private sphere and delegates patriarchal power and mastery within it. The sexual contract within social contract theory produced the private and public spheres.[26] Thus the social contract is the founding of *two* sovereignties, one nested in the other: a sovereignty over political society and a sovereignty within the private sphere.[27] The distinction, for example between "political violence" and "domestic violence," follows this division.[28] Second, the private sphere is constructed and regulated publicly. It is an integral terrain of state sovereignty, power, and legitimation.[29] Finally, the contracting of women into the public sphere and into the category of "man" is often produced through racial subjection.[30] In most cases, these lenses have been constituted as *secular* theories of power. Sextarianism, on the other hand, is neither secularist nor theological. It circumvents liberal epistemology and methodology that reproduce the public/private divide as the constitutional foundation for citizen and property. These divides have long obscured the complex figures of power that operate in the borderlands between religion and the secular on the one hand and sexual and political difference on the other.[31] If liberal states envision, regulate, and discipline political society through the heuristic of the public/private, sextariansim focuses our attention on how sovereignty is amplified by crossing, delineating, nesting, securitizing, and rupturing the so-called public and private spheres.

Sovereignty has also been theorized as the ability to decide on the state of exception. The sovereign is that which can remove itself from the jurisdiction of its primary technology, the law—even though it must usually perform this sleight of hand through a legal procedure.[32] While the state of exception is a temporal order in which the sovereign identifies itself as such, sovereignty is more and less than the drama of the state of exception. The state of exception is neither a rupture nor a grand reveal, and perhaps that is the point. Military and necropolitical rule were and are mundane—both as forms of colonial, settler colonial, and neocolonial rule and within states against their own racialized and classed subjects.[33] Generations of political leaders, citizens, and refugees have ruled, enriched themselves, struggled, lived, and died under "emergency" law. Individuals and populations have been killed without sacrifice, and entire populations have been killed *as* a sacrifice to modernity or manifest destiny. As Elizabeth Povinelli writes, there is nothing much to report on the terror of sovereignty—this is simply our world.[34] Moreover, the right *to* a body itself, let alone a body that matters,[35] is not distributed equally.[36] The body, as both a material and ideological edifice, is formed through a history of race, speciesism, economy, sex, colonialism, and science.[37]

States and nonstate publics also perform sovereignty as a reiterative series of practices.[38] These practices may be legal, carceral, economic, medical, biopolitical, or unfold and fold a terrain of intimacy.[39] Crucially, sovereignty also requires reiterative consent, even if that consent is expressed by an everyday *lack* of resistance.[40] Audra Simpson has theorized settler colonial forms of "nested sovereignty"—whereby distinct sovereignties are nested and practiced within the larger structuring sovereignty of settler states.[41] These nested sovereignties have genealogies that precede the settler state, yet are state authorized and adjacent. Settler sovereignty, moreover, requires formal nesting of indigenous sovereignties as a marker of tolerance, pluralism, and supremacy.[42] Both preceding sovereignties and sovereignties incited by contact with state power are suspended—surrounded by the background sovereignty of the nation-state. Simpson's elaboration of nested sovereignty can be employed in contexts where preceding sovereignties are ingested, bordered, transformed, and authorized by nation-states. Lebanon and other postcolonial states like it may be new, but competing transnational legal systems and sovereignties are not. Nor are preceding and competing transnational sovereignties ever confined to the past. For example, Lebanon is a former colony of France and a former territory of the Ottoman Empire, and its legal system carries the markings of both. However, once restructured in a modern liberal and independent state, the very same legal structure may mediate/produce different ideological tenets. While an Ottoman system of legal pluralism at the level of family law mediated an ideology of pluralism and Muslim tolerance,[43] the Lebanese state's legal pluralism at the level of personal status law mediates and performs an ideology of liberal secularism. A key step in this transition was a French Mandate–era demotion of Sunni Islam to the status of one sect among many, all of which were to be nested within the sovereignty of the colonial state.[44] Central to that process was personal status law.[45]

Personal status laws regulate and help produce the stakes and compulsory nature of heterosexuality.[46] Personal status laws, whether they are religious or civil, regulate heteropatriarchal kinship relations—they are an iteration of family law. They cannot be understood outside the framework that gives them legal force: that of the nation-state. Lebanon ties state recognition of sectarian difference to a personal status law, and the political system and mode of governance is based on power sharing between sects. The recognition of religious difference is an act that both performs and amplifies secular state sovereignty.[47] Lebanon, a country that is only 10,452 square kilometers and where about seven million people live—four and a half million of whom are citizens—has the highest number of personal status laws in the world. Personal status is key to the production and regulation of both the so-called private and public spheres.[48] In fact, it is the production of the private sphere via personal status law that produces the public sphere of civil and criminal law—laws that all citizens must adhere to regardless of sect or sex. Personal status laws also perform the secular "equality" of different sects within the public sphere, even between sects for whom executive power is reserved and those that are small and amalgamated into the one parliamentary seat designated for "minorities." Though different sects enjoy political power based on their demography, they all equally share, with the state, the right to legislate and regulate kinship relations, sex, and sexuality.[49] State power is articulated and amplified by regulating the private sphere and by *declining* to intervene or regulate aspects of the private sphere, such as in cases of marital rape or inequality between men and women within personal status law.

I use "sex" throughout this book because sex is the operative legal and bureaucratic category in state practice. Moreover, feminist and queer theorists have suggested that too often "gender" is used to refer to cultural/social/intersubjective processes, while "sex" continues to be used to refer to biological or chromosomal "truth"—as if scientific processes and truths can be divorced from social, political, historical, or economic processes. The maintenance of a strict binary between sex and gender forms a disciplinary feedback loop that continues to privilege sexual dimorphism as well as the power of science to determine sexual truth. My use of "sex," as opposed to "gender," follows the terminology and categories used by the Lebanese state; I do not subscribe an inner truth or an intersubjective register to that category. When it comes to Lebanon, academic work has focused on the categories of sect and, to a lesser extent, region when revisiting the 1932 census and its structural and ideological afterlives. Sex and marital status have been overlooked. And yet sex, sect, and kinship status cannot be alienated from each other because it is their imbrication that produced the everyday conditions of Samera's life in 1932, just as their imbrication continues to produce the conditions of everyday life today. Sex and sect always already contain each other ideologically, legally, and bureaucratically. The ideological registers of "sext" are present every time men's experiences of sect and of sex—so starkly different from women's—are used as ungendered evidence through which to theorize or historicize sectarianism, citizenship, religion, revolution, war, and the Lebanese state. Similarly, "queer" is experienced, structured, and regulated in starkly different ways when it comes to women and men. In the eyes of the state, queer men and women are not very different from straight men and women in that the seam of sexual difference sutures the regulation and experience of citizenship, law, family, property, and sexuality. The lives of queer men and women are regulated differently by the state due to their assigned or changed sex status, that is, because they are men and women in a sextarian system. It is easier (though still difficult) to envision LGBTQ Pride marches in Beirut than marches demanding women's sexual freedom and autonomy *as* women of any and all sexualities.

Sextarianism unpacks how heterosexuality, the sex binary, and civil and criminal law are key to secularism's management of sexual and religious difference. Secularism's investment in sex is multiple; it manifests as the regulation of straight *and* queer sexualities *and* a sex-gender binary system. Throughout this book, I use "sexual difference" to describe the productive and disciplinary relationship between the state, the sex binary, and sexuality.[50] In academic work centered in the Middle East, the study of sexuality is often collapsed with the study of sexual minorities and, in particular, queer people and sexualities. On the other hand, work that focuses on gender inequality often takes for granted the categories of "man" and "woman," and rarely theorizes heterosexuality as a productive, regulated, and securitized form of sexuality.[51] *Sextarianism* traces the regulatory relationship between heterosexuality and homosexuality,[52] and elaborates how the stakes of both are different for men and for women. The chapters of *Sextarianism* (1, 3, and 5) that feature people who are queer or that focus on the regulation of sexuality seek neither to *explain* queer life in the Middle East nor to argue over authenticity and representation. Rather, to the extent that queer politics and people animate the pages of *Sextarianism*, they do so as they do in life: fully. Queer people play an integral role in the sociopolitical life of state power, activism and social movement building in Lebanon. For decades they have been leaders, foot soldiers, intellectuals, knowledge producers, lawyers, antagonists, and protagonists in various political, legal, and activist campaigns and processes.

Could ungendered theories or histories of sectarianism, citizenship, the state, queerness, or religion focus solely—or even mostly—on the experiences of women? Sextarianism, thus, has methodological implications. When we look for histories and presents of "sect" or "sex" or "sexuality" in the archives of state institutions, in bureaucracies, or in people's experiences, we can and should anticipate and theorize how they always already contain and exceed each other. If biopower modulates the relationship between the individual and the population through sexuality and securitization,[53] that power is only amplified when epistemological and methodological silos map onto governmental ones.[54] In many ways, *unseeing* the braid of sexual and sectarian difference demonstrates how women bear, and are, the analytic cost of the myth of the universal subject.[55] Women are variations, clauses, parenthesis, or footnotes to the subjects and actors of history and theory, who are gendered precisely because they are framed as ungendered, as universal. Sextarianism in Lebanon has undergirded state power since at least 1932, when the census elaborated sex and sect as stable and discrete, yet impossible to untangle in their daily, legal, and bureaucratic effects. In these ways, the 1932 census—conducted under military curfew—was both law making and law preserving.[56] However, in the case we now return to, jurists at both the Greek Orthodox Court of Appeals and the Plenary Assembly at the Court of Cassation presented the census as potentially law *bending*. They introduced skepticism and multiplicity into the census itself.

Truth as Lies

The Greek Orthodox courts ruled in Jean's favor—he was, in fact, Samera's "legitimate" son. They argued that in cases involving two sets of contradicting documentation, evidence preceding the 1932 census had more legal weight than the information documented on the census itself. This was for two reasons, both tied to the question-and-answer methodology of the 1932 census. First, the census takers did not know anything about the people they were taking information from, while religious institutions were well acquainted with their community members. Second, census takers had no way to verify the information being given to them,[57] even if those answers subsequently became law and bureaucracy. They noted that the absence of a marriage certificate in state registries did not mean that a marriage had not taken place, particularly if the marriage had taken place before centralized, state bureaucracy and during a period of war, famine, and disease. They described this period of history as a *nakba*, or catastrophe. How could people file papers while they were sick, starving, and running for their lives? Jean won his case. Armed with a decision from the religious personal status courts that restored his dead mother's honor and rendered him her "legitimate" son, Jean was confident he would inherit Samera's estate in the civil personal status courts. But in 1981 his distant cousins turned to the Plenary Assembly at the Court of Cassation,[58] the highest court that citizens have access to in Lebanon.

The Plenary Assembly is composed of the presidents of the different chambers of the Lebanese Cassation Courts and the president of the Cassation Court itself.[59] The Plenary Assembly's decisions are final and public, and form jurisprudential, authoritative interpretations of Lebanese law.[60] The Assembly rules on cases against the state when judges are accused of violating legal procedures and in any case that fundamentally challenges Cassation Court jurisprudence.[61] The Assembly also hears cases that implicate or contravene jurisprudence and final decisions from personal status courts that include substantive violations of procedural law that may impact public order.[62] Finally, it decides proper jurisdiction in cases where more than one judiciary court, a judiciary and a personal status court, or two personal status courts have issued decisions, and in cases where a plaintiff alleges that a final decision issued by a personal status court lacks proper jurisdiction. Structures like the Assembly perform the sovereignty of the state as that which respects, preserves, recognizes, and transcends the rights of religious communities to share in the regulation of sextarian difference.

Jean's cousins appealed the decision of the Greek Orthodox Personal Status Court in front of the Assembly, claiming a conflict of jurisdiction between a civil and a religious court. Shouldn't the civil personal status court rule on Samera's estate, as it did for the estates of all Christians in Lebanon? If so, what role did the Greek Orthodox personal status court have in authenticating an almost sixty-year-old marriage that had never

been registered with the Lebanese state? They argued that the Greek Orthodox courts were themselves out of order because the Greek Orthodox patriarchate of Antioch in Damascus, and not a Lebanese court, had
convened them.[63] The Plenary Assembly was not impressed by this line
of argument. Other religions also had courts of appeal that were not
within the borders of the state, and the Lebanese state had to treat all
religious court systems equally in the name of public order. To challenge
the authority of the patriarchate of Antioch in Damascus would necessitate similar challenges of the Catholic Rota courts, at the Vatican, for example. The Lebanese nation-state, as a legal system, had been erected on
and intervened into preexisting legal and religious transnational systems.
Both sides had to adapt. Thus while some religions had legal authorities
outside the borders of the Lebanese state, the state set the terms and organized the forms and enforceability of that transnational relationship.

The Assembly agreed with the Greek personal status courts: In cases
where there was a contradiction between information recorded in the
1932 census and information recorded prior to the 1932 census, documents preceding 1932 were more legally persuasive. There were two
Sameras: one who had never been married, and one who had been married and had a son, Jean. Other narratives bubbled up alongside the sectarian, at the apocryphal moment of the founding of the state. A cunning
was introduced to both the intentions of the people being surveyed and
those of the surveyors. People may have purposely given information to
the census takers that was untrue, may have used the world-making technology of the census to make new worlds for themselves. A lie became
the basis for an origin story parallel to that of the state—a woman leav-
ing a bad marriage behind and starting a new life as single. Doubt and
skepticism shadowed this juridical reading of the census—just as they,
alongside fear, probably shadowed the experience of people like Samera,
who opened a door and answered questions. The power relationship inherent in a colonial census was slightly recalibrated. Census takers did
not know, and perhaps did not have the capacity to know, that they were
being lied to. Or perhaps they did know, but truth was never the point
of the exercise. The ideological foundations of the Lebanese state—that
the census merely reflected an age-old, religious, sectarian, patriarchal

truth—were thrown into disarray by the lies people may have told. The lies that became bureaucracy. The lies that became law.

Secularism

The Plenary Assembly is often asked to assess whether somebody is lying. In cases that are centered on religious conversion and its legal and bureaucratic effects, lying comes up regularly. The plaintiffs may be a Christian church or a Muslim charitable trust accusing someone of converting to Islam for financial benefit, or a wife accusing her former spouse of converting to marry someone else without bothering with a divorce. The Assembly's jurisprudence on religious conversion is clear: The state does not have the right to interrogate or demand evidence of religious sincerity. The state must maintain an equal, dispassionate distance from all religions and sects. Bureaucratic procedure is key to that goal.[64] Bureaucracy, not faith, practice, or intent, is the evidentiary terrain for religious conversion. The state does not have the right to assess whether someone lied to a sheikh or priest to convert, even if that lie created new bureaucratic and legal subject positions for the person and, if he were a man, his minor children.

Religion is inescapably tied to biopolitical power, particularly in states where religious categories are regulatory categories.[65] From the vantage point of Lebanon, sectarian subjects, male and female subjects, Muslim subjects, secular subjects, straight, gay, and Christian subjects all have one thing in common: They are shaped through institutional, bureaucratic, discursive, and legal practices that build and manage the intersections between sex and sect. Regardless of faith or politics or individual identification, sex and sect are regulatory categories that are coercively assigned at birth. The assignment of one modulates the practice of the other, and the legal and bureaucratic infrastructure of secular citizenship forms through their articulation. The hypervisibility and the compulsory nature of categories of religious, sectarian, and gendered difference in Lebanon in fact produces and ensures—in the state's eyes—a right to opacity within the freedom of religion.[66] This is the right to *not* identify as what the state identifies you as. When it comes to converts, the state's position on religious freedom is clear: Not only is religious freedom the freedom to decide between religions and sects, it is also the freedom to *not* identify with any of the compulsory categories the state uses to produce political difference.

Secularism is the framework or, as Hussein Ali Agrama calls it, the "problem space" within which debates on religion, citizenship, and modernity are articulated. Secularism is also the framework within which sexual and religious difference is regulated and debated.[67] Following Talal Asad's injunction to write about secularity as it is embodied and practiced, it proved impossible to write only *one* account of secularity in Lebanon. Instead, two narratives of secularism emerged. The first narrative, that of the Plenary Assembly, emphasized religious pluralism and the rights and duties of Lebanese citizens. The practice of secularism was the state's impartial management of religious pluralism via the legal system and the stymying of religious conflict through the state's right to interpret and enforce public order. The regulation and experience of religious conversion pointed to the banality of religion as a category of secular governmentality. In this narrative, the bureaucratic, compulsory, banal, and hypervisible nature of sextarian difference is key to the sovereignty of the state.

The second practice of secularism that *Sectarianism* traces is what I term "evangelical secularism," activism aimed at transcending a "culture of sectarianism" and fostering a "culture of secularism." Evangelical secularism theorizes the pedagogical registers of activist movements that believe that cultural and ethical change must precede political change. It was opposed to sectarianism and aimed to save religion, and the state, from its corrosive forces. Evangelical secularists saw themselves as belonging to a minority community that identified as secular/liberal, one that was disrupting normative sectarian space while expanding the existing community of secular liberals through acts of *da'wa*, the Arabic term for proselytizing, or inviting, to Islam. Their motive was to shape a counterpublic that would disrupt what they saw as a hegemonic sectarian space. Evangelical secularism drew on Islamic practices and models of religious activism; was steeped in the global, missionary character of state modernity; and was informed by the structural, historical, and ideological resonance of Christianity in Lebanon. In its 2010–2013 Laique Pride iteration, evangelical secularism was also informed by a queer politics of visibility—coming out as secular; marches taking over public, normative space; and an emphasis on the heterosexual freedom to marry someone from a different sect. Evangelical secularism had Muslim, Christian, statist, leftist, and queer genealogies and elaborated how secularism operates and circulates as a set of cultural and ethical practices. Secularism served as an identity and as a litmus test that separated those who have achieved *real* citizenship and those who were *still* sectarian.

These two articulations of secularism—state and evangelical secularism—were informed by each other. State secularism was expressed through the ability of citizens, including evangelical secularists, to both transcend sectarian institutions and maintain an opacity between religious/sectarian categorization and religious conviction. Evangelical secularism sought to reform the secularism of the state, which it viewed as atrophied and unable to cope with the challenges of contemporary Lebanon. Both articulations of secularism were affectively informed by the ever-present possibility of civil war in Lebanon.[68] The state's protection of religious pluralism and its insistence on the legal harmony of the religious personal status system was framed as a way to ward off conflict. Evangelical secularists, for their part, feared their lives and work would be colored, consumed, and marred by war, just as war had defined the life and work of the jurists who sat on the Plenary Assembly in 1983 and decided Jean's case.

History and Contingency

In the hundreds of pages of Samera's case file, we meet a woman who used the French Mandate census in 1932 as a vehicle to escape a bad marriage while avoiding a costly divorce. We found the highest court in Lebanon claiming that the census on which the state and its bureaucracies grew was methodologically flawed. We saw the possibilities—the abundance that must be entertained once we understood that both census planners and takers may have used this technology to make new worlds for themselves. The stakes of sexual difference—being married or unmarried, a woman or a man, a legitimate child or not—consumed three generations of one family. It was only through claiming sovereignty, or jurisdiction,

over matters of sexual difference that sects—in this case Greek Orthodoxy—became legible to, were stakeholders in, and practiced a nested
sovereignty within the Lebanese state. Lebanese state sovereignty came
into view as a bounded entity through asserting jurisdiction over personal status courts and over the ability to define public order. The scaf-
folding of sexual difference to sectarian difference is the origin story of
political difference and of the nation-state in Lebanon. It is this scaf-
folding that makes the identification, management, and governance of
populations—whether sects or their aggregates, citizens—possible. Sectarian and sexual difference are co-travelers, and they are both ongoing
disciplinary projects—often produced through the same technologies of
biopolitical power, such as the 1932 census or the postcolonial bureaucracy of the state. To understand how political difference is structurally
reproduced we have to take seriously the ways that reproduction is not
simply a metaphor of state power or hegemony. The regulation of reproduction is at the very heart of political difference.[69]

Contingency frames much of what we consider to be the historical
record and much of academic knowledge production itself.[70] The categories that the colonial state chose as relevant and that the postcolonial
state continues to rule through—sect, sex, region, kinship status—*were
choices*. Sectarianism here, to follow Anjali Arondekar, may be a foundational fiction—and it is also a frame that we must use with skepticism
or "hesitance" while conducting research.[71] There is an epistemological
hubris to the categories we use to conduct research, whether archival or
ethnographic. We think we know what sect, sectarianism, sex, secularism,
sovereignty, or even history and theory are, for example, and we think
we will know them when we see them. We assume the coherence of our
questions, and thus we actively cohere them. This cohering of an analytic common sense reflects and amplifies the power relationship between
methodology and epistemology.[72]

Rather than reading the results of a colonial census as reflecting anything more than what colonial power and postcolonial state institutions
methodologically stage as vital data—data vital for power to know—we
can read the census with Samera. This reading would stress the cunning
at both sides of this vignette: the census worker and Samera, answering

questions about her marital status—questions indelibly linked to her sectarian and sex status. Because she knows how difficult and costly it is to divorce under her sect's personal status laws, she says she is single. Because she says she is single, her son is cleaved from her legal and bureaucratic person. These are not moments of truth or important events in the history of a coherent and unitary sectarian subject, the unfolding of the inevitability of the nation-state. Instead, these moments introduce contingency, opacity, and unknowability as central to the consolidation and experience of state power.[73] The experience of state power, moreover, includes the experience of its aporias. The 1983 Plenary Assembly ruling was not the end of the story. After Jean's death in 2005, his children again turned to the Assembly to authenticate their inheritance, asking to receive an official photocopy of Jean's file, to append their names as Jean's heirs, and to receive a certificate of the decision with the list of appended heirs.[74] They returned yet again in 2008 to fix a mistake: One heir's name was left off the official documentation issued by the Assembly and the civil courts in 2005. That same year, violence between different political camps broke out in Lebanon, what some called a "mini" civil war. In 1983 when the Plenary Assembly first decided the case, outside the walls of the Ministry of Justice and the Beirut Courthouse was the green line—snipers, sandbags, car bombs, and checkpoints. Israel still occupied one-third of the country, a president-elect had just been assassinated, and massacres against Palestinian refugees and Lebanese citizens had been committed. Outside the walls of the archive continued the Lebanese Civil War, which began as an attempt to maintain or change Christian political hegemony in the Lebanese state—a hegemony legitimated by the facts "revealed" by the census.

Violence, Sovereignty, and an Epidermal State

The relationship between law, sovereignty, and violence is multiple. From the viewpoint of the modern Middle East, the stakes of the debate on sovereignty are not abstract. The diagnosis of having "failed" opens states, territories, and the people who live in them to war, invasion, and occupation. Lebanon, it seems, is forever on the precipice of failing. In fact, "almost failing" seems to be the stable temporality of the state, as well as its preferred mode of governance. Complete failure, or the presence of a civil war or a foreign invasion, is what keeps ordinary people desperately attached to the *almost* failing state. Moreover, just because a state lacks the hegemony over the means of violence does not mean that it is not violent; the Lebanese state daily exerts violence and violates vulnerable populations including refugees, prisoners, and migrant laborers. Instead of viewing this or that state as "failing" to live up to a particular unitary model of sovereignty, hegemony, or domination, we are better served studying how, where, and *when* states and citizens invest in acts of sovereignty and sovereignty-announcing violence, in ideological fashioning and permeation, in nationalism, and in discourses and practices of the better state, the better citizen, the *better* relation to power.[75]

Central to evangelical secularism was the desire for a stronger state, a state that was sovereign over all aspects of citizens' lives and over the use of violence. But what do calls for a stronger state sound like from the site of sexual difference? The third conceptual tool that *Sextarianism* offers is the epidermal state, a state that performs its sovereignty by materializing the sextarian stakes of bodies and sexualities through securitization, violence, and law. The term "epidermal state" evokes the role of state power in producing and regulating the body as a contained, felt, and visible truth of sex and sexuality. The state is materialized as a bounded, contained, felt, and sovereign entity as it turns inward, exerting violence against people positioned differently, and at various levels of precarity, in a sextarian system. Epidermal sovereignty unfolds at the sites of sex, sexuality, race, and legal status. It is modulated by the sextarian architecture of state power in Lebanon. Violence and sovereignty are experienced and *felt* differently by different genders, by citizens and noncitizens, and across the axes of race and class. In a sextarian system, the state shares the regulation and materialization of women's sexuality with parastatal actors such as the heteropatriarchal family, but it retains the sole right to regulate and materialize the stakes of men's sexuality. The concept of an "epidermal state" allows us to center the relationship of violence, sovereignty, and the materiality of the body at the site of sexuality and sex, and invites us to rethink the state's sextarian investment in regulating and stabilizing sexualities across an intersectional political economy of violability.

The chapters of this book theorize sextarianism and its companion concepts—evangelical secularism and the epidermal state—across different sites, using ethnographic and archival research. All three concepts invite a rethinking of sovereignty, secularism, and state power along the axes of sex, sect, religion, class, legal status, and race. Chapter 1, "Afterlives of a Census: Rethinking State Power and Political Difference," traces the suffusions between sex and sect bureaucratically, legally, and ideologically. Seen through the lens of sextarianism, political sectarianism emerges as a technology of securitization that centers sectarian demographics, women's sexuality, racism, classism, and violence. The production of sextarianism as a mode of power threads the legal and bureaucratic apparatus together, erupting epistemological boundaries often made between religious personal status law and other arenas of state law, between the religious, the sectarian, and the secular. We will meet several Sameras throughout this book, people whose actions are inflected with and informed by the sextarian stakes of everyday life.

Chapter 2, "A Fire in the Archive: History, Ethnography, Multiplicity," focuses on the lived history of the Beirut Courthouse, and the archive of the Plenary Assembly at the Court of Cassation. I went to the archive looking for the relationship between sectarianism and secularism as seen through religious conversion. Instead, the people I studied and the archivists who led me to them offered sextarianism. The Court of Cassation archive was burnt in a fire that started after a mortar barrage on the Ministry of Justice in 1985. This fire has had structuring effects on the past, present, and future of the court. It has also consumed the archivists that work at the Court of Cassation. Almost forty years later, the fire is still burning in Lebanese jurisprudence—shaping decisions, engendering acts of sovereignty, influencing the working relations and the lives of archivists, and affecting academic research. Samera's case file, for example, was badly damaged by smoke, and its edges were fire eaten. It was also not a file I had asked for. The multi-authored nature of archival research is evident when we focus on the relationships between archivists and academics. When I asked the head archivist of the Plenary Assembly what cases *she* thought were important, she introduced me to Samera, Jean, and others we meet in chapter 2. I offer a method and framework for archival ethnography that emphasizes contingency, opacity, and multiplicity.

Chapter 3, "Regulating Conversion: Sovereignty, Bureaucracy, and the Banality of Religion," demonstrates how religious conversion, and sometimes reconversion, is essentially a conversion between regimes of sexual difference. I present cases from the Plenary Assembly that concern religious conversion alongside ethnographic research with religious converts, one of whom also described himself as a "convert to secularism."[76] Sextarianism inflects both state secularism and discourse that propose secularism as a set of values, aspirational practices, and a hierarchy of modernity.

Chapter 4, "Are You Going to Pride? Evangelical Secularism and the Politics of Law," is an ethnography of evangelical, or *da'wa*, secularism and controversies over religious and sexual minorities that clustered around its formation. Evangelical secularists believed that the Lebanese state had imposed an injurious and dangerous form of sectarian misrecognition on them. They demanded the state create a mechanism for people who did not want to be identified by a sect, end corruption linked to sectarianism, legislate a civil marriage law, and protect the freedom of expression and the rights of women. Only then would the Lebanese state be "truly secular." Evangelical secularism was an ethical project aimed at transcending sectarianism. The heyday of evangelical secularism was the 2010–2013 Laique Pride march.

Chapter 5, "The Epidermal State: Violence and the Materiality of Power," follows the deployment of anal and hymen exams against vulnerable people to securitize sex and sexuality. We begin with a successful LGBTQ rights campaign against the use of anal examinations as "evidence" of sex between men within criminal courts. This success story, however, was and is shadowed by the intersectional experience of vulnerability and state violence, particularly when it came to Syrian refugees and migrant laborers targeted and arrested for engaging in "unnatural sex." We then turn to a divorce and alimony case at the Plenary Assembly that pivoted on the conditions and results of a hymen exam. The states' investment in the regulation of sexuality, in this case women's heterosexuality, become clear. Staying with hymen exams, we end with an ethnography of an Internal Security Forces interrogation room where forced hymen exams were deployed as a threat against an LGBTQ activist and human rights worker. By focusing on these exams and their sextarian deployment in criminal, civil, and personal status law, one can glimpse the articulation of an epidermal state, a state that performs its sovereignty by materializing bodies, sexualities, and their stakes through securitization, violence, and law.

CHAPTER I

Afterlives of a Census

Rethinking State Power and Political Difference

IN 2011 AND AGAIN IN 2019 I conducted an experiment. I drew up a chart of religious institutions in Lebanon and began cold calling them. Each time, I asked to speak with the sheikh or priest responsible for conversion. In both years, a majority of the phone calls resulted, without prompting, in a question of whether I was marrying a man from that sect or religion. During the phone call to a Shiʻi sheikh responsible for conversions, he assumed—based on my last name, which marked me as Sunni—that my husband and I had not been "blessed with a son" and thus wanted to become Shiʻi to better ensure our daughter's inheritance. When I called the Armenian Orthodox Church, I was asked—with a laugh—who the lucky Armenian man was. All these responses were initiated by one question: "Can you please let me know what procedures are required for joining your religious community?" These phone conversations highlighted the importance of three factors as they relate to religious conversion: sexual difference, personal status law, and money. The context of our conversations, the taken-for-granted background, was heterosexual marriage, the different sextarian legal regimes that govern heterosexuality and the binary gender relations therein, and sextarian-specific rules over capital accumulation. An entire political economy of conversion centers on inheritance, wealth, and gender. This political economy points to an understudied primary function of personal status law: the reproduction of capital and of wealth.[1] The sextarian state is the framework that enables, compels, and defines religious conversion in Lebanon.[2]

Seen through the lens of state power, "sexual difference" is not only a set of relations between and within gendered subject positions but also a process by which a binary *and* a hierarchical regime within and between sexualities is coercively upheld. Revisiting sectarianism through sexual difference, I argue that sexual difference is also sectarian, political difference. The very category of "sect" is a patriarchal inheritance, a fact that has received scant analytic and political attention in conversations about sectarianism or political confessionalism.[3] In the eyes of the state, what makes someone Muslim as opposed to Christian, or Sunni rather than Shi'i, is not religious conviction, communal cohesion, political persuasion, or sectarian investment—instead what matters is what sect your father was. In Lebanon and in other states that build and organize political power through sectarian governmental categories, sectarian difference *is* sexual difference: to be a legitimate, distinct, and measurable sect requires the legal infrastructures of personal status law and of census data regimes that entrench sexual difference. To that end, I consider personal status laws—laws governing marriage, divorce, inheritance and other kinship matters—laws of sexual difference. To be more precise, personal status laws are laws of sexual difference just as criminal, civil, and constitutional laws are. This naming highlights what personal status laws *actually do* in the framework of a secular state and simultaneously refuses to amplify the ideological tenet that the regulation of the heteropatriarchal family is personal or private.

Important research has and continues to be done on women, gender, and "the family" as they relate to religious personal status laws in the Middle East, and my work is indebted to this body of literature.[4] I join this conversation by focusing on three aspects of personal status and how they help construct and regulate sexual difference. First, I suggest personal status laws are key to the production and management of sexuality: in this case, heterosexuality. Second, I trace how personal status laws are integrated into, and are critical components of, a larger secular system of law. Finally, I argue that personal status laws are crucial to the production of political difference precisely through tying and untying the knot of sex and sect. Religious personal status laws are one technology among many that the state employs to stabilize sexual difference.[5] For example, Lebanon, in addition to having fifteen different religious personal status laws and court systems, also has a civil personal status law and court system. This court adjudicates inheritance matters for non-Muslims as well as aspects of "the family" that are not covered in religious personal status courts: changing one's family name, settling cases involving children allegedly born outside of a marriage, and changing the assigned-at-birth sex of a citizen or resident.[6]

Sextarianism does not privilege the analysis of "religious family law" in the management of sexual difference, though this is the role that secularism has defined for religion, as Saba Mahmood notes.[7] It follows the example set by feminist legal scholar Lamia Rustum Shehadeh in stressing the entirety of the Lebanese legal system as it shapes and produces gendered modes of citizenship,[8] and argues that the regulation of sexuality is inextricable from this process. Sextarianism focuses our attention on how religious *and* civil laws and census bureaucracy stabilize the sex binary and different sexualities across different technologies of state power. Muslim majority states such as Lebanon are no different from any other state in their investment in an expanded view of sexual difference. Moreover, "Muslim majority states" may itself be a misnomer. Lebanon, Egypt, Pakistan, Indonesia, Morocco, Turkey, and Saudi Arabia are all "Muslim majority states," and they all regulate sexual difference differently, even in the arena of Muslim family law. The Lebanese legal system has more in common with the Israeli legal system than it does with most Muslim majority states. What Muslim majority states have in common is something they have in common with all states: the management of sexual difference itself.[9] Where they differ is in the historically specific tools and strategies to manage sexual difference. Sextarianism argues that liberal, secular, and nonliberal or secularizing states share an investment in the regulation of sexual difference. Indeed, it underlines how the mandate to secularize, as well as practices of secularization, are key vectors of state power. Sextarianism focuses on technologies of power that nation-states share regardless of their ideological, structural, or national inflections: bureaucracy, law, and the production and management of political difference through regimes of kinship. Lest we forget, citizenship itself is a regime of kinship based on the inheritability of status from parent to child.[10]

Law and Bureaucracy in Lebanon

Lebanese citizenship and statecraft are constituted along two axes of political difference: sectarian and sexual difference. To be a Lebanese citizen with a full set of attendant rights and duties, one must be a member of one of eighteen legally recognized religious sects. Official state discourse identifies all of these sects as minorities, a governing strategy used to negate any discussion of actual demographics. These minorities form the basis of power sharing in the Lebanese state. Personal status law, and with it the assigning of each citizen to a particular sect, is the primary mechanism of legal recognition by the state for separate sectarian groups, which then form the terrain for representation and participation in the state. French colonial authorities first established this system of recognition in 1936 with the implementation of administrative and civil order 60 LR, by which the state recognized different sectarian communities in Lebanon based on their adjudication of a separate personal law for kinship relations.[11] Citizens and residents inherit the jurisdiction of different personal status laws, regions, and religions from their fathers. In this way sectarian belonging itself is defined through sexual difference and patriarchal kinship regulations. Not only is sect a paternally inherited biopolitical category, citizenship itself is also exclusively inherited patrilineally.[12]

The three highest offices of the state—president, prime minister, and speaker of Parliament—are distributed to members of the three numerically largest sects—Maronite Christian, Sunni Muslim, and Shia Muslim. Parliamentary seats are allocated on a 1:1 ratio between Muslim and Christian members of parliament, the result of the post 1975–90 civil war settlement. The previous division of parliamentary seats was set under the French Mandate and favored Christian citizens over their Muslim counterparts. The logic of sectarian allocation is that equal political representation ensures sectarian harmony and protects Lebanese diversity and secularism. In effect, this logic suggests that political sectarianism emerged as a power-sharing agreement between preexisting antagonistic sectarian communities, and that the state is the neutral arena of compromise and debate between these preexisting political communities. But the state is not and has never been merely an arena of compromise. Instead, state power is deeply invested in producing, maintaining, and multiplying political difference as a practice of sovereignty.[13]

Academic literature on the Lebanese state has focused on the historical developments and operations of sectarianism, political sectarianism, regionalism, and, to a lesser extent, the production and protection of class interest.[14] This body of literature suggests that the management of sectarian difference is the primary mode of Lebanese statecraft and sovereignty[15] and theorizes political violence through a focus on sectarian violence,[16] Israeli-Lebanese violence, or Lebanese-Palestinian violence.[17] Notable interventions by feminist scholars have outlined how gendered and sexed differences have developed historically and in conjunction with sectarian differences in the arenas of law and state practice.[18] However, much of the literature on sectarianism in Lebanon, and in the Middle East more generally, does not engage with the role of laws that govern reproduction, sexual difference, and kinship. In other words, sectarianism does not appear as an embodied and biopolitical category. But sectarian citizens do not sprout, like mushrooms, from the ground. Instead they are structurally produced through laws and bureaucracies that regulate sexuality and gender. Sectarian and sexual differences are not two separate spheres of production and management, one of which can be added or subtracted from the other analytically or politically.

Sex and sect are themselves biopolitical categories:[19] They are defined at birth and categorized, quantified, and managed through state law and institutions at the level of the individual (citizen, noncitizen) and at the level of populations (sexes, sects, citizenry). One is not a cypher of the other. Sex is not an analytic frame to unlock or understand sect or vice versa. Instead, sect and sex are mutually constitutive modes of political difference. The "state effect," and indeed Lebanese sovereignty itself, emerges from the management of these modes of political difference.[20] The intractability of sex and sect manifests in law, legal practice, and in the regulation of citizenship and noncitizenship as multiple modalities of structural difference. In what follows, I build a theory of sextarianism across different arenas of Lebanese law and state practice: census bureaucracies, and personal status, civil, and criminal law. While I focus on the legal and bureaucratic registers of sextarianism, knowledge of the broader political, economic, social, and gendered dynamics at play in Lebanon is key. These broader factors often shape how laws are practiced in a courtroom, in judges' chambers, in lawyer's offices, and within civil and religious institutions. Furthermore, these dynamics are not static. Their historical movement continues to shape the practice of the Lebanese legal system. Thus, for example, the past fifty years of feminist advocacy as well as growing rates of women's employment and independence, including in the judiciary, have influenced the interpretation and application of law in Lebanon.[21] The 2019 uprising, in which feminist groups and demands played prominent roles, also reinvigorated debates on citizenship, census bureaucracy, and personal status law. More recently, Lebanon's financial crisis has pushed women's rights activists to demand economic reform such as equal pay and the right to financial guardianship over minor children. All of these demands would necessitate reforming a quilting point of the sextarian system, the census regime.

The Elementary Structures of Sext

Census registries are an integral biopolitical technology of the modern state, and the Lebanese state is no different: Census registries both individualize citizens and produce the citizenry as a unitary population and as a group of populations (sectarian, regional, sexed). They make possible birth, death, marriage and divorce, sectarian, and regional statistics. Censuses are methods that produce and reflect particular forms of knowledge. They are a dense site through which to think about the relationship between research and theory, on the one hand, and methodology and epistemology, on the other. This relationship creates a feedback loop.[22] A population census gathers and produces knowledge among a particular group of people, but the knowledge that informs a census itself decides whether a group of people is a population and what categories are relevant to know about that "population." Censuses are critical to the emergence, legitimization, and practice of state power.[23] They are also technologies of surveillance and securitization. The 1932 census made a "Lebanese" population legible for measurement, taxation, discipline, and securitization across a bounded piece of territory and diaspora. It produced a "national population" that aggregated clearly defined sectarian populations, sexes, and kinship relations—registration numbers were issued by heteropatriarchal family. The census also produced "populations" that were not citizens——most notably at the time, Kurdish stateless people.[24] The 1932 census claimed to reveal, but in fact produced, the "reality" of sectarian diversity.[25] The census evidenced an already existing—and competing—sectarian reality on which the state would be built as a zone of "compromise." The census bureaucracy that grew around the 1932 census normalized its disciplinary nature by using appeals to a "traditional" and patriarchal family structure, all the while constructing, regulating, and quantifying kinship and political relations through the axes of sexual difference. Sexual difference, for example, defines the collection, storage, and analysis of census, electoral, and demographic data. The census regime in Lebanon is the bureaucratic roadblock to women's ability to grant citizenship, is the mechanism through which sectarian status is reproduced via patriarchal inheritance, and is the basis on which regional origin/political representation is frozen in time. For these reasons, changing the census regime is critical for both anti-sectarian and anti-sexist activists.

Census data is stored and announced on a citizen's census document (*ikhrāj al- qayd*), one of three official documents issued by the state to citizens. The census document, the national identification card, and the passport are interchangeable for many bureaucratic procedures, but there are important differences between them. While passports assign an individual serial number to each citizen, census documents are organized by family, such that individuals from the same extended heteropatriarchal family carry the same registration number.[26] Each municipality has a census office that records and stores the data of citizens that belong to it.[27] An individual can request two types of census documents: an individual census document and a family document. Lebanese citizens are registered in their respective local census offices according to the organizational metrics of region of origin, kinship and/or marital status, personal status/sect, and sex. These four metrics determine which folder an individual's census information is placed in. Beirut is the only governorate that is not subdivided into districts. In a subdivided governate, the census information of the towns or cities that comprise it are aggregated and stored separately. However, in all governates citizens are disaggregated according to sect and placed as extended patriarchal families into separate digital and physical folders. It is on the basis of this shared sextarian folder that extended patriarchal family serial numbers are issued. Individuals who choose to remove their sect as a form of political protest[28] are still categorized in the larger sectarian folder because their family registration number does not change. Census records note when citizens have removed their sect, but thus far no structural change has been made to accommodate citizens without sects in the census registries.

Men and women—the only options offered by the state—are both registered according to the same organizational metrics: region, family, personal status, age, and sex. A citizen's sex, however, determines how this data is recorded and aggregated. For example, because serial numbers are distributed on the basis of extended patriarchal families, women citizens cannot be considered heads of families, circumscribing their ability to be considered legal and individual guardians of their children. They are either recorded into state registries as daughters of their fathers or wives of their husbands. In fact, when a female citizen gets married she is removed from her family serial number and added to that of her husband, a bureaucratic transfer that is reversed in case of divorce. Women can only be added or subtracted from these patriarchally organized databases of extended families; as mentioned earlier, they cannot be heads of families or individuals outside of patriarchal relations. As in the rest of the world, you must be registered to receive a birth certificate from the state and to be legally legible and traceable by state bureaucracy and institutions.

When women citizens are married and adopt their husbands' family serial number, they are automatically counted as "from" their husband's region.[29] This determines where they will vote in parliamentary and municipal elections, making the pressing need for a nonsectarian and one-district electoral law a feminist issue.[30] As it currently stands, women—a majority of eligible voters—are shuttled between their fathers and husbands in terms of their electoral agency and political representation. Children are automatically incorporated into their fathers' family serial numbers, "inheriting" their father's municipality and his sect. If the father changes his religion or sect or legally changes his municipality, his minor children's sectarian and/or regional status are automatically changed. A father's religious or sectarian conversion effectively places legal barriers between a mother and her minor children—unless she was initially from the different sect that he is converting to. A mother's conversion has no legal effect on her children, minority or otherwise.[31] Citizens who are assigned as female are registered and quantified in relation to male citizens as wives and/or daughters, while citizens assigned as male form the nodal points around which legal, bureaucratic, and kinship relations extend and contract.[32]

Citizenship law is intimately affected by and tied to the sexual regime of the census registries. Because women cannot be heads of families, they cannot "add" non-Lebanese husbands to their family serial numbers. Instead, Lebanese women who are married to non-Lebanese men are listed as "married" on their natal "family census document." However, they cannot initiate a new family census document for the family they create with their foreign husband. In contrast, non-Lebanese women who marry Lebanese male citizens are automatically incorporated into their husbands' family serial number through which they may file for and receive citizenship. During fieldwork I collected the life history of a young man who was trying to change his census registration from woman to man—a process that required him to sue the state for gender misrecognition. He told me the story of his friend who had succeeded in changing his sex in the census registry and was, with the help of his lawyers, hoping to marry his non-Lebanese girlfriend and grant her citizenship. This was not something he was able to do when he was identified as a woman in the census registries.[33] However, nationality law contains a loophole. If a woman citizen gives birth and nobody claims paternity over the child, the child in question can be incorporated into the maternal grandfather's family serial number and thus be eligible for citizenship.[34] This loophole exists only for children who are "unclaimed" by their natal fathers.[35]

Children of Men: Lebanese Citizenship Law Examined

Citizenship is a constellation of and a conduit for biopolitical techniques and power.[36] In practice, citizenship is an assemblage that is contingent, tense, and often articulated through contradiction. While citizenship is performative, it is always a marked form of citizenship that is being practiced and/or iterated. Theoretical abstractions such as the universal and unmarked citizen are fantasies of a mythical kind of state power that functions without governmentality, structural difference, or securitization.[37] The ideal of citizenship is always in the making[38] and never actually achieved. State power is produced and derived from the ability to define the normative ideal of citizenship and then measuring citizens' and residents' deviations from that ideal. States maintain the ability to measure, the authority to find wanting, and the power to discipline that which they have decided is wanting. Only through repetition across a disciplinary matrix does the stability of the category of the citizen appear (and disappear).[39] Crucially, the citizen can emerge as a legal and embodied subject position only if its negation, the noncitizen, is present. Lebanon has one of the highest refugee-to-citizen ratio in the world. For every three citizens residing in Lebanon, one refugee seeks shelter from wars in Palestine, Syria, Iraq, Yemen, Sudan, and elsewhere. Their movement and residence in Lebanon traces an arc of political violence—invasions, colonization, displacement, refugee securitization, and civil wars—that people in the Middle East have been living through for decades. In addition, hundreds of thousands of migrant laborers and expatriates live in Lebanon. The racialized, classed difference between the terms "expatriate" and "migrant laborer" refers to where workers migrate *from*, as well as the kinds of work they do. The difference is legally constructed, mainly because domestic workers are expressly excluded from labor law. For example, both an American professor at a university in Lebanon and the Ethiopian woman he hires to clean his home are migrant laborers, but race, class, and nationality inform their experience in Lebanon, and the categories used to refer to them—expatriate (professor) and migrant laborer (housecleaner). By 2022, the overall ratio between noncitizen and citizen residents was about 1:3.

The modern state, through biopolitical, governmental, and necro-political technologies of power, produces, quantifies, and regulates individuals and groups with individuating and totalizing identifiers: region, gender, name, sect, sex, religion, age, race, refugee, and citizenship. A citizen's sect, class, region/municipality, and gender together structure and contingently frame each practice of citizenship. Biopolitical power, after all, is not something that discrete subjects, or groups of subjects, are formed through or subjected to. Rather, biopolitical power functions at the interrelated national, transnational, and international scales. It works through abstraction, massification, and modulation across a given population; at heart, it is relational, about patterns in the modulation of securitization, reproductivity, and capacitation.[40] If biopolitical power and analysis tunes our attention to the making and measuring of normative and nonnormative bodies and groups, populations that are capacitated and debilitated, and statistical models of sectarian demography, then it also reveals these categories as existing only in relation to each other.[41] Biopolitics is the logic and praxis of that relation.

The majority of Lebanese citizens cannot grant citizenship to their spouses or children. This majority is diverse in terms of sect, income bracket, race, sexual orientation, religious belonging, and political affiliation. Despite this diversity, they have one thing in common: the Lebanese state characterizes them as "women."[42] Thus while a Lebanese woman could both theoretically and legally become the prime minister of Lebanon, under the current legal system she would have to be married to a Lebanese man to reproduce children who are Lebanese citizens. Even a woman who occupies the most privileged political, social, and economic positions cannot practice a right that every Lebanese man takes for granted.[43] The structural contradiction between the constitutional principle of equality and citizenship law was emphasized by Lebanese lawyer and civil rights activist Nadine Moussa when she announced her candidacy for the Lebanese presidency in 2016, making her the first-ever woman candidate for the post.[44] Moussa is married to a non-Lebanese man; her children are not Lebanese citizens, despite having lived their entire lives in Lebanon. Women's rights activists have argued that the Lebanese constitution's guarantee of equality to all citizens is contradicted by Lebanese nationality law because only the foreign spouses of men citizens are eligible for naturalization.[45]

The denial of full citizenship rights to women carries legal, economic, and social consequences. The children of Lebanese women and non-Lebanese men must have a visa to enter or reside in Lebanon, pay more to access public education, and require a permit to work legally in the country. This paperwork and its regular filing, storing, and processing are economic, psychological, and emotional burdens. Additionally, laws limit how much property non-Lebanese residents can own and how that property is inherited.[46] Because they are considered Palestinian by the state, the children of Lebanese mothers and Palestinian fathers are not allowed to work in most professional fields, nor are they eligible for government aid in times of crisis. The stakes of these exclusions became clear in 2020, with Lebanon caught between a global pandemic and an economic meltdown, necessitating both the need for aid and for health and first aid professionals. The economic and legal distinctions made between the children of Lebanese men and women—the difficulties that children of Lebanese mothers face—are not neutral. They are coercive. Lebanese law discourages citizens who are women from marrying foreigners, while there are no legal barriers to Lebanese men marrying non-Lebanese women of any nationality.[47] However, General Security has imposed security measures on foreign women from specific nationalities, namely Syrian and Palestinian women and women who have worked under either an artist[48] visa or a domestic worker visa. When Syrian or Palestinian women marry Lebanese men, General Security attaches a note to their names in the database of foreigners in the country. This security note is removed and the woman granted citizenship only after three years of marriage and after the woman has given birth to a child. If a woman has not given birth to a child, she must submit a medical report. The timeframe for women on an artist or a domestic worker visa who have not given birth is extended to five years instead of three. These regulations are illegal, racist, and sexist. Still, they have been imposed by General Security and implicitly accepted by civil personal status courts. Feminists and women's rights activists have been fighting for a woman's right to grant citizenship for decades, and it was a demand that feminists centered in the October 2019 uprising. These feminists and their allies deployed a slogan that indicted the sextarian nature of citizenship law: To hell with sectarian parity.

The specter of sectarian balance saturates current debates and efforts to amend Lebanese citizenship law. Political leaders, op-ed writers, and ordinary citizens frame women's citizenship rights as a back door to the naturalization of Palestinian refugees and, more recently, Syrian refugees. The anxiety around potential refugee naturalization is predicated on demographic fears and realities in the sectarian power-sharing system.[49] Xenophobia, classism, and racism directed at Palestinians and Syrians inflect this demographic anxiety.[50] Sextarianism, as a biopolitical modality of power, shapes and genders the ways that birth, marriage, and emigration patterns produce demographic anxieties. The debate on granting Lebanese women rights equal to their male counterparts is refracted through the question of sectarian parity and the declining share of Christians in the country's demography. Within this framework political leaders who are for women's citizenship rights are accused of sectarianism by political leaders who are not. This accusation is based on the fact that the Sunni sect in Lebanon would grow if Palestinian refugees were naturalized and would double if Syrian refugees were naturalized. The sextarian panic over the settlement of refugees and their potential impact on the demography inflects the highest law of the land, the Constitution of Lebanon. The constitution's preamble links the unity of Lebanon and to the principle of nonsettlement: "Lebanese territory is one for all Lebanese. Every Lebanese shall have the right to live in any part thereof and to enjoy the rule of law wherever he resides. There shall be no segregation of the people on the basis of any type of belonging, and no fragmentation, partition, or settlement of non-Lebanese in Lebanon." If the majority of Palestinian or Syrian refugees in Lebanon were Christian, the debate over their demographic "danger" might look different. After all, most Christian Palestinian refugees *were* naturalized (via presidential decree) and have by now held Lebanese citizenship for generations.[51]

Lebanese citizenship law was amended in 2015, but not to grant women the right to pass on citizenship. Instead the reforms ensured that foreigners of Lebanese origin could apply for and receive Lebanese citizenship. Many hoped the amendment would further buttress the number of Christian Lebanese citizens, as Christians form a majority of the generations-old Lebanese diaspora.[52] The former minister of foreign affairs and member of Parliament, Gibrān Bassīl—a popular target of the 2019 uprising for his xenophobia, sectarianism, and alleged corruption—made clear that amending the nationality law to grant equal rights to women is a sextarian problem. Far from rectifying the sextarian bargain made at women's expense, the 2015 amendments to the nationality law preserved and extended it by making it applicable to the Lebanese diaspora.

The challenges of extending the right to pass citizenship status to the children and spouses of Lebanese women are grounded in the structural conditions of sexual difference and the masculinist state. Women's exclusion from full citizenship rights is due to the ideological praxis of political sectarianism as a secular regime that centers religious pluralism and equality, the sectarian number crunching inspired by that regime, sextarian bureaucracies, and a sexist discourse that places the "needs" of sects above the equality of Lebanese women. Giving women the ability to pass on citizenship would be a step toward assuring that all citizens have equal political, economic, and civic rights, at least on paper. However, extending full citizenship rights to women would require a complete overhaul of the census regime and how it defines, regulates, and produces sextarian difference.

The discursive and structural functions of sextarianism, as seen through Lebanese citizenship law, demonstrate women citizens' conditional incorporation into the state. They inherit citizenship from their fathers but cannot bequeath it to their children. Instead, they reproduce the sexual and sectarian exception that Lebanese nationality is predicated on.[53] Moreover, the debate over "giving" Lebanese women full citizenship rights revolves around sextarianism. Women's marriage and procreative choices are said to endanger Lebanon's sectarian balance. The same concern over demographic balance is never issued over the fact that Lebanese men have been marrying non-Lebanese Muslims (and Christians) and granting them and their children citizenship for generations.[54] Specifically, granting Lebanese women married to refugee and stateless men in Lebanon the right to pass citizenship to their children and spouses is framed as a sectarian demographic "problem." Political sectarianism is not simply a regime that represents the political concerns of citizens. It is a regime of securitization that defines populations that can *never* be citizens. The "sex bargain,"[55] alongside the "sect bargain," produces and stabilizes citizenship and nationalism. Lebanese statecraft and practices of sovereignty emerge from the management of conflict emanating from the sect and sex bargain within Lebanese law. While gendered pacts entrench sectarianism and sectarian practices in Lebanon, I suggest, with Suad Joseph, that the relationship cuts both ways. Sectarian pacts also entrench gendered pacts and heteropatriarchal sexual ideologies and practices.[56]

Sex, not sect, is foundational to Lebanese law. Criminal codes distinguish between the rape of a stranger and the rape of a wife. They also afford leniency to crimes against women under the rubric of "passion" or mitigating circumstances.[57] Civil law and bureaucracy register women citizens as legal dependents of their fathers or husbands. Women's political representation and electoral agency are determined not by where they live but by where their husbands or fathers are identified as originally "from." Nationality laws and procedures ensure that women cannot pass citizenship to spouses and children. All fifteen personal status laws distinguish between the rights and duties of men and women identified persons. Labor law grants women the right to resign from their jobs when they gets married and still be entitled to severance pay, a right that men do not have. Article 14 of the National Social Security Fund law states that social security covers both the insured and the insured's family members. However, insured male spouses can extend coverage to their wives without conditions, whereas insured women can only grant coverage to their husbands if they over 60 years old or are incapable of providing for themselves because of physical or mental disabilities. It is difficult, if not impossible, to study Lebanon without enumerating the various ways that sextarian difference shapes daily life, law, power, politics, and the economy.

Personal Status and Sexual Difference

Kinship regimes are a political technology that shape and give legal form to ideologically inflected and coercive forms of intimacy.[58] Each of the fifteen current personal status laws distinguishes between the rights and duties of men and women. Civil, criminal, and nationality laws—laws that apply to all citizens—also differentiate systematically between these categories. As such, there are almost thirty articulations of structural sex-based differentiated Lebanese citizenship. For example, a Sunni Muslim woman and a Maronite Christian woman cannot transfer their Lebanese citizenship to their foreign husbands or to their children. However, the

Sunni Muslim woman will inherit one-half of a share of her father's or mother's estate according to Islamic inheritance laws, whereas the Maronite woman will inherit a full share under a civil law that adjudicates inheritance for non-Muslims. While both Maronite and Greek Orthodox men can legally coerce or force their wives to have sex, Maronite men cannot divorce them. The modern Lebanese state regulates the intersection between rights, sex, and kinship through the simultaneous application of civil and personal status law and through civil institutions that provide oversight over the legal system as a whole. The interstitial nature of personal status, civil, and criminal law makes possible one of the main functions of the nation-state: to produce a body of people who, although differentiated by sex and sect, are unified under the overarching category of Lebanese citizenship.

There are important differences between the incorporation of Christian personal status courts and Muslim personal status courts into the state. Christian courts are institutionally separate and enjoy a greater measure of independence. The lack of state oversight can leave Lebanese Christians in a more vulnerable position than their Muslim counterparts. Muslim courts include a public prosecutor and an inspector, who are supposed to play supervisory roles in court proceedings.[59] Muslim citizens who are divorcing have the right to demand that a civil representative review legal proceedings to ensure that the rights of both plaintiffs are respected. Christian citizens do not have this right. Similarly, the fees associated with legal proceedings at Muslim personal status courts are standardized across the country, while the cost of initiating a divorce in Christian personal status courts can differ dramatically. Perhaps most importantly, all Lebanese citizens are allowed to enter Muslim personal status courts because they are considered an aspect of the Lebanese legal system and thus cannot discriminate against citizens based on sectarian affiliation. This is not the case for Christian courts, which have the right to demand that those entering the court or practicing within it are Christians, and often Christians of the same sect.

Many argue that the solution to the problem of sexual difference in personal status law is the adoption of an optional, secular personal status law.[60] While the adoption of such a law would indeed be a great benefit to the many Lebanese couples in heterosexual relationships who could choose to be under its jurisdiction, the law itself would be promulgated under the precepts of French Mandate era 60 LR.[61] Directive 60 LR, and its afterlives within Lebanese law, affects Muslim and Christians differently. Colonial and postcolonial law created a system in which Lebanese citizens can marry anywhere in the world and register that contract with census authorities, and Lebanese judges at the civil personal status courts must adjudicate all conflicts resulting from that contract according to its original precepts. On any given day, the civil personal courts in Lebanon may be adjudicating laws that govern divorce in Cyprus, Germany, France, Turkey, or different states in the United States of America. But if the couple in question are both Muslim, personal courts hold jurisdiction regardless of where the marriage contract originates from.[62] To make things even more complicated, most international secular marriage laws do not include custody or inheritance, and any areas not explicitly within marriage law return to personal status jurisdiction. The differences between a marriage law and personal status law—both laws of sexual difference—are key to these lived realities. Ultimately, any optional, or compulsory civil marriage law should be judged on its content and not its civil or secular packaging. A civil law marriage law, for example, may still legislate different marriage ages for men and women, differentiate financial settlements and obligations in divorces based on sex, or define marriage as between a man and a woman. Finally, the adoption of an optional law will not affect the structural nature of sexual difference to personal status, civil, nationality, or criminal law. It will not disrupt or transform the sectarianian organization and bureaucratic praxis of the Lebanese state. An optional civil marriage law, depending on its content, is a necessary measure to meet the needs and rights of couples in heterosexual relationships. But moving the state's exercise of power away from sectarianism necessitates reconfiguring the entire legal and bureaucratic system and the ways it coproduces sexual and sectarian differences.

The constitutive nature of sexual difference to the Lebanese legal system is evident in cases involving religious and/or sectarian conversion. In fact, sexual difference often engenders the choice and ability *to* convert. When both members of a married couple convert to the same sect, the new sect's personal status replaces the previous as having the force of law. For example, a Maronite couple may convert to Greek Orthodoxy together to apply for a divorce. However, if the husband alone converts to Islam, he may marry a new wife under Ḥanafī (Sunni) personal status or Ja'farī (Shi'i) jurisprudence, while his first wife remains married to him under Maronite law.[63] Similarly, a Sunni man who has daughters but no sons can convert to Shi'a Islam to assure that his daughters inherit the majority of his estate.[64] Thus religious conversion is also effectively a conversion between structurally produced modes of sexed citizenship. In fact, many of these conversions are done with the express purpose of changing one's gendered rights or duties. The Plenary Assembly rarely overturns conversions, even those that seem obviously done in order to remarry, divorce, or bequeath, despite the fact that conversion with the intent to manipulate law is illegal.[65] In fact, when women plaintiffs sue their spouses and ex-spouses for fraud due to their conversion and subsequent use of a different set of gendered rights, the Lebanese state protects those conversions on the grounds of freedom of religion and the nested independence of personal status courts, a subject that chapter 3 turns to. Thus claims of fraud and discrimination in the application of personal status law are rerouted by high court jurists toward the state's role to protect religious freedom, the harmony of the legal system, public order, and sectarian coexistence. These discursive and legal acts produce the state's sovereignty and secularism.[66] The protection of Lebanon's sectarian diversity, and thus its practice of secularism, is articulated through the maintenance of multiple and modular forms of sexual difference.[67] The principles of "public order"—used by the Assembly in cases related to conversion, divorce, or inheritance, and "public morality"—used mainly in criminal cases to securitize sexuality—reveal the sextarian nature of the legal system as a whole. Of course, only the sextarian state, via its courts, has the right to define the content of both public order and public morality.

Criminal Law

Conflicts over the "sex bargain" are fought, managed, and resolved across all areas of Lebanese law: constitutional and nationality law, personal status law, civil law, labor law, and criminal law. The sextarian institutions of the state have been a battleground for feminists and women's rights activists, a contradiction familiar to feminist organizing the world over.[68] For years, feminist activists and their allies have lobbied the state to take domestic violence seriously, a campaign that resulted in the passage of a domestic violence law in 2014,[69] a national domestic violence hotline, and domestic violence sensitivity training for security forces. Yet migrant domestic laborers, a highly racialized and precarious category of labor performed mainly by women and girls from countries in sub-Saharan Africa and South and East Asia are excluded from the protections of the family violence law and thus any other new state service resulting from it. They are not included in the definition of "family members" whose protection falls under the domestic violence law. While the law applies to migrants within their own families, it does not apply to their workplaces, where they are also excluded from labor laws. Migrant domestic labor is employed under the Kafala system of labor—a system that activists in Lebanon and across the world have characterized as legal enslavement. The refusal to fold domestic laborers into the protections of family violence law is in contradiction to their growing centrality within Lebanese families. These women are critical to the production and maintenance of Lebanese domestic space—the so-called private sphere. The system of Kafala recenters the "family" as a sextarian political unit by ensuring that foreign domestic laborers are racialized and constitutive outsiders.[70] Thus while the labor that produces Lebanese families is increasingly transnational and multiracial, only Lebanese citizens in that family unit are granted the right to claim domestic violence before the courts. Differences exist between people who can appeal to Lebanese courts and who are only subject to them, whether in theory or in practice. These differences are key to understanding how sectarianism reproduces political society across an intersectional grid that includes not only sexes and sects and citizens and noncitizens, but modular and multiple articulations of all these categories—which are all embedded within a system of relation. Thus even though Syrian refugee labor and migrant domestic labor are governed by the same system of Kafala, racism and anti-blackness animate the differences between experiences of Kafala, as does gender and the *site* of labor.[71] Syrian refugees (men, women, and children) working under a Kafala system labor on farms, as doormen and building superintendents, in construction or in sanitation. Women migrant workers are multinational and multiracial, and labor mostly inside the home. Men who are migrant workers are rarely employed inside homes. Critically, Syrian refugees are not separated from their families and social/economic/intimate networks through Kafala [they may be by war] precisely because they are not travelling to Lebanon in order to work; and if they do, the distance is a matter of an hours' long car or bus ride. The racializing effects of the Kafala system are perhaps best understood in relation to Lebanese "sponsors," who through their mastery over another person's labor and residency status participate in a global regime of racial capitalism—one that helps produce transnational whiteness as the ability to consume, exploit, master, and securitize the labor of others.

Criminal law in Lebanon differentiates between men and women in important ways, sometimes prescribing different sentencing precepts or regimes of evidence for men and women who are accused of committing the same crime. For example, adultery is a "crime" for both men and women, as well as grounds for divorce in personal status law—but loopholes exist for adulterous husbands, not wives, in personal status laws. Similar to "adultery," "honor" is a legal category constructed across multiple bodies of law. Article 562 of the criminal code, which provided a framework for lesser sentences in crimes committed out of concern for honor, was targeted by feminist activists and successfully repealed in 2011. Article 252, however, which provides lesser punishment for a crime if it was committed "in a state of anger" because of a dangerous act done by the victim, remains on the books and in practice. While this article is open to broad interpretation, it has been used to provide lesser sentences to those who commit "crimes of passion," a crime classification that in practice is deeply gendered.[72] Additionally, abortion is illegal in all cases except to save a mother's life, but a lesser sentence is possible if the abortion was undertaken out of concern for family status or honor. "Unnatural" sexual acts, largely interpreted by Lebanese jurists to indicate sex between men or between women, is illegal. A woman who cohabitates with a man or who lives alone can be investigated or, more likely, threatened with allegations of prostitution, a tactic that has been deployed in rent disputes between women tenants and their landlords.[73] Heterosexual marriage is the only licit sexual venue for citizens who are women—but even within heterosexual marriage women's sexuality is not autonomous. The family violence law of 2014 law[74] makes an exception for marital rape, a form and practice of violence not recognized as a crime in any body of law.[75] Through this nexus of law and extra-legal practice, the state constructs and regulates the heteropatriarchal family as the ideal form of intimacy and as the only legitimate sphere for women's reproductive sexuality. This heteropatriarchal family is deeply masculinist: Men are the heads of families in census registries, the conduit for the citizenship of children, and the de facto legal guardians of their minor children. The constitution of women citizens as the legal dependents of their husbands or fathers, coupled with the state's legalization of forms of gendered violence, in effect distributes those forms of gendered violence to the heteropatriarchal family.[76]

Rarely is gendered violence considered political violence.[77] Yet like sectarian violence, gendered violence emerges from a complex knot of legal, historical, social, and economic factors. Like sectarian violence, gendered violence is distributed across and articulated through law, bureaucracy, and, as Paul Amar and Suad Joseph have elaborated, parastatal actors.[78] In the case of gendered violence, the heteropatriarchal family should be understood as parastatal actor, a structure that operates as a satellite of state norms and power. The state maintains its sovereign right to produce and regulate sexual difference and sectarian difference, but distributes and shares its sovereign right to regulate sexual, national, and racial difference to parastatal actors within a shared heteropatriarchal ideological space. The Lebanese state and the heteropatriarchal family are joined in the regulation, application, and experience of the system of Kafala, for example. Under Kafala, the state vests the heteropatriarchal family with the power to operate as a satellite of labor, immigration, and criminal law. The state and the heteropatriarchal family are also conjoined carceral sites for migrant domestic workers. Employers regularly confiscate the travel documents of migrant domestic workers, lock them into rooms or houses, and deny them freedom of movement, of sociality, and of intimacy. The Kafala system allows employers to "test" migrant domestic workers for pregnancy, and if they test positive they are deported by the state.[79] There is a general lack of accountability for sexual, physical, or psychological abuse—or for withholding salaries from their Kafala employees. But Lebanese jails and detention sites are filled with African and South and East Asian women migrant workers accused of stealing from, lying about, or hitting/harming their employers (often in self-defense). When women escape from one carceral site—the home—employers can call on the state, and the state often incarcerates them again for having broken their Kafala agreement. Chapter 5 explores more fully the heteropatriarchal family's role as a parastatal actor.

Given the constitutive nature of sexual difference to Lebanese law, citizenship, and statecraft, the passage of a family violence law in 2014 was a watershed event. Yet precisely because the logic and praxis of sectarianism is hegemonic and expressed both through the hypervisibility of difference *and* its intersectional effects, legal reform may take us only so far. Imagine, for example, laws that make sectarian killings a "hate crime" in a sectarian political and legal system. Such a law might make killing a Sunni because she is a Sunni a crime, but it would do nothing to address how material and legal conditions produced and identified this citizen as "Sunni" to begin with.[80] Similarly, the removal of the "sex bargain" from Lebanese citizenship as an entire edifice of rights, laws, and duties necessitates an overhaul of criminal, civil, personal status, labor, procedural, and nationality laws. Racialized national and sectarian "outsiders"—most prominently domestic and migrant labor, and Syrian and Palestinian refugees—hold the legal and bureaucratic architecture of sectarianism together.[81]

Sectarianism is a theory of state power that does not separate or privilege sectarian difference from sexual difference and emphasizes the traffic *between* religious and secular modalities of power when it comes to regulating sextarian difference. Parastatal actors such as the heteropatriarchal family are also actors in a sextarian system, in that patriarchal laws and bureaucracies scaffold that formation. The fact that sexual difference is an integral part of political difference is not unique to Lebanon,[82] nor are the ways that kinship and intimacy are regulated as parts and parcels of state power.[83] Lebanon represents a site of intensification, not exceptionalism. The "social contract" is not only an origin story for political practice and theory, but the initial signers of this social construct—posited in classic political theory as rational, individual, property owning, and disembodied actors—gendered male and deracinated—are just as mythological. Indeed, as feminist and queer theory has taught us, citizens have *bodies that matter*,[84] bodies that both operate in the political sphere and are constructed and regulated through political processes. Sextarianism follows this feminist rethinking of political theory and practice, recenters it in colonial and postcolonial frameworks, and rethinks the diffuse relationships between the religious and the secular outside of the binary of private/public.

Grounding a theory of sextaranism in Lebanon draws attention to the centrality of sexual difference to and for state power, and to how sectarian and religious differences are structured as modalities of sexual difference.[85] Sextarianism inspires and articulates demographic, democratic, and ideological fantasies, contradictions, and practices. Sextarianism makes possible the nationalist ideal of "coexistence"—through the making and cohering of quantifiable sects and sectarian demography—and forms the ideological and legal basis of political inclusion and exclusion in service of that ideal. A sextarian reading of political sectarianism, for example, emphasizes how it manifests as a securitization of women's reproductive and marriage practices through an exclusionary citizenship law. Approaching the Lebanese state through a focus on sextarianism allows us to think more capaciously about sectarian political difference, by highlighting the ways in which sectarian difference is dependent on, emergent with, and articulated together with sexual difference and the regulation of heteronormative reproductive sexuality at the level of law and bureaucracy. And yet, while so much academic work about Lebanon focuses on sectarianism and political sectarianism, very few studies actually explain how "sect" is structurally reproduced. The hesitance to do so, this unseeing, may be in part because it would be impossible to do so without studying its relation to sex. This unseeing is active: It creates a universal political subject emptied of the conditions of their historical production, and it constructs male experiences of state power and of sectarianism as universal. A focus on law, bureaucracy, and everyday experience, however, reveals that there is no practice of sectarianism, sovereignty, or citizenship that is not marked by sexual difference. The structures and institutions of the state produce multiple variations of sextarian subject positions that are legally and bureaucratically bound, and socially, politically, and economically refracted. Only when we bring sexual and sectarian difference together in our analysis can we understand, and transform, the ideology, arrangement, and effects of state power.

CHAPTER 2

A Fire in the Archive

History, Ethnography, Multiplicity

"You remember that, don't you?"

—Mona, to me, in conversation

I MET THE PRESIDENT OF the State Shura Council when he gave a lecture on war and justice in Lebanon at Columbia University's law school. This jurist, whom I will call Youssef, became an important interlocuter throughout my fieldwork. Our relationship began with an argument. In Lebanon, Youssef has been publicly accused of corruption in relation to postwar reconstruction. In his talk, Youssef recounted his support for a private corporation, Solidere, to seize much of downtown Beirut under a form of eminent domain, after a fifteen-year civil war. At the time, Youssef headed committees that determined the amount of compensation given to real estate owners and tenants forced from their properties.[1] Today it is easy to forget that 80 percent of the old city was demolished by postwar reconstruction and not by the war itself.[2] At the time, the civil war had just ended, and downtown Beirut—long a middle- and working-class commercial and residential sector—was part of the "green line" that had separated the city's two halves during wartime. Following decisions taken by the judiciary and Parliament, Solidere, under the leadership of then prime minister Rafik Hariri, confiscated the vast majority of privately owned shops, apartments, and land of the old city.[3]

During the question-and-answer period, I asked Youssef about his role in and support of eminent domain to dispossess more than 100,000 "claimants"[4]—property owners, residents, and renters—just after they had survived fifteen years of civil war, and transform downtown Beirut into a playground for wealthy tourists and members of the Lebanese

FIGURE 2. Photograph of Roman statue inside Ministry of Justice/ Cassation Courthouse, 2019. Papers and a pack of cigarettes can be seen.

diaspora. At the time, Columbia University was threatening to use eminent domain to expand into Manhattanville. The specter of a powerful, rich, and elite university mobilizing its considerable resources to dispossess its poorer, less white, and less powerful neighbors was a political issue on campus and in New York City. Throughout this battle I had Beirut on my mind, and I linked the two in my question to the jurist from Lebanon. After a back and forth, I was invited to join him, my professor at the law school, and his son for drinks. We had a lot of fun. We continued to debate and argue our way around a bottle of wine,[5] our laughter as loud as our disagreements and sometimes indistinguishable. Youssef and I were decades apart in age, were from different regions and religions, and had vastly different politics. But we did have some things in common: We both spoke multiple languages, enjoyed the art of a good argument, and were passionate about the same area of research: law. He was pleased that social science research would be conducted at the judiciary, a sentiment multiple people expressed throughout my fieldwork, and he took me under his wing.[6]

I called Youssef when I arrived home. He invited me to his office at the Ministry of Justice and Beirut Courthouse complex, the scene—alongside long lunches at restaurants and cafes near his workplace—of our meetings. We were sipping coffee in his office one day when he called the archivists at the Court of Cassation and introduced me as a PhD researcher. The court's chief archivist and clerk, Evelyn, introduced me to Mona, the archivist of the Plenary Assembly and the person I worked most closely with during my research. Mona and I quickly discovered that we were from the same neighborhood in Beirut, *tarīq al jadīda* (new street).[7] There are multiple ways to describe *tarīq al jadīda* and indeed all of the different areas of Beirut, but sectarian and classist discourse fixes the neighborhood as a tightknit community wary of outsiders. In this discourse there is only one kind of insider or outsider: a sectarian one, and *tarīq al jadīda* is described as the city's "Sunni bastion" of the working and middle classes. It turned out that Mona had been my aunt's neighbor for years and knew my cousins, many of whom still lived only a block or two away from her. This neighborly connection shaped our interactions at the archives. I was now accountable to my family for my comportment at the judiciary, a form of accountability more immediate and pressing than my distant dissertation committee. To Mona, I represented someone from the neighborhood she could be proud of for getting a PhD abroad and being a young woman living all by herself in New York City. Our exchanges folded us deeper into an archive of shared experience[8] and an economy of favors that had linked our families for years. Mona and I formed an "us" who debated over the best bakeries in *tarīq al jadīda* and who were about specific forms of rootedness despite our different mobilities. Mona and I were not only from the same sect, we were both women in that sect. We shared a sextarian positionality vis-à-vis the state, and at times, she seemed to be offering me advice on how to navigate that position. For example, she once outlined the specific clauses Sunni women could add to marriage contracts to make them more equitable, as she handed a divorce case file to me. When we were discussing a particularly nasty custody case, Mona remarked that only women with more wealth or status than their husbands stood a chance at evening out the sextarian system. "Make sure to marry a poor man," she said to me, laughing.

Youssef and I had a different kind of "us"—one based on social class, educational status, and transnational mobility, even though he and I did not share the same sectarian or sexed positionality vis-à-vis the state. His sextarian position came with more civil, political, and economic rights than either Mona's or mine. When I asked them separately about the necessities of legal reform, at the forefront of Mona's mind was nationality law. She was angry that a group of her relatives were not Lebanese because their mother had married a Palestinian man. On the other hand, Youssef believed administrative reform was necessary to bolster the efficiency, transparency, and legitimacy of the judiciary. They were both right, but their delivery also told a story. Mona was angry and personalized the effects of the nationality law; Youssef, who shared a loud and gregarious personality with Mona, was coolly analytic. Both Mona and Youssef were powerful figures at the judiciary. One had control over the archive of Lebanon's highest court, and the other over an entire regulatory branch of the legal system. Their power manifested, circulated, and was compensated at different scales, but both were critical figures in the state apparatus. Some mornings I would follow Mona as she worked, breaking for cheap coffee poured into a small plastic cup; later I would have lunch with Youssef at a chic café near the Ministry. They were both invested in teaching me the ways of their world, and the three of us shared a sense of humor. This intimacy allowed us to broach difficult subjects that often became heated disagreements about contemporary politics and politicians. With both Mona and Youssef, it was intimacy that facilitated argument, and argument that facilitated more intimacy.

I have been conducting ethnographic and archival research at the judiciary on and off for more than a decade. Mostly, this has meant spending time in the archives and clerk's offices[9] at the Beirut Courthouse and the law library of the lawyer's syndicate. Although I began my research focused solely on religious conversion, my interests expanded and shifted the more research I conducted and the more sectarianism came into view with every court case and conversation. Early on I asked my interlocutors—archivists, judges, and lawyers—to share case files that they thought were important or that had occupied and weighed on them. What case files did *they* think reflected the work of law and of the court system, the aporias of sovereignty, and the stakes of religious conversion? Mona and her boss, Evelyn, both suggested Samera's case to me, but for different reasons. Evelyn wanted me to see how such an important case had almost been burnt to a crisp, and Mona wanted me to see Samera. Knowledge production and theorization are always already collaborative efforts that are embedded in power relations. Expertise functions and shapes any given arena of research; a court clerk/archivist might illustrate the workings of the Lebanese state through a different case file than an anthropologist or a historian or a nonacademic activist would. Marking this difference places academic expertise alongside, and not above, a different form of expertise that makes much of our work possible: that of archivists themselves.

The archive of the Court of Cassation is not a room you can enter and exit: except, of course, it is. You could identify a case, ask an archivist for it, watch her walk into a room, emerge with a file, and then read that case alone in a corner at the Beirut Courthouse. Instead of staging archival and ethnographic research as a set of extractive and authorial encounters, I suggest a research and writing practice that centers not the archival object itself but the assemblage that makes *that thing*, the archival object, both legible and knitted into a larger economy of knowledge production.[10] Archives *are* this assemblage of people, paper, processes, temporalities, desires, economies, memories, arguments, and affects—all open to the reversals of time.[11] Giving up control—or perhaps, giving up the *fantasy* of control—can potentiate research as a line of flight[12] rather than as a goal or a point of departure.

This chapter focuses on two case files held in the Cassation Court archive—cases that Mona suggested to me. She offered one case file of a notorious civil-war time militia leader who is currently the head of a political party well represented in the Lebanese Parliament—for reasons I still cannot fathom. That case was decided by the Judicial Council. The other file Mona shared to help me illustrate the work of archivists and was from the Plenary Assembly at the Court of Cassation. Mona was the archivist of both courts. The Plenary Assembly case began in 1982—the year the Israeli army occupied Beirut. It concerned inheritance claims. Because the family in question was Christian, their case was heard at the Civil Personal Status Court, and the sons and daughters, and their heirs, would inherit equally. After a decision was issued, the case file was burnt in a fire at the court archives following a night of intense fighting and rocket barrages. The family began a new case, asking for certification of their personal photocopy of the decision as an original, and thus actionable, legal document. Once certified as the original, the photocopy would be refiled in the archive and become a citable source for both addendums to the case itself and to the jurisprudential and historical record of the Assembly. In its 1992 iteration, the case focused largely on bureaucratic practice—the Assembly's ability to differentiate, decide between, and authenticate legal documents. The second, Judicial Council case file Mona shared with me is infamous in Lebanon; it was the case against Samir Geagea for crimes committed during and after the civil war. To date, Geagea is the only militia leader to have spent time behind bars. Almost every leader in the civil war era has either been assassinated, has died, or is "in" politics. Upon being pardoned in 2005, Geagea joined his war-time brethren as a postwar political leader. In both the Plenary Assembly and the Judicial Council case files, that of the photocopy and that of Geagea, the civil war was an active subject, setting, and experience. I draw attention to the multiplicity of narratives, social worlds, and actions as they relate to war, archives, and ethnography. Meaning is indeterminate, opaque, and unknowable. Indeterminacy opens insights into the historiographic, political, and affective realms of archival and ethnographic research and theory. By indeterminacy I mean the multiple and sometimes contradictory meanings, intentions, and effects that exist within one interaction, action, or statement[13]—and the ways that multiplicity is often disciplined into linear and professional productions of history through technologies of archival curation—or the archival disciplining of *what might have happened* into regimes of truth.[14]

A Life in the Archive

Mona began working at the judiciary in 1985. She is a trained archeologist and classicist, a mother, and a grandmother. During the years I conducted fieldwork, Mona was responsible for maintaining the archives and the ongoing cases of the Plenary Assembly at the Court of Cassation and the Judicial Council. While the Assembly is the highest court that ordinary citizens have access to, the Council is an originating and final criminal court that has jurisdiction over crimes committed against the internal or external security of the state, such as political assassinations, and crimes against the public, such as terrorism. The judges that sit on the Plenary Assembly and the Judicial Council are both drawn from the Cassation Courts and overlap, and the same clerk works in both courts and their archives. Mona's professional responsibilities and her work life did not begin and end in courtrooms, offices, and in archives. She also spent hours offering legal advice, quoting jurisprudential tenets, remembering the history of the court and its jurists, and sometimes providing a shoulder to cry on. Everybody—from jurist to lawyer to clerk to coffee delivery boy to plaintiff—knew that she was powerful. Early on in my research, Mona told me she was going to convert from Sunni to Shi'i Islam. I told her that I found her impending conversion to be a funny coincidence, given that the case files I was researching and that she was helping me find were specifically about religious conversion and the Plenary Assembly's role in arbitrating between personal status courts. She threw up her hands and said, "What can we do? We only had girls, and I'm not going to allow my husbands' brothers to take my money," in a reference to the different inheritance laws practiced by these two Muslim sects. As an archivist of Lebanon's highest court, she understood the sextarian system inside out. She knew that conversion can be the easiest and cheapest way to ensure her daughters actually inherited the entirety of her and her husband's estate.[15] In this regard, Mona and her husband were not alone. While there is a regional and national fear in Lebanon over a sectarian Muslim civil war (*fitna*), most married Sunni couples I knew had converted when they had "only" daughters. At the same time, I didn't know one Sunni couple who had a son and had converted, because in the presence of a son the inheritance rules of Shi'i and Sunni Islam are the same: Sons inherit one full share to a daughter's half. The banal, sextarian nature of religious conversion troubled narratives of hardened sectarian difference and simultaneously revealed how state practices of religious coexistence and secularism in Lebanon function through the maintenance of unequal regimes of sexual difference.

Tracing the life worlds of the archive challenges dominant historical narratives of civil war, occupations, and invasions by emphasizing the daily workings, as opposed to the failings, of a wartime state.[16] For fifteen years, the warring factions of the Lebanese Civil War killed upward of 150,000 people, mostly civilians, and maimed many more. Thirty percent of the prewar population of 2.576 million emigrated, and another 33 percent were internally displaced. Four percent of the resident population were wounded, and about 19,300 people forcibly disappeared during the civil war.[17] Throughout these years, citizens continued to turn toward the judiciary to adjudicate the mundane and the quotidian—and the judiciary continued to answer that call. Wartime legal argumentation and the life world of the Cassation Court archives reveal the place of memory, or the act of remembering, in constructing and living continuity in Lebanese jurisprudence and history. This life world unfolds archives as threshold places of war and peace, of history and anthropology, and of theory and methodology.

The analytic and political common sense has been to layer a history of destruction, invasion, war, and authoritarianism in the Middle East alongside a history of destroyed, constructed, weaponized, strategically deployed, colonized, and kidnapped archives. The relationship of violence to history making appears linear through this layering, and archives serve as a metaphor or as a coherent technology for historical processes and the consolidation, ruptures, and machinations of political regimes. And yet, archives, people, and power are never as coherent as the stories they tell about themselves. In the case of archives, they are never as coherent as academics present them. I build an archival, ethnographic theory and method that centers the life worlds and knowledge production of archivists, and suggest that archival destruction, corruption, and recuperation reveal archives as abundant, contradictory, and indeterminate spaces. Law, history, jurisprudence, method, theory, and violence curate truths out of abundance, destruction, and indeterminacy.[18] What we make of archives, and what archives make of us, reflects and inflects the impossible desire to render the unknowable rational and predictable—and to fix that meaning in time.[19] Seen this way, historical or theoretical coherence is in fact the compulsive drive *to cohere*, to epistemologically and ideologically fold the reversals and unpredictability of life, death, and everything in between into a narrative that stresses continuity, predictability, and the surety of a recognizable future.

An ethnography of the archive as a physical space, coupled with an ethnographic reading of the documents that archives hold and circulate,[20] troubles the division of labor between cultural and academic production.[21] Such an approach presents embodied knowledge, memory, abundance, and affect as sites for the writing and reading of history and ethnography. The practices of the art collective led by Walid Raad, the Atlas Group, have shown that the distinctions between historical and fictional narrative, and between historical events and subjective experiences of those events, are multiple, compulsive, and contradictory. We dwell in a constitutive contradiction: a lack of organized historical/archival documents and a lack of a public history of the civil war, coupled with the hyperpresence of civil war in the built environment of Lebanon and within the memory and futurescapes of people who live in or come from Lebanon. How can war be both everywhere and nowhere at the same time? How can war and violence continue to animate political, social, economic, and urban fabrics across the country, and yet be excluded by official narrations of history, including national history curricula? Omnia El Shakry has persuasively demonstrated that to perform decolonial history is to grapple with destruction and a lack of documents, and to turn toward other sources, methods, and affects of history making.[22] The burning of the Cassation Court archives during the civil war was a catastrophe, and yet catastrophe, as Sherene Seikaly reminds us, is never an ending. Catastrophe is a temporal, affective, and archival order.[23]

Lebanon is not an exceptional site of archival destruction. The Middle East is a space where archives and documents are routinely damaged and targeted by war and occupation practices—most infamously the targeted removal of the Iraqi state archives from Baghdad to Qatar by US occupation forces and the targeted removal of the PLO archives from Beirut to Tel Aviv as a tactic of Israeli warfare during the invasion and occupation of Lebanon. I join Shakry, the Atlas Group, and Seikaly in arguing that a *lack* of organized sources and official archives are motivation for thinking otherwise, looking elsewhere, and writing/creating multiply about and for history. In line with Marisa Fuentes, Anjali Arondekar, Michel-Rolph Trouillot, and Saidiya Hartman, [24] I also suggest that factual fictions, or what we might call historical "ficticity," are often constructed not through a lack of documents but within an abundance of historical documents, narratives, and archives. Desiring or mourning archives and documents as unique and prized sources for passive, "lying in wait" truths recirculates the power and coercion that colonial archives and authority are both constructed by and construct.[25] Destruction, in fact, is a process of abundance.[26] I do not only mean the ways that archival destruction or creation is a theoretical metonym for an origin story about sovereignty or a metaphor for power more broadly, but also the abundant affect of mourning and of loss that animates much writing and reading about archival destruction or creation.[27] I am interested in the affective pull toward insurrectionary or recuperative research, what we might call, following Lila Abu-Lughod, the romance of archival resistance,[28] along with the pleasure and careers that come with archival "discovery." Lebanon is a site of archival aporia and absences, on the one hand, and a surfeit of documents, on the other. Lack and excess exist at the same time, and this is neither a contradiction nor a unique feature of archives or archival research in Lebanon.

The abundance of archives—even as they are being destroyed or serving as sites and technologies of destruction—is tied to their material and immaterial forms. Archives are life worlds, and thus even the material destruction of an archive facilitates abundance and creation—the work needed to save, remember, reorganize, and substitute originals for copies. Archivists, and not only archives, are the repository of institutional memory and of history making. While academics are obsessed with lost and found archival objects, it is archivists who are curating and embodying the relationship of archives to power.[29] Moreover, the destruction or the loss of archives and archival objects are quotidian events; archivists and academics curate, rearrange, forget, stain, steal, and lose archival objects all the time. Archives are workspaces filled with colleagues and bosses to navigate and commutes and lunch breaks, laughter, and arguments. Archivists are public sector employees who in many parts of the world, including Lebanon, are chronically underpaid, threatened with layoffs and digitization, and accused of everything from corruption to government bloat, inefficiency, and being holdovers from an analog past.[30] The material conditions of the archives of the Court of Cassation are inextricable from their geopolitical context. The documents have been burned in a fire; they are housed in a dark and musky room, in a building—the Beirut Courthouse—deemed structurally unsound by civil engineers and literally sinking into the ground.

A Fire in the Archive

At the time of my research, the archive of the Cassation Court was divided into three locations. The first, containing the most recent and active case files, was a large L-shaped room facing the archivists' office, which was also L shaped. The lip of the "L" housed the archival files of the Plenary Assembly, and the much smaller archive of the Judicial Council, on one side of the hallway and the office of Evelyn, the head archivist of the Cassation Court, on the other. Both Evelyn's office and the Plenary Assembly archive were alcoves jutting out from the large shared room of both the archives of the different branches of the Cassation Court and the archivists of those courts, mirroring each other across a hallway. In a space between the second and third floor—something between an attic and a crawl space—was another set of archival files from the Cassation Court, these dating from the 1940s to the 1967. Getting to those files required a chair or stepladder, and Mona had once broken a bone in her hand jumping down from the attic with a file tucked under the other arm.

A third set of files, dated from 1967 to 1985, were stacked in an underground depot near a parking lot and the judiciary café, a "mountain of case files" (*jabal malafāt*, according to Mona), which I saw the first day of my research at the judiciary. Evelyn had asked for the files to be taken to this separate location, but she was furious at how the workers had treated them, and said that it was as if they had "worked for Sukleen," the dominant waste removal and treatment company in Lebanon. She accused the workers of treating historical documents as refuse, but there is (always) another story here. The majority of men who collect trash in Lebanon are migrant workers, and they are subjected to racism, classism, and xenophobia. In fact, migrant laborers help create a community and a sense of who Lebanese are: people who are from diverse religious, sectarian, class, and regional backgrounds, but people who are discernably different from the people who pick up their trash or clean their homes. When I returned to the underground depot in 2020, it had become an archive that joined and housed all but the most recent and active Cassation Court cases in filing cabinets organized by year. This had been Evelyn's project, her passion, for more than a decade, and she was proud of her work's fruition. The Assembly files that Mona had tended to had been given their own locker, just as they had previously been granted their own shelves and mountains and piles, alongside and apart from the Cassation Court writ large.

All case files found in the Assembly's archive contain the court decisions that are being appealed, lawyers' arguments to all concerning courts including the Assembly, copies of evidence and fees submitted to courts, proof of legal representation, and in many cases the handwritten notes of judges, archivists, and clerks at every stage of the case. They

FIGURE 3. Plenary Assembly files in newly organized
Cassation Court archives, 2020.

demonstrate the legal, bureaucratic, and financial ladder that must be climbed for cases to reach the jurisdiction of the country's highest civil court. The case files perform a legal practice uniquely inflected with competing discourses of secular and religious jurisdiction and the nature and role of the Lebanese state. They also articulate the rights and duties of citizens toward religious and civil institutions and toward each other. The Assembly, a civil and secular body composed of the highest-ranking judges at the judiciary, practices a unitary sovereignty over the Lebanese legal system, a legal sovereignty that enacts that of the Lebanese state.

For stretches of time there was no working lightbulb in the small room that housed the case files of the highest court that citizens have access to, the Plenary Assembly, and the files of the Judicial Council, which defines and rules on crimes against the state and the people writ large. When the electricity would cut out or the lightbulb would not turn on, Mona and

I used the weak flashlights built into cigarette lighters to navigate the room. The files were arranged on metal shelves roughly by decade, and each case file was summarized on the manila folder that contained it. The thinnest file I saw while conducting research contained only 5 pages, but the fattest was more than 1,100 pages and bulged against the many layers of twine that held it together. The room itself was dusty, dark, and smelled like old paper. My eyes scanned for inevitable cockroaches. When I asked Mona why there was no lightbulb in the room, she remarked that the archivists had collectively decided to stop buying lightbulbs until the state had reimbursed them for past purchases. That had been months ago, she added. The state (*dawle*) had not reimbursed them, and had not bought light bulbs. Archivists also paid for the upkeep of their bathroom and their offices, Mona told me. The state only sometimes stocked the bathrooms with toiletries.

The case files contained in this section of the archives corresponded to "after the fire of 1985." The fire in question had begun after a vicious bout of shelling[31] during the civil war, a night when 3 people were killed and 17 were wounded, one night in a two-week battle in Beirut that killed 89 and wounded 467. Amin Nassar, president of Lebanon's Supreme Judicial Council at the time, described the fire as "the greatest catastrophe"[32] of the war up until that point—a period that included massacres, aerial bombardment, invasions and occupations, and mass displacement all over the country. He continued, "all files with no exception have been burned, and the rights of citizens from all religions and sects have turned into ashes."[33] The burning of legal paper was equated with the ashes of citizenship, and not any citizenship, but the community of citizens from different religions and sects that are diverse but equal as *citizens* before the judiciary, and perhaps equal nowhere else except the judiciary, during a civil war. A gaping, burrowing, burning hole in the heart of Lebanon, its legal history and capacities, its promise of citizenship as the protector of religious difference, harmony, and coexistence. Of course, "coexistence" is sextarian and predicated on sexual difference and inequality, on the one hand, and forever securitized Muslim majority refugee populations, on the other. Given the centrality of Palestinians in Lebanon during the civil war period statements that center "citizens" are not neutral—they construct the history of civilian life in Lebanon, especially during the war, as particularly *Lebanese* rather than multinational.

There is a common misconception that militia leaders became state officials and politicians after the civil war. In fact, during the war politicians and statesmen became militia leaders, and militia leaders sometimes became politicians and statesmen. The line between militia leaders and political leaders has always been a blur rather than a diagnostic between pre– and post–civil war eras. Nabih Berri, who served as minister of justice from 1984 to 1988, and who has been speaker of Parliament since 1992, is just one example of many. The year 1985 saw the fire at the Beirut Courthouse, which neighbors the Ministry of Justice which Berri headed, but it was also the year the militia he led at the same time, Amal, launched "the war of the camps" and besieged the Palestinian refugee camp in Shatila. There was fierce fighting in *tarīq al jadīda* not only because it neighbors Shatila and Sabra but because it mirrors them: Lebanese and Palestinians living together and in many cases fighting together for what they perceived to be common causes and common enemies.[34] This is one history, one multiple multinational history that frames Lebanese and Palestinians as symbiotic, part of a common project and life world, rather than as adversaries. This is decidedly *not* the historical narrative highlighted in the postwar era.

From 1975 to 1990, state institutions regularly came under fire by design and mistake. Still, the barrage of mortars that struck the Cassation Court archives in 1985 seemed, to the archivists, to be aimed at the archive itself. When they discussed the fire of 1985, archivists at the Court of Cassation refused to speculate on or fix where the shelling came from. Such speculation would implicate "which side" shelled the Ministry of Justice—and the six archivists came from all possible sides in Lebanon. When I pressed the archivists about the fire of 1985, refusing to believe that they had no idea who shelled them and their colleagues, a collective story emerged: Whoever gave the order to shell the archives that night had a divorce or criminal case file they wanted expunged from the record. The archive must have been targeted in its capacity *as* an archive. The archivists rendered the shelling that started the fire personal, impossible to rationalize, and safe from political affiliation or implication. Perhaps they didn't want to get into an argument in front of me, so they settled on a narrative they could perform together. I was skeptical of this story of sour divorces and notoriously imprecise mortars precisely aimed at the Cassation archives, and I said so. In response, the archivist of the Criminal Chamber of the Cassation Court waved vaguely westward and said the shells must have come from West Beirut.[35] Mona immediately slapped my shoulder and joked, "See? She thinks it came from *our* side [of the city]." The stakes of this interaction were clear. While war requires the mobilization of collective memory, post-war terrains—particularly post–civil war terrains—require either a selective forgetting or a necessary lie. It may not be true that these archivists have no opinion as to where the shells came from that night or that the culprit would be difficult to uniquely identify. *Making* it true and insisting on that truth enables the room to function and the archivists to remain friendly coworkers. They perform post–civil war coexistence. The refusal to remember, or the insistence on creating a memory together, the highlighting of a collective feeling and experience of war—these are all political choices, although they are meant to intentionally avoid discussions of politics. The archivists built sociability around a collective sense and a sensibility of what cannot be said, and how in fact it *can* be said: Of course a militia member managed to precisely aim his rockets at the archive, and of course he did it to expunge one particular file from history—it was a targeted burning. The personalization and the intentionality of violence is perhaps more comforting than the alternatives. After all, the rockets could have been a political decision taken by a wartime leader who is now a politician currently supported one of the archivists in this postwar work environment. Or a different wartime leader turned politician, who played a role in appointing a particular archivist or their boss, could have ordered the rocket barrage. Worst of all, the rockets could be evidence of violence *without* intentionality, a reminder of life lived within the reality of death without consequence, your loved one's life and death as someone else's mistake, a mechanical error, the 150,000 deaths that pardons have been issued for. Perhaps the militiaman giving the orders that night didn't actually care about the archive at all. Maybe he didn't even know it was there—the rocket just happened to start a fire in that room. Maybe it was someone launching the rockets who got carried away, or two defective rockets following their own destiny,[36] and we are still here decades later, finding and performing narratives, making this room, and the Cassation Courts, and the archive, work.

The Beirut Courthouse and the Ministry of Justice sit at the seam of majority-Christian East and majority-Muslim West Beirut and formed part of the "green line." This makeshift border of checkpoints, snipers, overgrown trees, car bombs, mines, and barbed wire separated the two halves of the city at varying levels of intensification throughout the civil war. To get to work, Mona would cross Barbir Bridge and its shifting checkpoints. The place of the Ministry on the green line, between warring halves of the city, is key to Mona's memory of her work life during the war.

FIGURE 4. Photograph of checkpoint at Barbir Bridge, 1984. Image by Nabih Nassar. Sign reads: "We must exit the borders of sectarianism to enter the nation, for the nation is more welcoming and more generous and capacious." Reprinted with permission from Zaven Kouyoumdjian.

MONA: We were used to the bombing. We used to go to the parking garage, and when the shelling got worse, we would go *under* the garage. When all of this was burned [points around the room], we sat in the big hall over there [points across the hallway], we put our desks and our files and our cabinets and we sat, and we would be exposed to sniper fire there. Because around here [the Beirut Courthouse] it is East/West, we were in the middle of the green line.

MAYA: You used to come here every day?

MONA: Yes. I would come walking from *tarīq al jadīda*. From the East side, they come in their cars, it is close [laughs]. Not like us, they didn't have to do that zig-zag of opened and closed streets, official and unofficial checkpoints. But those in the East side, if they wanted to come to the West side, yes it was the same . . . the same process, same problems. From my house . . . sometimes my husband would give me a ride to Barbir, Barbir was all sandbags. Sandbags up to here [points to her neck]. You remember that, don't you? They must have been taller than you! [laughs]

MAYA: Yes, I remember that . . . were there ever . . . I mean, did you used to tell the *shabab* [militiamen/boys] that you worked at the judiciary? Did you have any problems or . . . ?

MONA: No, nobody ever assaulted me or shot me, I was never exposed to anything dangerous. Ever. Quite the opposite. Maybe they used to make it easier on government employees . . . I don't know . . . there are people . . . maybe they were crossing but they weren't employees with a purpose, those that used to pass through these places could have been kidnapped, robbed, exposed to sniper fire . . . I don't know, but for me thank God [*hamdillah*], not one day, and throughout the entire war I would cross.

MAYA: Thank God [*hamdillah*].

MAYA: Did you ever have to sleep here?

MONA: No, when the bombing would let up [even if late at night] I would leave. Sometimes . . . there is a day I will never forget. It was a Monday. The shelling started from the mountains to here [points out the window and mimics the trajectory of a mortar, tapping her finger on her desk to illustrate impact]. We went down [to the parking garage]. I had my transistor radio. They always used to give out the flashes [on the radio]. You remember those right? [I nod] So we went downstairs. And my car was here that day because I was sick and I drove. I waited a little bit until 11 [pm]. It was quieter so I got into the car. I drove on to the museum. Once I got to the military court, a shell landed near the museum [a distance about 300 meters] . . . then another. I felt as if the ground under the car was opening up. How I passed, I don't know—but I did . . . There was a checkpoint there too. I stopped. I just stopped the car and got out on the road and fell in front of that checkpoint . . . I was feeling as if . . . there is a mountain on my back and I want to . . . I couldn't anymore I wanted to just throw that mountain off . . . I arrived yellowed. The shabab/militiamen ran to me. They told me what's wrong with you, *khalto* [auntie]?[37] What happened? Are you okay, *auntie*? I told them nothing. I crossed the road and a shell landed behind me. But as you know all of this was nothing compared to others' experiences. People like us were very lucky.

This moment and others like it made it clear to me that Mona considered she and I to form an "us," particularly when talking about the past and specifically when discussing the violence of the civil war. This "us" was tied to our neighborhood with all of its sectarian and class connotations, but it was not contained by it. The intimacy of sharing civil war memories is a larger "us" that many in Lebanon construct, conversation by conversation. There is an "us" who are here to share stories, an ability informed by the contingency of our presence and hence, luck. Mona's narration also points to the contradictory intimacies that flourish around violence: the militiamen who may have extorted Mona or harassed her at a checkpoint called her auntie when they thought she might be having a heart attack. Or perhaps she actually was their auntie, someone these militiamen believed, or willed and drugged themselves to believe, that they were protecting by terrorizing others. She hated them, or at least she said she did, but in that moment their concern stood out to her enough that she remembered and narrated it to me more twenty years later. Through-out our conversation Mona kept asking me whether I understood the language she was using, whether I remembered checkpoints and sand-bags, transistor radios and the feeling of luck, then and now. This was an "us" that Mona did not have to explain. Mona and I were a different "us" when discussing the 2006 Israel-Lebanon war. In that context, "we" represented everyone who had stood against Israel during the war and re-mained "steadfast," with the implication that there were other Lebanese who had supported Israel, echoing earlier experiences of war when some Lebanese allied with Israel or with Syria against other Lebanese. Some-times "us" was anyone who had not left Lebanon to live abroad during the civil war,[38] and at other times "us" didn't include me at all—it was used to mark a difference between the "us" of civil servants and myself, a researcher in their workplace.

Archival files are inseparable from the embodied expertise of archi-vists and clerks, whom lawyers, plaintiffs, judges, and researchers call on to explain the significance, the logic, the system, and the history of this or that case file. They mediate and shed light on the relationship between truth and violence, a relationship that functions through multiple scales: the social, material, methodological, epistemological, and ideological. Archives, even when destroyed, kidnapped, transplanted, or burned, con-tinue to function because their power is immaterial: An empty archive is still full, as Arondekar writes.[39] The ethnographic space[40] of the ar-chive, moreover, is an actual, physical space—it does not exist without an archivist sharing a file or a document with a researcher, whether by delicately holding a case file about custody or throwing a war crimes file on the floor. It is government employees who have already curated the material we use to curate truths out of an archive. What if our theory centered the material conditions and experiences of those that curate and create the spaces that academics conduct research in: archivists, clerks, employees? At the very least, academics—and nation-states—are not the only, the primary, or even the most authoritative victims of archive fever. Seen this way, archive fever is less a theoretical metonym for compulsion and desire and more the people working tirelessly to save an archive from a fire in Beirut in 1985, in Nablus in 2002, in Baghdad in 2003, or in Rio De Janeiro in 2018, putting themselves in danger of mortars and flames and smoke and water damage. These images and memories indicate the power of archives, both practically and ideologically, in their role as warehouses for the curation of multiple futures. As Mona explained it to me: "If *we* didn't rescue files, there would be no record of anything left—and then what would happen?" Archives, after all, do not merely produce and perform sovereignty; they are also archives *of* sovereignty.[41] Merely having them is a claim to power, and importantly, to a history of power and the power of history and of historical coherence.[42] The working conditions of government employees who run archives are part of that history and the fabric of knowledge production. We see them—we rely on them—pushing their desks away from a window before it shatters, driving through a checkpoint to get to work, walking into a room of embers, inhaling smoke, pulling smoldering files with their bare hands, breaking their arms retrieving documents, collapsing feverishly and in pain. None of this is metaphorical.[43]

Economies of Scale

The six archivists share one large room, with their boss, Evelyn, the head archivist of the Cassation Court, occupying the only separate office within that space. They are each in charge of a different branch of the Cassation Court and are diverse in terms of gender, sect, age, and regional origins. In fact, their sectarian diversity is engineered—keeping in line with state practices that ensure equitable sectarian representation in lower-level state bureaucracy and institutions.[44] The principle of sectarian "diversity" and aversion to monosectarian state life extends from the highest offices off the state—where the president must be Maronite, the prime minister Sunni, and the president of Parliament Shiʻa—to the higher posts in the judiciary, including the one Youssef occupied—the man who had made the phone call that got me into the archivists' offices. Despite the sectarian "diversity" of the archivists of the Cassation Courts, there is a unifying characteristic: they are all from middle- and working-class backgrounds, and many are from generations when a government job guaranteed entry into a professional middle class, economic stability, and a comfortable retirement. Some were hired during or before the civil war, some before the devaluation of the Lebanese pound and its pegging to the US dollar in 1997, and many during and after neo-liberal market reforms introduced by then Prime Minister Rafik al Hariri, which destroyed the middle class. These reforms led to hyperinflation and to Beirut consistently ranking as one of the most expensive cities in the world. In 2020 the dollar peg collapsed, and with it the spending power of everyone except those with foreign income streams.

All six archivists attended public schools and public universities. Before the dollar peg collapsed in 2019, they were paid a low salary and benefits package scaled to seniority. Today, in 2022, their salaries rise and fall on the black market along with the value of the Lebanese lira. But before the financial collapse of 2019, the economy worked for the benefit of the few and to the detriment of most. Three of the archivists at the Court of Cassation had attended law school but could not afford the unpaid three-year "internship" required to take the bar exam and enter practice. The favors they sometimes gained from lawyers in return for their services were in part a recognition that they could not live on their salaries and, perhaps more important, a recognition that their salaries did not reflect the value of their work. I witnessed exchanges between archivists, lawyers, and judges conducted in several currencies. While paper money was common, lawyers with closer relationships and histories with the judiciary also brought archivists olive oil and kilos of fruit from their family farms. The most popular currency was the favor and the delayed reciprocity expected in any gift-exchange.[45] In fact, what we might call an economy of favors accomplished two things. First, it produced a cycle of exchange that used several commodities and currencies to ameliorate the ravages of an "official economy" marked by war, inflation, and post-war neoliberal market restructuring. Second, sociality traveled at each point of this cycle of exchange, creating ties between people occupying different positions in the sociopolitical space of Lebanon. Thus archivists, who were economically disadvantaged in relation to judges and lawyers, gave favors knowing that they would be paid back in kind at a later date. These favors ensured the continuation of intersectarian and interclass exchange in a country where ordinary citizens were convinced their politicians were leading them to another civil war. In times of war, such exchanges and relations can ensure the safety of one's loved ones. In times of economic collapse, this economy of favors offers and enacts a variety of currencies that people can draw from. The more stress on the "official" economy the more critical the economy of favors becomes precisely because people escape, or appear to escape, the corrupt financial or political leadership in the country.[46]

The thickness of this exchange and the commodities involved—economic, social, bodily, strategic, agricultural, favors—are often pointed to by civil society activists and by local and international NGOs as evidence of corruption and sectarianism at the Judiciary and the Beirut Courthouse. Discourses on corruption flatten these complexities and aim to bring everyone under the "official" and international monetary economy. Millions of dollars have been spent promoting "good governance" in Lebanon. The premise of these programs and reformatory projects was that Lebanon is a failed state that operates through corruption and cronyism, both of which were refracted through and bolstered sectarianism. Sectarianism was framed as opposite, and corrosive, to nationalism. In this argument, sectarianism leads to corruption and war, while nationalism engenders dignity and civil peace. These discourses comment on the *correct* way to be a citizen and a "productive" member of society: a citizen who cannot be bought. A correct citizen is autonomous, tied to and reliant on only the meritocratic state and private sector for her needs. A correct citizen trusts the state and embodies the very dignity—and sincerity—of citizenship. Many anti-corruption campaigns target bureaucrats and workers as opposed to political leaders. They speak the language of good governance—not of political change or political accountability.[47]

Digitization looms large in debates over corruption in government institutions. Before I began my research, the Ministry of Justice had received a grant from USAID to further "the rule of law" in Lebanon. Digitizing court archives, substituting type for handwriting, and standardizing the filing and retrieval system was part of the vision of increasing transparency and judicial independence.[48] Mona's boss Evelyn was in favor of these reforms, but her subordinates were not. They feared they would lose their jobs because they could not master the new computer programs. Mona had an additional, more political concern, telling me that she would not allow "other governments [meaning the US government]" to control how Lebanese court files are managed, retrieved, or categorized.[49] She did not even trust Lebanese politicians to understand or change the system, or logic, of the archive. So how could she trust another state?

Digitization and modernization transform archivists from people whose handwriting, legal advice, and memories cannot be disambiguated from court files into workers who adhere to international standards of training and professionalism. This process of digitization and the economy of digital knowledge moves power from middle-class government employees such as clerks and archivists into the hands of "experts." Their job description will be clear, their hours and tasks regimented, and they will be easily fired, hired, and replaced—or, most likely, *not* replaced. Debates about digitization and standardization are sites of power struggle. The stakes of this struggle are the regime of the archive, the way research is conducted, and the relationship of memory and feeling—shared or oppositional—to knowledge production.[50] They implicate and threaten jobs and socioeconomic class. Neoliberal visions of the public sector contain fewer employees and different forms of employment; they shift embodied expertise to contingent forms of labor. Digitization is not merely a copy; it is a new economic, and epistemological, order.[51] Under digitization, the possibility of loss, of losing this or that file, is assumed to disappear. In this way, the files will no longer be texts that can be comprehended only by acts of active and ethnographic reading.[52] The files will circulate outside of the life worlds that they both build and are built by. They will become texts that can be removed from their immediate physical context and still be comprehensible to readers who are rendered more passive.[53] In addition to reshaping research methods, these changes will have an effect on jurisprudence itself, which, at times, requires acts of collective memory and sensitivity to life's contingencies and reversals to be experienced emotively and collectively, rather than electronically. Digitization promises immortality but cannot deliver it. It promises transparency and openness but works to censor and erase.[54]

The Legal Life of Memory

One day, to illustrate the effects of the fire of 1985 on the archive and the need for digitization, Mona handed me an inheritance case file that included decisions from Roman Catholic and civil personal status courts. In 1992 a group of siblings—men and women—presented a case to the Plenary Assembly. In his brief, their lawyer wrote that his clients were the heirs of a man whose case was presented to the Assembly in 1982— the year the Israeli army occupied West Beirut. That year was also the year of the Sabra and Shatila massacre, in which members of right-wing Christian Lebanese militias[55] raped, murdered, and mutilated thousands of Palestinian refugees and Lebanese under the capacitating eye of both Israel and the United States.[56] The beach resort case was decided in 1985. But the file was "lost" in the fire, and the siblings needed the case to ward off a group of cousins who were suing them for shares of the beach resort. The case file consisted of the legally binding ruling, arguments by both the plaintiff and the defendants, evidence presented to the court, and copies of every step of this case as it was heard and ruled on at two different civil personal status courts before being appealed at the Plenary Assembly. Because the case file was "lost to the fire" and, the lawyer argued, the archivists had been unable to find either its remnants or the ledger that indexed its presence, he asked the court to certify a photocopy of the decision, held by the siblings, as legally binding. A case file is definitively closed and enforceable only if it can be found and reproduced in the Cassation Court archive.

To reach a decision in this case, the judges analyzed handwriting, questioned archivists, and both separately and collectively *remembered* the case and the search for fire-eaten remnants of files and ledgers. They also remembered the judges presiding, the archivists employed at the time, and their handwriting to decide whether the siblings' copy *was* an untampered copy of the original, which, they write, was "lost with many others" in the fire of 1985. The judges wondered about their duty as jurists and representatives of the state regarding documents, decisions, or files lost to the war. The war and the fire were referenced in only the passive voice.[57] The case file was thick with historical narratives. It was the history of a family, of a beach resort, and of careers made and retired at the judiciary. The same judges climbed the ranks of the judiciary over the course of the case. One can even read the history of Mona's employment and that of her predecessor, as the photocopy of the original file carries the signature of a different archivist, but the pages that certify the copy as the original are marked with her distinctive two-letter imprint.

This and other cases adjudicated during the Lebanese Civil War contain lawyers' briefs that directly impress on judges, archivists, and researchers the shared reality of terrifying, and in many cases terrifyingly arbitrary, violence. The cases insist on and call forth an activation of memory, a bubbling up, a breaking of the surface. Reading them, one is struck by the quotidian ways in which life and law continue during a war where an estimated one in eight residents in Lebanon were killed or critically injured—one in three residents were casualties if we consider emigration, displacement, and disappearance analogous to physical injuries and deaths. Some cases seem tragic and surreal: What is a murder case, after all, in the middle of a civil war if not an insistence that lives still *matter* and that killing is still a *crime*? By referencing the war to judges, who were also living and working through it, the briefs make an appeal: *We are all in this together, and together we all refuse to be in it. We are an "us."* The briefs were excess information within the genre of legal writing, and their excess is precisely how I read the community making of citizenship during a civil war. They performed "acts of citizenship"[58] at a time when formal citizenship, alongside the state, was fraying under a civil war and under foreign occupations. These acts of citizenship, moreover, insisted on a community of citizens—a community manifested in a shared lexicon of war regardless of political affiliation, sectarian identification, or regional location. They signaled a refusal to seek redress from militia justice, at a time of war, a turn toward the state.

But the briefs are also legal appeals made on behalf of clients in ongoing court cases where they may be defendants or plaintiffs—they are a legal strategy: My client could not come to the courthouse because there was a militia checkpoint at the mouth of the road: This man has perverted Christianity and Islam and turned them against each other through his manipulations of religious conversion—a danger to the spirit of the Taif peace accord that ended our brutal nightmare of civil war. These statements activate shared archives of experience and press them into the present.[59] They are forms of address that both affectively and *knowingly* call a community into being. These statements also place the court in the world and the war, and insist that the law must bend to, and acknowledge, the realities of the world, but at the same time must also transcend them, remain above them. It must be at once impartial to and contingent on life outside the court—life that jurists and ordinary people share when not structured by the context of legal encounter. The "us" of citizens is always exclusionary. The price of a post–civil war order is the sanctity of citizenship and the banishing of noncitizens from political community, including the community of legal memory. The files that contain these appeals, moreover, are all in this burned and shelled building, rendering the archive an artifact, a museum, a repository, an abundant affective realm, and a threshold of war.

The geopolitical context of the Middle East, and the lived experience of that context, is an effervescent site from which to rethink the relationship between archives and history. The order and location of what we consider spectacular and nonspectacular violence shifts when we think, for example, that archives cannot account for people who could not get to court or muster the resources needed to pursue a case, or if public prosecutors did not investigate or charge rape, murder, racketeering, or assault during a war. What cannot be found in wartime archives is a meditation on the relationship between violence, law, and history. Archival absence is overflowing with people doing the quotidian work of surviving a war, with the violence that is never legally structured as a crime. War is often thought of us as a seismic event, a rupture of the everyday. Yet anyone who has lived through a war knows that given enough time, war and destruction are everyday contexts that people not only die in but live through. Archives—particularly archives in countries where war is a recursive temporality rather than a rupture in time[60]—may in fact demonstrate an indeterminacy to the temporal and epistemological borders between war and peace, on the one hand, and of theory and method, on the other.[61]

Legal files are a particular genre of writing—highly formulaic, governed by a different set of rules, and modular. Lawyers, often with the advice of archivists such as Mona, orient their arguments to particular sets of audiences that are both embodied (judges, juries) and temporal. They write and argue their way into a tradition and a history via citational logic, and they write and argue with an eye toward the future—being a citation in a future case or supporting an appeal. The record left by legal procedure is necessarily incomplete; we encounter stories at the middle and before they end, we start somewhere and never return there, and we encounter subjects narrating and being narrated by and toward archival truths that are violent and violating.[62] The force of the state compels one to narrate according to formal procedures and within particular discourses. In a case file, we read the ultimate authority of the state that can license truth statements and give a document, a photocopy in this case, the force of law.[63] In certifying a copy as the original, the Lebanese state performed its sovereignty and scripted its own history of civil war as a history of legal procedure and the continuation of professional life at the judiciary. In doing so, it acknowledged the aporias of sovereignty itself, its power, and its vacuums. The lack of sovereign authority to protect its own archive from fire engendered and produced new sovereign acts: a photocopy that has to be certified by the judiciary to stand in for the original.

Describing War

To understand war, one has to pluralize both the wars themselves and the actors involved in them. In Lebanon, Lebanese nationalists, allied with the United States and in some cases Israel, and Arab nationalists, allied with Egypt and in some cases Palestinians, have fought a civil war. Arab nationalists allied with Syria have also fought against Arab nationalists allied with Iraq. In fact, at different points everyone was both an ally and an enemy of Syria. Protectors of the political status quo and supporters of Palestinian liberation have fought a war, fascists and socialists have fought a war, people who supported and opposed political sectarianism have fought a war, capitalists and communists have fought a war. Christians have fought Christians, and Muslims have fought Muslims for reasons ranging from the ideological to the profit margins of racketeering and militia "taxation" of areas under their control. The Israeli, US, and Syrian armies were part of the civil war from 1975 to 1990. Yet despite these complex and rapidly shifting alliances and counteralliances, the popular imagination and memory of these wars reduces and simplifies them to Christians versus Muslims—to a sectarian civil war. Memories of life—of shared life—during the wars are a tangle of intersecting and diverging descriptions. Some histories of the war, such as the sexual violence that made life for Lebanese women "hell"—in the curt words of a female militia member I interviewed—have yet to be broached.[64]

The post–civil war era, meanwhile, is also war filled. Political assassinations inaugurated the Taif Accord peace deal and with it the era of the Second Lebanese Republic. A full quarter of the country was under Israeli occupation until the year 2000, while 1996 saw the "Grapes of Wrath" Israeli war campaign against Lebanon. In 2006 came yet another Israeli invasion and Lebanon-Israel war, more than 1125 hundred people in Lebanon were killed, the vast majority of whom were civilians and approximately 30 percent of whom were children.[65] Another seventy people have been killed by Israeli cluster munitions left behind in South Lebanon since the end of the war, with more being killed each year. One year later, in 2007, the Lebanese army launched a military campaign against Fath Al Islam, an Islamist militant group. The campaign lasted for months and included the army besieging and shelling Nahr El Bared, a Palestinian refugee camp that the militants had taken over, with the majority of Palestinian refugees displaced and traumatized yet again by the fighting. More than 500 soldiers, militants, and civilians are estimated to have died. Another year later, in 2008, armed clashes between political parties/militias killed at least 71 people.[66] No fewer than 30 bombings, political assassinations, and attempted assassinations seized the country from 2004 to 2015.[67] The Lebanese army and its allies fought a war with ISIL and Nusra from 2014 to 2017; since 2012, political, social, and economic life in Lebanon has been largely defined by war in Syria. Amid this past and present multiplicity of violence, the Taif Accord was and is a technology of archival curation.[68] The Taif Accord produced the authoritative, sectarian account of the Lebanese Civil War.

The economic, social, gendered, ideological, and national "wars within wars" were silenced.[69] The reforms envisioned were narrowly sectarian. Peace deals such as Taif shape and curate the wars that precede them, and, as Hiba Bou Akar terms it, the wars yet to come.[70] The history of political violence in Lebanon is recursive and tragic, but it is not exceptional. Iraq, Syria, Palestine, and Yemen are also war filled and have been for decades. Any Iraqi, Syrian, Palestinian, Kurd, or Yemeni reading this will recognize how the terms "war," "peace," and "ceasefire" fail to account for experience. These words, if anything, index a vanishing point between violence and stability, rather than a border. If only Lebanon were exceptional.

When we study or recount events that seem overburdened or over-signified/saturated with meaning, we should be attentive to the multiple descriptions that any one act can fall under. Only when we start with multiplicity can we understand conditions under which one of these descriptions will become hegemonic or authoritative.[71] Arondekar has cautioned us away from a heuristic of loss and melancholia—orientations toward the archive that demonstrate our attachment to historical categories (the power effects of the archives)—and toward an attentiveness to the abundance of the archival object itself.[72] This attention to abundance may allow us to destabilize not only the singularity of truth but also our own investments in the singular nature of truth.[73] With these insights in mind, we turn now to our final ethnographic vignette.

One day while I was at the archives, Mona picked up a file that I had not asked for and remarked that it was *the* Judicial Council case against a Maronite Christian militia leader, Samir Geagea. Geagea is the only wartime leader to have served time for crimes committed during the war and after the Taif Accord. He was arrested in 1994 and faced four separate Judicial Council trials, for attempted and completed political assassinations during the civil war and the bombing of a church that killed nine people after the war had ended. He was convicted of all crimes and sentenced to death. He then had his sentences commuted to life in prison, was pardoned in 2005, and swiftly reentered political life. Geagea, an ally of the United States and Israel during the civil war, and still a political leader and ally of the United States and, now, of Saudi Arabia, is responsible for brutal wartime violence. He was a leader of the Lebanese Forces, a group of which committed the Sabra and Shatila massacre under cover from their allies, the Israeli army,[74] blocks away from where Mona, my parents, and my two-year-old self lived at the time. A few years earlier a sniper from that same militia shot my grandfather twice (he survived) as he went to check on his shops on the green line of downtown Beirut, shops that he would lose not during the war but after it because of a series of legal actions that paved the way for a corporation's "eminent domain." Geagea was still a militia leader when both Mona's family and my family were displaced, alongside many others, because an army general who later became president launched a war against Syria—a war that included a vicious war within a war against the Lebanese Forces led by Geagea. Twenty years later, Mona asked me whether I wanted to see his file. Before I could answer, she threw it pointedly onto the dusty floor. I had never seen her handle archival documents with such disrespect. I was surprised, curious, jolted—emotions I papered over with a performance of professionalism. I told her I was interested only in the files I had actually requested—that were about religious conversion.

Why did I not look at the file? Or rather, *how* did I not look at the file?[75] Was I really, as I explained it to myself at the time, worried that she would doubt my professionalism or stated academic reason for being in the archive if I took Samir Geagea's case file or even just looked at it? More likely I did not want to know, could not bear to research the only case of "war crimes" and the only alleged "war criminal" in a war full of crimes and criminals, all pardoned—but never forgotten. How can anyone forget when their faces and insignias still populate the country, now cloaked in the respectability of electoral paraphernalia? Maybe I did not want to feel all the dust Mona had kicked up inside of me, could not dare to breathe it in. I froze. I said no. Mona looked back at me, smiled faintly, and shrugged as if to say "your loss." She went back to the files.

Years later, I struggle to explain the density of this action and my reaction to it. There are several ways to describe Mona's throwing the case file of the warlord-turned-politician at my feet. For example, Mona threw this politician's case file at Maya's feet; or, Mona threw Geagea's file at Maya's feet as a statement of disrespect; or, Mona threw his file because he is the most famous name in that archive, the case in question is infamous, and Maya is, after all, a researcher. Or, Mona threw Geagea's file at Maya's feet because he was a leader of a wartime Christian militia and Maya and Mona are from a "different side." In this discourse, Mona and Maya can discuss Geagea's war crimes only if they make equivalences and engage in both-side-ism.[76] Or, Mona demonstrated her unprofessionalism—brought forth by corruption, sectarianism, and family connections—by throwing a file that Maya had not officially requested across a room, at her feet. Maybe Mona threw Geagea's file because she was building another "us"—an "us" that cannot believe that our past is still our future. All of these explanations describe the same act—throwing an archival file documenting a war leader cum politician's treason case at a researcher's feet. All of these descriptions are accurate. But only some are statements. The discourse that licenses these statements anticipates the act of throwing a file and reads it as reflecting corruption and sectarianism. Moreover, this discourse—truth—can reach back into the past to place previous unrelated action and memory under the twinned signs of sectarianism and corruption—a process that Hacking calls "semantic contagion."[77]

In this ethnographic vignette, Mona was throwing the file during an American-led "war on terror" that killed more than a million people and spawned the multiple wars on terror that authoritarian leaders are currently waging across the Middle East targeting political dissent. A few months after Mona threw Geagea's file, the Arab uprisings would begin in Tunisia and roll like a wave across the region, just as securitization, authoritarianism, and wars would roll through on the uprisings' heels. A few months before she threw the file, there were parliamentary elections in Lebanon, and Geagea was an ally of the Sunni political leadership, led by Saad al Hariri, the son of the assassinated prime minister, that claimed to speak in mine and Mona's name. Mona and I had marveled at the spectacle of the son of an assassinated prime minister allying with a man who infamously assassinated another prime minister, Rashid Karami, whose murder is one of the "war crimes" that Geagea was convicted of by the Judicial Council. Geagea currently warns of the "dangers" that Syrian refugees pose to Lebanon and regularly threatens to "return"

them, just as he spoke of Palestinians during the civil war. The more we
zoom out of this ethnographic scene, the more the descriptions multiply,
intersect, and depart. As I initially wrote this archival ethnography, a civil
and transnational war two hours away, across the border into Syria, was
raging. Ten years into that war, almost 400,000 Syrians have been killed
or wounded, twelve million more have been displaced; the strongest military force in Lebanon—Hizballah—played a decisive role in that war, in
propping up the Asad regime.[78] Syrian refugees in Lebanon are targeted,
securitized, and attacked just as Palestinian refugees were during the civil
war and continue to be. The year 2021 was Lebanon's centenary, two
years into a popular uprising, and by then the country had imploded
economically, politically, and financially. That same year, 2021, I looked
up the Judicial Council's decisions related to Samir Geagea and noticed,
for the first time, Mona identified as the clerk and archivist. And again,
the descriptions proliferate. Maybe Mona wanted me to see the role she
had played in the case. Maybe she wanted me to see her signature affixed
to the conviction of Samir Geagea—one of the most infamous and conse-
quential cases in the history of the Lebanese judiciary. Maybe I hurt her
by refusing to see her signature, by not speaking with her about what she
thought or felt as she sat there, taking notes and filing papers during the
trial and, later, tending to the case files' place in the archive. Maybe she
wanted to be asked questions. There is indeterminacy, then and now, to
Mona's action and my writing of it: One cannot know which combination of motivations made the act of throwing the case file possible—or
the motivations that informed my perceptions then, and continue to inform my perceptions now, of that act. Archival context is not only about
the past. Archives are also functioning *in time*, as is archival research
and ethnography. If the archive is a temporal order, so is our relationship to it.[79] What we look for, what we want to find, and how we dwell
with what we have found all change in time. The thickness and complex-
ity of this exchange of gestures—just like the previous thickness of an
economy of favors at the archive—is fixed and flattened by the discourses
of sectarianism. Sectarianism is one technology of archival curation, but
it vibrates with the prehensive force of historicity and futurity. Everything that has happened, everything that may happen, and even things

that did not happen can and are and will be curated through the lens of sectarianism.

Once fixed and curated this way, Mona's action can be understood only as evidence that together we are sectarian toward our common sect, a sectarianism manifesting in the singling out of one militia leader cum politician from a different sect, and that together we are performing the corruption in state institutions that this sectarianism fosters. But there is only one such file in this room, and I am only *in* this room because of a meeting at a bar near Columbia University law school with the president of the State Shura Council, a meeting mediated by my relationship with my internationally well-respected US constitutional law professor. This is a connection based on class and professionalism and success within an economy that is deeply polarized. It is a form of nepotism that circulates within transnational networks of class and privilege (perhaps sites of class warfare) that are not read as "dangerous" or inherently violent or corrupt. After all, there is no transnational industry of expertise devoted to "fixing" the problem of class-based bias, Ivy League networking, or the violent production and circulation of wealth. Academia revels in producing knowledge about a sectarian or authoritarian or corrupt or classed or monarchial Middle East, yet almost never addresses the ways that academics sometimes use these same networks to produce that research. Many books that use archival methods never point to and explain how exactly they were able to *access* particularly hard to reach archives: instead they reproduce the myth of objective meritocracy, a myth that scaffolds and resignifies structural inequality as individual genius, tenacity, and achievement.[80] These myths do work in propping up a vision of the academy as a meritocracy precisely when—in the face of neoliberal austerity, restructuring, and public defunding—prestige, pedigree, and the class system within academia become ever more pronounced.[81]

The archive is not a room that the lonely researcher enters and exits to extract research. Such an approach ensures that both the archival object and the trope of the intrepid researcher remain stable. Citational practices do much to create this stage. To the extent that archivists or bureaucrats or photocopiers or cleaners enter the stage, they enter as a good fieldwork or research story, usually via a footnote or during an academic lecture. Yet the conversations I have had with Youssef and Mona are part of what makes the Assembly archive a legible object, as are the built-in lighter flashlights we used to look for particular cases, as is the toilet paper that archivists bought for their office because the government did not provide it. The ordinariness of the archive *is* the fabric of knowledge production, and if we shift our attention away from the archival object and toward what makes it so we find ourselves in the middle of the story each time, and yet not as its primary authors or its primary audience.

We will end here, on Mona's performance of indeterminacy, with this gesture: Mona throwing the case file of a warlord-turned-politician across the floor of an archive full of dust, cracked walls, and, at the time, no electricity. This is happening in the archive of Lebanon's highest court: a repository of memory and state action and networks of living together and apart during war and postwar worlds; a place where judges remember the handwriting of their dead colleagues and where lawyers construct an affective bridge, a legal strategy, a place I came to look for insights into the rule and ruptures of law, armed with theory and history and ethnography; a place of work. A place I had to unlearn to learn sectarianism. This room struck by mortars and the site of a fire, these rooms that may soon be replaced by digital files, software, and workers without tenure. In my mind now, I imagine, or choose to think, that Mona is throwing the file across the threshold between memory, ethnography, and history, of archive and Archive, and war and postwar worlds. Years later, the judiciary will be in the crosshairs of political and economic upheaval, accused of corruption, nepotism and perhaps even worse, of being ineffectual, hobbled, and lame. But in this moment, years earlier, Mona perhaps knows what her action indexes to readers: corruption, sectarianism, unprofessionalism, the failure of state institutions. She knows because she has been to training sessions, has read the civil society literature, follows the news that corrupt politicians want to cut the benefits of public employees as a first step to fighting their own corruption, feels the threat of immanent replacement, and is waiting to retire. But in this moment, in *her* archive, holding a warlord turned politician's file and looking toward me, Mona does not care.

She throws it anyway.

CHAPTER 3

Regulating Conversion

Sovereignty, Bureaucracy, and the Banality of Religion

"It [Christianity] was a piece of paper. . . .
[W]hen I was done with it I threw it away."
—Zahra

I VISITED DAR AL-FATWA with my parents in 2011. Decades earlier, they were married at a justice of the peace in Michigan. They had met in college in the United States and moved to Lebanon almost 10 years later, with two children and a third (me) on the way. Now, after living in Lebanon for 30 years, my mother was going to convert to Sunni Islam. As long as she was categorized as a Christian by the Lebanese state, she could not inherit from her Muslim husband or children, nor they from her. Outside the complex, my mother and I loosely covered our hair with scarves. My father rolled down his sleeves. The three of us entered the office of the sheikh with whom we had made an appointment. My parents were nervous, my father because he is generally distrustful of and somewhat allergic to clergy, and my mother because she wanted the whole affair to be over. My parents and I had argued earlier when I suggested that since my mother was becoming a Muslim *after* marriage, the standard Sunni marriage contract would now apply to their marriage. This contract, I explained, would mean that my father could divorce my mother at will and marry other women. They were furious at the suggestion that this might happen, but I was at that time one year into my fieldwork and was obsessed with legal facts and processes. I assumed that everyone, including my parents, would find these details as fascinating as I did.

Seated across from the sheikh, my father explained that he and my mother had married decades prior and that my mother had then twice professed that that there is no God other than God and the Mohammad is the Prophet of God (*shahada*). This was not true. My father, always looking for ways to evade clerical authority, hoped that my mother allegedly converting in private would be enough for the sheikh, and that we would soon be on our way with the correct paperwork in hand. We had rehearsed this line of argument at home, but it was to no avail. The sheikh was not convinced that there had been a "personal" conversion that had not been registered. He wanted to know why my mother had not converted earlier despite having been married into "a Muslim family" for decades and having "Muslim children." He asked her if she wanted to become a Muslim. After my mother had said yes, he then asked her, in English, if she knew that "Muslims also believe that Mary was a virgin." My mother, who does not consider herself religious and is certainly not Catholic, managed a polite "Oh really? That's interesting" in her best teacher's voice. The sheikh, clearly believing that he had *just* convinced my mother to convert, asked her whether she would be willing to attend Islamic classes, held at Dar al-Fatwa. My father was growing increasingly frustrated. He suspected the sheikh was dragging out the conversion to extract a monetary donation to Dar al-Fatwa. Before my father could step in and, I feared, derail the whole mission, I interjected. "Sheikh," I said to him, "we are a Muslim family and my mother has already said the *shahada* and is ready to say it again in front of you." When he began to respond, I cut him off. "We also know what the law is, and that as long as she professed before you she has become a Muslim." At this, the sheikh laughed and asked whether I was a lawyer. My mother muttered "almost." She then repeated the *shahada* after the sheikh, and we were promptly sent to a different office with a signed paper, which a different sheikh told us to file with the census registry of Beirut. We paid the fees associated with conversions and drove home.

This ethnographic vignette illustrates how the sectarian entanglement of sect, sexual difference, and secularism "animates the question of religious conversion," as Attiya Ahmad puts it, in Lebanon.[1] A couple marries in the United States and registers this civil marriage contract with Lebanese authorities. They have three children, who the Lebanese state identified and registered as Sunni Muslim following a patrilineal system of religious and sectarian registration. Later in life, they realize that the cheapest and most efficient way to protect their assets and those of their children is to both be from the same religion. Because sectarian classification is a patrilineal inheritance, it is incumbent on the wife to convert to be recognized as following the same religion. The alternative would mean that four people—my father, myself, my brother, and my sister—would have had to convert to Christianity, a process that is also more complicated than conversion to Islam.[2] When my mother's census registration was changed to reflect her conversion, Sunni courts gained jurisdiction over her marriage. A new set of laws now governed the physical, emotional, and financial relationship between wife and husband and wife and children. What enables this process are a set of sextarian laws and bureaucracies that regulate the relationship between the Lebanese state, its religious and personal status institutions, and its citizens.[3]

Law is not the only factor at play in this vignette. My parents were, at the time, upper class professionals. My father was a well-respected dean at an American university and has a broad social network. My mother, a retired children's librarian, has a cooler and more curious disposition than most. She was bemused throughout the process of her conversion, while my father stewed and seemed embarrassed by the whole thing. Neither of my parents is religious, and neither has any great deference to clerics of any religion. Importantly, their daughter had been studying law in Lebanon for years and knew exactly what their rights and duties were and were *not* in relation to both Dar al-Fatwa and the Lebanese state. She had even by that point interviewed lower- and higher-ranking sheikhs at Dar al-Fatwa about religious conversion. Law does not function outside of the ability to leverage it, and the laws and bureaucracies governing religious conversion in Lebanon are not exceptional to this rule. I have been told of encounters with the same sheikh at Dar al Fatwa that unfolded very differently. In one case, a European man needed to convert to Sunni Islam to placate his fiancée's wealthy and politically powerful family. He (and his fiancée) did not know what the civil laws governing religious conversion were. In fact, they had assumed that there were no civil laws that regulated or legislated conversion. He paid for religious classes at Dar al-Fatwa for months before being given his certificate of conversion. Until our interview he had believed that this was proper procedure. In some cases, the price of not having legal information available is much higher. A few years ago a friend was going through an acrimonious divorce. She is a British citizen who met her husband, a human rights worker, in the United States while they were both in graduate school. The couple had three daughters and decided to convert to Shi'i Islam together (he was Sunni, she Christian) in order to protect their inheritance. At the time of their conversion, neither knew that the standard marriage contract would apply by default in case of divorce or marital discord. When they separated, the wife found that only her husband could "decide" that the marriage was definitively over. I asked her why she had not researched the legal implications of her conversion. She replied that she had thought that they were protecting their daughters and that she had never imagined that she would be locked in a bitter divorce with a man intent on utilizing all the patriarchal advantages enshrined in Ja'fari jurisprudence. This sentiment—that one does not enter a marriage thinking of a divorce—was one that I heard often while conducting fieldwork. "People who are in love," another friend told me, after I advised her to write an air-tight Muslim marriage contract instead of getting married in Cyprus, "aren't going to think about things like law when all they want to do is get married."[4]

Anthropologists have long been interested in religious conversion; in the role that religion plays in the production, maintenance, and circulation of cultural practice and difference, the relationships between conversion, colonization, and political dissent, and in the epistemic, structural, and affective contours of secularism.[5] Much of this work[6] has framed religious conversion, in Talal Asad's words, as something that "happens *to* people rather being something that they choose to become after careful thought."[7] Much like love, religion and religious conversion are framed as passionate states that inhabit, consume, blur, and ultimately transform us. Webb Keane has pointed to sincerity, predicated on the idea that acts in the world are accurate translations of internalized states and an interior will, as a critical aspect of what he names the "Christian modern"[8]—a term that points to the traffic between Christian and secular semiotic ideologies. Selim Derengil and Gauri Viswanathan have shown how political and economic concerns animate religious conversion, from tax evasion (Christian to Muslim) and escape from military service (Muslim to Christian) in the Ottoman Empire, to mass conversions of Dalits to Buddhism in colonial and postcolonial India to gain political representation in a secular and pluralistic state. There is a popular sense that conversion *out* of Islam is always met with violence and social exclusion in Muslim societies. As Ahmad notes, "The question of conversion is perhaps most acute in respect to Islam. . . . Hegemonic expectations of modernity and secularism produce an incitement to questions about religious conversions, especially Islamic ones."[9] I still remember the surprise of classmates when in a graduate seminar I said I knew Muslims in Lebanon who had converted to Christianity and who had neither been disowned nor shunned. "Apostasy" is not the only metonym through which to understand religious conversion, including conversion from Islam to Christianity in the Middle East. In Lebanon, religious conversion is a conversion into a different sextarian legal regime, and religious difference and pluralism are articulated as the sovereign right to have a nested jurisdiction over sexual difference. The ability to convert, the guarantee of religious freedom and religious "choice," is structured by the compulsory nature of the modern state.[10]

Thinking about religious conversion from the vantage point of Lebanon brings new perspectives and questions to the anthropological literature on religion, secularism, sexual difference, and sovereignty. This is not because Lebanon is an exceptional confluence of historical and contemporary factors. Instead, the Lebanese state represents an intensification of the relationship between pluralism, secularism, and sovereignty, on the one hand, and the contradictions of liberalism's articulation of this relationship, on the other. Above all, following religious conversion in Lebanon invites us to rethink secularism's management of religious difference by stressing the *banality* of religious conversion, and perhaps, of religious difference itself. By banality I mean the mundane, bureaucratic, opaque, and inescapable skein of religious difference *as* governmentality and as governance. Stressing the banal, sextarian nature of religious conversion at the very least troubles narratives of hardened sectarian difference and simultaneously reveals how state practices of religious coexistence and secularism function through the maintenance of unequal regimes of sexual difference. While perhaps these conversions do not index a shift in consciousness or religious conviction, they also do not need to, as the example of my parents and the following case from the Assembly demonstrate. In this chapter, I follow conversion archivally and ethnographically to better understand and theorize secular state power and its relationship to sovereignty, religious difference, and sexual difference. We begin with ethnographic readings of cases concerning conversion and converts from the Plenary Assembly archive, then move to the life histories of two converts. Marriage, inheritance, custody, and divorce animate the process and experience of religious conversion—underlining the sextarian infrastructure of property and intimacy.

Scenes from a Marriage

In 1988 a Lebanese Melkite Roman Catholic man and a Lebanese Sunni Muslim woman got married and received marriage certificates from both the Catholic Church and the Sunni Muslim religious authority, Dar al-Fatwa. They registered their Catholic marriage with the census offices run by the Ministry of the Interior. The couple had been given special permission from a Catholic bishop to have a "mixed," Muslim-Christian marriage, and the Sunni woman had not converted. Two weeks prior to the church wedding the husband had converted to Islam at Dar al-Fatwa, and six days after that church wedding the couple also signed and registered a wedding contract with Dar al-Fatwa. These multiple marriages are not uncommon as attempts to satisfy both families of a mixed-religion couple. Neither the husband's conversion to Islam nor the Muslim marriage contract was registered with the census office. For many years, the couple was in "crazy love," according to a ruling from the Catholic Court of First Instance in 2004.

In May 2003, the wife filed for an annulment, asking the Catholic courts to grant her both child support and custody of the couple's minor children. She claimed that her husband had been neglecting his physical and financial duties toward her and that he had also neglected his children. In arguing for an annulment, the woman stressed that she was a practicing Sunni Muslim and as such did not and had never believed that marriage was a sacrament. Instead, she had always believed in the right to divorce. She brought up the fact that she had insisted on her right to initiate divorce in the Muslim marriage contract, the contract the couple had not registered with the state. Besides, she and her lawyers wrote, she had neither been baptized nor officially converted. She relayed statements from family and friends attesting to her conviction that Islam was a more just religion precisely because Muslims could divorce their spouses. Her lawyers used this evidence to argue that the Catholic Church should annul her marriage. The husband did not argue against the annulment, nor did he seek custody. Instead, he argued that he should not be required to pay alimony because *she* was seeking an annulment and because he was "surprised" to discover that she did not believe in the sacrament of marriage, as he did. He did not request custody over his children. The couple's case put the Roman Catholic court in a quandary. The children were legally Catholics, yet a self-professed practicing Muslim was asking for an annulment, alimony, and custody, claiming that her children's Catholic father was an unfit parent and husband. Meanwhile, the Catholic husband had objected only to the amount of alimony his wife was requesting. In December 2004, more than a year after her initial appeal, the Court of First Instance granted the Muslim Sunni woman an annulment, awarded her guardianship over her minor Melkite Roman Catholic children, and required the husband to pay for all legal expenses, child support, and the children's medical and school expenses.

In February 2005, three months after the Catholic court issued its decision, the husband registered his 1988 conversion to Islam with the Ministry of Interior and the census offices. He also obtained a certified document claiming that, in the eyes of Dar al-Fatwa, he had been a Sunni Muslim since his 1988 conversion and thus his children had been born Muslim, as children inherit the personal status of their fathers.[11] One month after registering his conversion, the Sunni Court of First Instance granted him a divorce and custody over his children. In response, the wife and her lawyer returned to the Catholic Court of Appeals. This time, the husband and his lawyers claimed in legal briefs to the Roman Catholic Court of Appeals that his wife had "tricked him" into converting to Islam back in 1988, that she had refused to raise their children as Christians as he had wanted, that she had forced their children to fast during Ramadan, and that she had urged him to work abroad so that she could be with her boyfriend in Lebanon. As further proof of her corrupted and corrupting character, he claimed that she enjoyed oriental dancing (belly dancing) in public, taught oriental dance lessons, and had also taught his daughters "this dancing style" despite his objections. Throughout his lawyers' legal briefs to the Catholic court, he did not mention that he had already appealed to and been granted a divorce by the Sunni court system.

But she did. She submitted evidence, in the form of the family's census IDs, that he had only just registered his conversion to Islam, thus stimulating a change in the status of his minor children, *after* a decision by the Catholic courts had been issued. Because of this, her lawyers argued, the jurisdiction of the original, Catholic marriage certificate held, even if she and her ex-husband were now both Sunni Muslim in the eyes of the state. In mid-2005, the Catholic Court of Appeals certified the verdict issued by the Court of First Instance and again granted the wife an annulment, guardianship, and child support. At this point the woman had been awarded two favorable verdicts, and the man one, from two different personal status court systems.

The husband appealed to the Plenary Assembly that same month, asking it to decide on the proper jurisdiction of their marriage contract and hence divorce or annulment. The husband and his lawyers argued that because they were both (*now*) Sunni Muslims, the Sunni personal status court had jurisdiction. The wife and her lawyers argued that because they were married under Roman Catholic law and because the man had only registered his 1988 conversion to Islam with the state in 2005, *after* Catholic court proceedings had begun and indeed after a decision had been issued, the jurisdiction remained with the church.[12]

The Assembly decided the case between the two personal status court systems on procedural, not substantive, grounds. The husband's lawyers, if we recall, had argued that because he had converted to Islam in 1988 both he *and* his wife were Sunni Muslim, and the Roman Catholic court lacked jurisdiction. He was, on the surface, correct; Lebanese law states that the proper jurisdiction of any marriage between two Muslim[13] citizens always lies in Muslim personal status courts, even when the marriage

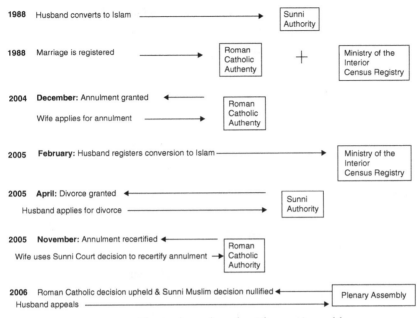

FIGURE 5. Chart of case heard at Plenary Assembly.

is conducted outside of Lebanon and through a civil marriage contract. In fact, his lawyers appended and submitted an opinion from the public prosecutor at the sharia court[14] to the Assembly. The non-binding advisory opinion argued that the proper jurisdiction did lie with the Sunni courts. However, the Assembly reiterated that Lebanese law clarifies that conversions go into legal effect only when they are registered with state institutions, that is, in the census registry. The husband had registered his conversion to Islam with Dar al-Fatwa in 1988, but not with the state until 2005. This meant that his children had also been Melkite Roman Catholic until 2005. Lebanese law states that the jurisdiction of a marriage contract is transferred when both members of a couple convert to the same religion or sect, but only if both members of a couple convert *at the same time*. This standard was put in place to protect against solitary conversions done to intentionally subvert the rule of law.[15]

The Plenary Assembly's decision was issued during the 2006 Israel-Lebanon war. The justices decided that the Roman Catholic courts had jurisdiction and noted that the man registered his conversion with the census authorities only after a legal decision related to the marriage had already been issued. If it allowed the Sunni court's verdict to stand, the Assembly reasoned, it would cause harm to public order and to the harmony of the personal status system. The Assembly noted that for the Sunni personal status court to have jurisdiction over this case, both husband and wife would have had to become Muslim at the same time. This was a moot point, given that she was, and had always been, a Muslim. His conversion should have been registered before any party approached the Roman Catholic court. The state and its institutions, the jurists argued, do not have the right to interrogate the faith or beliefs of a citizen. Instead, the state must limit itself to examining legal and bureaucratic evidence to delineate the proper jurisdiction of a case between personal status courts. The standard of conversion *must* be the equalizing temporality of state bureaucracy. The Assembly decided that the ruling of the Roman Catholic Court of Appeals stood and the ruling from the Sunni personal status court was voided. The Sunni Muslim woman was awarded custody over her (now Muslim) minor children, alimony, and child support by the Roman Catholic courts.

In the Name of the Lebanese People

The Assembly hears cases that are often spectacular, complicated, and substantive. Plaintiffs must have the tenacity and resources to advance their case to the Assembly, the country's highest civil court. For example, the lawyer who argued on behalf of the Sunni woman in the case above is, to put it mildly, a rock star of the legal world. When I first requested that particular case file from Mona, she tapped her finger on the lawyer's name and remarked "every case he takes, he wins." The first of many times I visited that lawyer in his office, I marveled at his photographs with a pope, bishops, the presidents of world powers, Lebanese politicians and Arab leaders, and other international, regional, and national movers and shakers. He has presented cases in front of the Vatican Rota, published books in Arabic and French, and lectured and taught at universities locally and internationally. Needless to say, his expertise, inseparable from his connections, is not cheap.

Decisions by Lebanese courts, including the Assembly, begin with "In the Name of the Lebanese People." This sentence is not merely a rhetorical device. It is a form of address that calls into being a national public and announces that national public as the ultimate source and author of state sovereignty. "In the Name of the Lebanese People" cites the authority of a preceding and stable national sovereignty even as it performs it into being and stabilizes it,[16] demonstrating the past-future temporality of the nation-state.[17] Nation-states are not alone in performing this temporal trick—citing a preexisting sovereignty to reconstruct it through an authoritative legal framework. While civil courts such as the Assembly ground their sovereign authority in a body of people—a nation—religious courts ground their sovereignty in both a Lebanese national framework *and* a transnational religious one. For example, while Roman Catholic Courts of First Instance and Appeals are located in Lebanon, their final appeals court is in the Vatican. The Shiʿi (Jaʿfari) courts are fully in Lebanon, but cases advanced to it sometimes append or cite opinions from ayatollahs not in or from that country. Sometimes those opinions are taken into account, and sometimes they are not.[18]

The Assembly is often tasked with deciding whether a Lebanese personal status court or a foreign marriage/family court has jurisdiction. Muslim personal status courts, as we saw in the divorce case from the Assembly archive, retain jurisdiction between two Lebanese Muslims (with the exception of the Druze) anywhere in the world, a jurisdiction that can be enacted on the ground via a court case. Many cases in the Assembly archive feature husbands who traveled to Lebanon to begin a divorce case after having already received one in their country of residence. The Assembly has reviewed cases that include divorce, separation, or alimony proceedings from a broad array of countries including Australia, Canada, Egypt, France, Iran, Kuwait, Turkey, the UAE, and the United States—basically anywhere the Lebanese diaspora resides. Lebanese civil and religious personal status laws are knitted into transnational legal frameworks; religious transnational legal frameworks are partnered with transnational civil frameworks dedicated to the regulation of blood kinship relations and "families."[19] The same day a judge at the Lebanese civil personal status court adjudicates a divorce based on Cypriot law,[20] an annulment decision by the Rota courts is recorded into and enforced by the Lebanese state.[21] National bodies such as the Assembly are nodal points in the disentanglement of international laws, jurisdictions, and rulings into actionable and territorially bounded ones. The Assembly is a window into the scalar nature of sovereignty and into how national sovereignty is enacted alongside, within, and above transnational civil and religious legal frameworks. As the Assembly nests the jurisdiction of personal status courts within its own, it is also a conduit and mediator of supra-national jurisdictions that in some cases supersede the jurisdiction of the nation-state.

A case decided by the Assembly in 1993 clearly illustrates how the court enacts and defines the sovereignty of the Lebanese state as that which surrounds and delimits the jurisdiction of personal status courts. The Assembly also performs sovereignty by insisting on the state's primary and indivisible right to interpret civil, criminal, and constitutional law and jurisprudence. The court makes clear that it is a line of defense for converts who are coerced or pressured by the religion they have left. The jurists distinguish themselves from the limited jurisdiction of personal status courts and describe their work as protecting the constitutional right to freedom of religion. The protection of religious freedom is thus a logic and articulation of the state's sovereignty.[22]

"We have left you your hegemony over us"

The Maronite Church is often before the Assembly in cases involving converts for two interrelated reasons: The church and the state disagree on how to measure the validity of a religious conversion, and a concern that too many Maronites are converting to other forms of Christianity or to Islam because of the specific difficulties of divorce in Catholic law. The language of a case from 1993, in which the Assembly weighed the validity of a decision issued by the Maronite Court of Appeals in 1989 (the last year of the civil war) explicates the state's power over religious institutions and communities. It also lays bare the frustration of the Maronite Church over how the state, through the Assembly, adjudicates and structures religious conversion.

The case concerned a man and a woman who got married in 1981 in the Maronite Church. The woman had converted to Maronite Catholicism from Greek Orthodoxy prior to their wedding. It was not a happy marriage, and the couple did not have any children. Years later they both converted to the Syriac Orthodox Church and obtained a divorce within a week. He then converted to Greek Orthodox Christianity, married again, and had children. After her ex-husband's remarriage, the now ex-wife converted "back" to Maronite Catholicism and filed a case with the Maronite Court asking to be considered an abandoned spouse with rights to financial support. She alleged that her conversion to the Syriac Orthodox Church (but not her first conversion, to Maronitism from Greek Orthodoxy) was done under duress and threats of violence by her then husband. This pressure and coercion violated the constitutional principle of freedom of religion, as well as the laws that regulate religious conversion. Both the Maronite Court of First Instance and the Maronite Court of Appeals subsequently granted her spousal support. This was despite the fact that the divorce from the Syriac court as well as her ex-husband's subsequent conversion to Greek Orthodoxy and marriage had been registered in the census registry. In its decision, the Maronite Court of Appeals implied that it *wanted* this case to reach the Assembly.

In the opening pages of the 1993 decision, the Maronite Court of Appeals offered a short history of the tension between the Maronite Church and the judiciary. It referenced a strike by the Lebanese Bar Association in 1951. That strike was both in favor of a civil marriage law and against a 1951 law that determined the jurisdiction of Christian and Jewish personal status courts.[23] The court wrote, "Are these positions [on conversion] to spite confessional authorities for having these rights, after the lawyers strike for three months, and which are less comprehensive than another well-known community?" This was a veiled reference to Muslim sects, whose personal status courts also adjudicate inheritance.[24] They also relayed a conversation from the 1950s that supposedly took place in a coincidental meeting between the head of the Maronite Court of Appeals and his "good friend" who subsequently became the president of the judiciary, which would have also made him a jurist on the Assembly. In this conversation, the president of the judiciary supposedly expressed his frustration that there was no civil marriage law, only religious personal status laws. He asked the Maronite priest "what have you left us?" in reference to the 1951 law and the jurisdiction of the civil judiciary. In this story, the Maronite priest supposedly responded that "we have left you your hegemony over us," expressing the nested nature of religious personal status jurisdiction within that of civil law.

The Maronite Court of Appeals went on to express its disappointment with the Assembly's record in cases regarding the affairs of converts. It historicized the Assembly's jurisprudence on conversion and insulted the current jurists who made up the Assembly.

> The Position of the Lebanese state, represented by the Plenary Assembly and the Cassation Courts to which it belongs, in its ability to decide jurisdiction, is not what it used to be; . . . In the past the judiciary investigated these kinds of [conversion] practices for subversion of law, and would take the opinion of the concerned sects,[25] but these days the Assembly refuses to listen to religious authorities and they have refused to consider the question of subversion of law, even though it is obvious and provable in some cases, as they have also ignored previous jurisprudence that was in the favor of confessional authorities, even though we cannot say that present Assembly jurists are any more educated, experienced, or wise than their predecessors.[26]

The Maronite Church was angry at the Assembly because it was not overturning decisions that the church or its constituents believed demonstrated that some were converting out of their community as a legal strategy.

The Assembly responded to many of the claims made by the Maronite Court of Appeals in its own strongly worded decision, issued in 1993. First, the Assembly noted that the Maronite Court of Appeals hoped this case would reopen debate on rulings concerning converts. However, it soon became clear that this decision would not make the Maronite Church happy. The jurists wrote that "The Cassation Court [of which the Assembly is composed] in its position of power does not question issues of faith or religious values," but it *does* decide if and when a religious court has issued a ruling on a case that it does not have jurisdiction over; this is a matter related to public order. Although the Maronite Church was refusing the jurisdiction of the Syriac court over anyone originally baptized in its church, "the confessional courts are limited in their jurisdiction to personal status issues, and that jurisdiction only extends to members of that sect." The Assembly then contrasted this limited jurisdiction with that of the state and the Cassation Courts that represent it, a jurisdiction that extends over the entire population of Lebanon. The jurists plainly stated that the Maronite courts overstepped their boundaries with serious ramifications that the Assembly could not allow to continue. It reiterated its sole right to interpret Lebanese laws and to produce jurisprudence for the national court system.

> In terms of the claim of subverting the law . . . In the first incidence, a sect that has been left by one of its sons cannot argue against his decision even if it has suspicions for his reasons of conversion, including a desire to remove himself from under their laws . . . It is not possible for a sect to keep him [the convert] by force under its laws and principles—and when it wants to, the civil powers cannot allow this kind of coercion to take place . . . and in the case of subversion and the question of a couple converting to another sect with the intention to change their personal status law . . . subversion of the law is not part of the Maronite Court's jurisdiction . . . The civil authorities cannot allow a sect to take it upon itself to decide what its jurisdiction is, or to deny the jurisdiction of others.[27]

The Assembly grounded its decisions on converts in the constitutional principle of freedom of religion. However, religious freedom here itself was plural and contested; whose religious freedom mattered? The freedom of the individual citizen to convert in and out of different religions and sects, or the freedom of religious authorities to adjudicate the "personal" affairs of its members? The Assembly answered this fundamental question by voiding the decision of the Maronite courts for lack of jurisdiction and noting that any subsequent decisions by it in this case should not be taken into account by any state institution.

Conversion and the Nesting of Sovereignty

Sovereignty and jurisdiction are fellow travelers. The sovereign claims to surround, organize, and permeate the nested jurisdiction of personal status courts.[28] The Assembly's power to decide legal cases that include competing sovereignties, its power to "protect" citizens from religious authorities, and its guarantee of religious freedom all express Lebanese state sovereignty. The Lebanese state is a productive space to think through the constitutive contradictions of liberal constitutionalism, its articulation through jurisdiction practices, and the background from which such formations emerge, the secular episteme.[29]

The 1993 case highlighted two critical aspects of sovereignty. First, sovereignty was defined by the Assembly as the resolution of conflict—a unitary sovereignty was performed as the ability to decide, limit, nullify, and authorize nested, contested, and multiple claims of jurisdiction. Here we can trace the productive relationship between conflict and sovereignty. Second, this case and others like it illustrated how unitary, secular, state sovereignties are formed through the production, bordering, performance, and regulation of a "private sphere." As Suad Joseph has written, "through legislation, through regulation of courts, through its practices as well as what it has not been willing to do, the state has invented the separations between the arenas of the "state," "civil society," and the "domestic" (what might also be called the arenas of government, non-government, and kinship)."[30] The private sphere evidences both the sovereignty of personal status courts *and* that of the state, which grants and limits this sovereignty. Here the term "nesting" points to the domestication of political and national alterity.[31] Personal status courts do not claim sovereignty over sectarian difference but over laws that govern sexual difference within different communities, over *sextarian* difference. Moreover, the state maintains the right to intervene in and arbitrate disputes that arise when the nested sovereignty of these courts affects public order. Of course, only the state can determine the content of the public order—just as only the state can define "public morality" and deploy it to securitize sexuality. The state's sextarian jurisdiction is always sovereign—it surrounds, overwhelms, intervenes, and interprets.

Conversion is a right granted to all Lebanese citizens; it is key to the practice of the freedom of religion and to the secular state's duty to equally defend the religious freedom of its citizens. Thus procedures for conversion are defined by civil law, the conditions of which must be satisfied for a citizen's conversion to take legal effect. This does not mean, however, that conversions that are not registered with the state are all exercises in religious insincerity; it merely means that these conversions have no impact on the bureaucratic and legal status of citizens or on that of their minor children, if the converts in question are fathers. In cases that concern unregistered conversions, the Assembly can decide that a citizen's religion may differ from personal status. In doing so, the Assembly maintains and practices the right to parse out the differences of religion, sect, and their personal status. It practices and demonstrates the secular sovereignty of the state as the ability to limit, define, and manage the place of religion in the body public. Secularism itself is practiced as a liberal form of governance—the promise of a space that transcends the calamity of religious difference through nesting and domesticating it in the private sphere.[32]

In a case decided by the Assembly in 2008, the Sunni Muslim charitable trust (*waqf*) of Tripoli alleged that a man had converted to Islam for financial benefit and thus "subvert[ed] the law." The case concerned the inheritance of an elderly man who converted from Maronite Catholicism to Sunni Islam decades earlier. This man was unmarried and had no children and no Muslim relatives. This meant that the Sunni charitable trust of Tripoli stood to inherit his estate. However, his nephew converted to Islam while his uncle was on his deathbed, which transformed him, he and his lawyers claimed, into his uncle's only legal heir. The trust accused the nephew of not *really* becoming a Muslim since he still attended church services. Obviously, the trust alleged, this man became a Muslim only to inherit from his uncle, who had "truly" converted from Maronite Christianity to Sunni Islam decades earlier. Ultimately, the case hinged on the fact that the nephew had not completed the bureaucratic procedures of his conversion in time for his uncle's death. In its decision, the Assembly examined the temporality of how and when religion, personal status, and sect are tied and untied. However, when responding to the trust's allegation that the nephew had subverted Lebanese law and offended religion, the judges argued that they could not interfere in a citizen's practice of the freedom of religion.[33] Despite the fact that conversion with the intent to subvert the law is illegal, the Assembly almost always rules that conversion is one of the quintessential rights of citizenship in a state dedicated to religious pluralism. Conversion should be judged by the citizen's *actions* and not by the *intention* motivating conversion.[34] To be more specific, the court argued that the evidentiary terrain of intent should be found in bureaucratic action, not in questions of faith or interiority. Thus at the time of his uncle's death, the judges at the Assembly reasoned, the defendant was a Muslim by religion and a Sunni by sect because he had professed faith in Allah and Muhammad in front of Sunni authorities. Yet in the eyes of the state, ultimately the eyes that mattered the most in this case, the nephew was a Maronite Catholic.

Personal Status/Sect/Religion

The divergences between personal status and sect are vital to understanding the sociopolitical realities of Lebanon and the myriad ways that citizens practice them. Suad Joseph has convincingly illustrated the tension between the sociopolitical realities of "sect" and "religion" in Lebanon.[35] I introduce here personal status as a third distinct form of identification and recognition that is collapsed with/in sect. The Lebanese state uses personal status to denote which one applies to each citizen—whether Muslim, Christian, or Jewish. One of the three official identity cards in Lebanon displays this information, where the category of *maddhab* corresponds to personal status law—Muslim Shi'i or Chaldean Christian, for example.[36] This is not because the state views personal status and sect as one and the same but because the state recognizes only one official personal status per sect. Sects that do not have their "own" recognized personal status and its attendant legal/bureaucratic apparatus follow that of the sect that they designate as closest to them, such as the case of the Alawite sect that follows the Ja'fari fiqh and the 1962 law regulating Sunni and Shi'i courts. The practice of conversion occurs at (and plays on) the jagged line of disambiguation between sect and personal status.

Religious conversion always engenders movement between personal status laws, but it does not always engender movement between sects or between religions. "Sect" is a larger and thicker category than personal status. It incorporates shared historical narratives, shared religious beliefs and practices, and, for many, shared political aspirations and anxieties. In the logic of the Lebanese state, a sect is (at least) three things: A sect is a historical community oriented toward a common past. A sect is a political community oriented toward a common future.[37] Finally, a sect is a biopolitical category, inherited from the father at birth via a regime of sexual difference that produces, identifies, and securitizes modular forms of political difference in a national framework. A citizen is recognized as belonging to a particular sect according to a much wider set of criteria than that of personal status. Lebanese history is filled with examples of "conversion" among the political and economic elite; from Emir Bashir to presidents, prime ministers, ministers and parliamentarians in the post–civil war era. At least one president and one prime minister have been converts, having left the personal status community that corresponds to the sect these offices claim to represent. Examples like this illustrate what is often neglected in Lebanese historiography and literature on sectarianism. A state's recognition of a citizen's sectarian affiliation through her personal status may not be the same as what that citizen identifies herself as; not what Lebanese society recognizes her as; and not what political party she votes for or even leads. Further, neither sect nor personal status necessarily reflects one's religious beliefs and practices. A citizen who converts to obtain a divorce may be an atheist recognized by the government as following the Greek Orthodox personal status but socially recognized as a Maronite.[38] Likewise, if a citizen chooses not to identify with her sect, she will *still* be sociopolitically and legally recognized by state institutions as, for example, a "Druze" woman. Personal status and sex are the technologies of recognition that the Lebanese census and the state follow. Sextarian status is *assigned*. It can change following religious conversion, but there is no outside the sectarian logics and structures of the state.

Colonial power has afterlives in postcolonial bureaucracy and politics.[39] Often postcolonial bureaucracy *is* colonial bureaucracy, and not only in former colonies but in imperial metropoles as well.[40] Census categories and legal, identity based categories themselves represent the disciplining of the unrelenting openness and messiness of assemblages, as Jasbir Puar notes, into regulatory categories that form and are governed by the coercive, unavoidable, and productive terrain of state power.[41] Liberal politics is a question of finding and calibrating the correct and least harmful relationship between categories of governance—a policy of harm reduction.[42]

Lebanon is a former colony and a former imperial node where political difference was produced and managed as a technology of rule.[43] Citizenship was not juridically constituted as a legally abstract and universal category; it was and is a serialization of political difference around the axis of sex/sect. Sectarian difference became hypervisible through technologies like the 1932 census and its ensuing national registry, a sectarian personal status regime. The hypervisibility of sectarian difference was constituted through the sublimation of its twin, sexual difference. While "sect" and "sex" are co-constitutive in practice, they are discrete census metrics that together form the legal and bureaucratic architecture of citizenship. Religious conversion is the recalibration and retying of the knot of sect and sex. State power and sovereignty move and build like kinetic energy, amplified and enacted through constituting, splitting, measuring, recalibrating, and regulating assemblages into intersections and intersections into knots. The Assembly is a juridical body that ties and unties the knots of sectarian difference.

The Public Order of Bureaucracy

Public order is ubiquitous in cases heard by the Assembly, but citizens and personal status courts define these notions in different ways. Citizens and their lawyers consider procedural missteps and omissions, as well as court decisions issued by the religion they have converted out of, violations of the public order. Personal status courts, however, will often advocate for their jurisdiction over a conversion case in the name of public order, arguing that this concept ensures the equal treatment and respect of all religious authorities by a neutral and secular state. The Assembly, in addition to considering the first two notions, has an additional understanding of public order that is couched in the anonymizing, banal, and reiterative nature of bureaucracy.

Anyone who has filled out a census form, applied for a visa or a travel document, or registered a marriage or a divorce understands something fundamental about state power: It is stultifying, and it is bureaucratic. Bureaucracy is a primary point of contact between people of multiple legal statuses as well as a singular nation-state and a global community of nation-states.[44] Bureaucracy also plays a key role in producing and managing this "global community." The promise of bureaucracy is its most frustrating aspect: anonymity. On the one hand, the anonymizing power of bureaucracy promises that you are not being measured unfairly or being judged by a different set of criteria than anyone else. In moments of bureaucratic failure, we blame ourselves (crap, I didn't fill out the form right!) rather than the process. On the other hand, the experience of bureaucracy is often an experience in *being* anonymous, an evisceration of the self,[45] the plotting of individuals into replaceable parts of a machine,[46] the mediation of chance and experience into a statistic.[47] The experience of bureaucracy often leads to the realization that to the state, which plays such a large and determining role in your life, you are literally nothing but a number.

When bureaucracy fails, when forms are not printed or run out, when government workers create years' long logjams by processing data late, and when disputes emerge between citizens due to a bureaucratic mistake, the answer is often *more* bureaucracy.[48] As Ilana Feldman has written, "Bureaucratic practice can appear as a hall of mirrors, each instance of such practice being judged in relation to other such practices, and which in fact may be simply the same practice duplicated endlessly."[49] For governments and state institutions, the power and promise of bureaucracy is clear. Bureaucracy makes statistics and the ever more efficient management of populations possible, in part by disciplining and representing the messiness of life as visible, contained, measurable, and intervenable. Bureaucracy stimulates a field of expertise, the bureaucrat, who represents the supposedly dispassionate "logic" of the state, rules and procedures on how to document, organize, measure, and represent life and death.[50] States and governments feverishly document their actions, up to and including genocide, through yet more bureaucracy.[51] Eventually this documentation becomes an archive where academics and others dwell, writing histories out of histories of power.[52] Bureaucratic power and the bureaucratic promise *to* power are at play every time a tired researcher rubs her eyes and wishes for more coffee as she rifles through reams of paper that meticulously record, for example, killing or torture.

Bureaucracy is an engine of governmentality and of biopower. Nowhere is this truer than in census registries. Census registries always claim to "record" relevant information, but in fact they produce that information. Census categories massify and individualize simultaneously through their organizational logics. State power can manifest as management of census categories (men's health indicators) and the management of the relationships *between* census categories (sectarian parity, percentage of citizens to noncitizens). At the most basic level, census categories are categories of securitization precisely because they represent the information a nation-state believes it *must* be able to know, measure, and modulate about people who live in a particular territory.[53] Bureaucracy is indispensable to modern state power because it produces vital information and promotes a form of meritocracy and equal access through depersonalization and massification. The reiterative and anonymizing nature of bureaucracy is key to a meritocratic promise in liberalism, equal *access* to equality. If liberal democracies' bureaucracies mediate structural access to equality, the foundational promise and aspiration of liberalism is an equality that never arrives, nor can it *ever* arrive.[54] Thus bureaucracy structures the compulsive relation between citizens and nation-states while ideologically mediating that relation. Everyone can be equal in the dispassionate eyes of bureaucracy, as long as *you* have the right to be equal, fill in the forms correctly, and pay the necessary fees. For these reasons, bureaucracy plays an important role in how the Plenary Assembly defines public order.

The Assembly uses bureaucracy and state census registries as evidence of religious freedom. They frame the state's refusal to interrogate a citizen's *reasons* for converting as protecting the freedoms of religion and expression. These protections stem from the liberalism of the state. The Assembly defines religious freedom in two registers: a citizen or resident's freedom of religion, and the freedom of religion guaranteed by vesting equal jurisdictional power in different religious communities via personal status courts. Public order can be protected and measured, however, only through ensuring that citizens *and* personal status courts correctly perform their bureaucratic relation to the state. Thus a personal status court issuing a decision in a case that it no longer has jurisdiction over is a threat to public order, as is a citizen's claim to be a convert while being unable to prove that proper and timely bureaucratic procedures related to conversion were followed.[55] The banality of conversion protects public order through the promise that everyone will be treated equally as long as the appropriate paperwork has been properly filed.[56] The forms are the same whether you are a man or a woman, from Beirut or a small village, or a Muslim or a Christian or a Jew or an atheist. However, while the paperwork may be the same, their gendered effects are not. The stories and life histories of Zahra, sixty-something divorced Lebanese woman, and Husayn, a thirty-something recently married Lebanese man, present conversion as an experience and a process predicated on the impasses between religion, personal status, and sect. They highlight the gulf that may be present or may open between assigned identity—by which I mean categories we are bureaucratically assigned at birth—and the *experience* and narration of identity. They also help ground the persons and personal stakes behind each life laid bare before the Assembly and later before a researcher, writer, and reader.

The Banality of Conversion: The Stories of Zahra and Husayn

At the beginning of our first meeting, Zahra quickly ascertained that we were both "real Beirutis" from "good" and "old" families, and that, more specifically, we were both Sunni Beirutis. She did not mean that we were practicing Muslims, which neither of us was. Rather, she meant that we came from a similar social class and that we shared an archive of experience, of narration, and of being narrated as a singular community. We were brought together by her close friend and colleague, my best friend's mother, who is neither Sunni nor from or residing in Beirut. Our multiple proximities allowed for an easy intimacy, and she proceeded to unpack her memories of wartime marriage, divorce, and conversion.

In the 1970s Zahra married a Shi'i Muslim under Ja'fari fiqh and had two children, a girl and a boy. Her husband used to gamble and physically abused her. They got divorced twice, and twice he convinced her that he would change and that she should return to him. When Zahra would escape to her mother's house after violent confrontations with her husband, her mother would mutter to herself in anger: "*wallah ta nasrinha*" (I swear to God I will make her a Christian). Hearing this often-repeated sentence, Zahra thought—erroneously, it turned out—that if she became a Christian, she could escape her marriage for good. She took her mother's words as intergenerational knowledge about how to navigate the sextarian system. After years, Zahra wanted to divorce her husband a third time, which according to the Ja'fari jurisprudence would have been the "final divorce" after which they could not remarry unless she married another man in the interim. Her husband refused her request and was content with the fact that only men can de facto initiate divorce proceedings in Ja'fari courts. Zahra swore to him (and to herself, she said decades later) that she would show him who the real decision maker was in their marriage[57] and would divorce him whether he accepted it or not. She finally received that divorce in 1990, ten years after the first of her three divorces. She explained: "Time takes its time during war."

Zahra hired a lawyer and asked him whether she could obtain a divorce if she converted to Christianity. Her lawyer responded that in such a case she could be considered an apostate and "outside" of Islam, a circumstance under which the judge could decide that the couple should divorce. Her lawyer, based in West Beirut, hired two other lawyers from East Beirut's to help obtain her conversion. The implication was that this second set of lawyers were Christian. Every week, Zahra would meet both her "East Beirut" and her "West Beirut" lawyers under the shade of pine trees near the Ministry of Justice, which used to denote a quadrant of the civil war–era "green line" dividing warring East and West Beirut.

Her high heels sunk in the dirt under pine trees today buried by buildings as she and her lawyers discussed her legal options. Once, during such a meeting, a mortar landed in eyesight. Neither she nor her lawyers moved because they were so engrossed in conversation and so accustomed to the war. More than twenty years later, sitting at a chic Beirut cafe carved into the Mediterranean Sea, Zahra recounted the smell of the pine trees and the explosion. Zahra chuckled: She hadn't even ducked for cover.

Zahra refused to be baptized or to say that she had accepted Jesus Christ as her savior—two requirements of conversion to Christianity. She was "just signing papers and paying money." Finally, she and her lawyers met a Greek Orthodox priest on the roof of hospital near the Ministry of Justice to finalize the paperwork. Every time the priest asked her a question about her religious beliefs, she refused to answer; her East Beirut lawyer tried to change the subject. Finally, the priest gave her a signed conversion certificate confirming that she was now Greek Orthodox. I told Zahra skeptically that it was rare for a conversion to take place without at least some interaction between the priest and the would-be convert, particularly if the convert was a Muslim. Zahra looked at me, pointed at the sea stretched before us, and asked:

See the sea? What color is it?
Blue, I answered.
She replied: If you add enough green [dollars] to the sea, it will change
    color. In Lebanon we do whatever we want.[58]

With the priest's certificate of conversion in hand, Zahra promptly drove to the relevant census offices and registered her conversion from "Sunni Muslim" to "Greek Orthodox Christian." Her West Beirut lawyer took a copy of her new census identity to the Ja'fari personal status court. He presented her new census document to the judge and argued that because Zahra had forsaken Islam, she should be considered an apostate. As an apostate she should not benefit from the rights bestowed on all Muslims, such as the rights guaranteed to her in a Muslim marriage. Zahra's husband, however, did not object to his wife's conversion, and the judge demurred, saying that Muslim men are allowed to marry Christian women. At this point her lawyer switched gears to focus on the husband's abuse, gambling, and drinking. He argued that her husband had made Zahra so desperate that she was willing to take drastic steps, including conversion to Christianity and out of Islam, just to get out of the marriage. The judge responded that Zahra was 75 percent on the way to a divorce, but that he needed proof that the husband was a gambler (but not, apparently, proof that he was abusive) to grant her a *final* divorce. The judge sent a court employee with Zahra to Beirut's horse racetrack, the Hippodrome. Zahra confided decades later that her husband watched the races but never bet on the horses. But in 1990 and from across the street, she pointed out her husband's bald spot as he exited the Hippodrome. The court employee nodded in acknowledgment, got into his car, and drove off. Today Zahra wonders whether she could have pointed at any bald man and gotten the same result.

Finally, the Ja'fari judge issued a divorce. Zahra felt victorious. Her next task was to reconvert to Islam because she knew there would be legal complications if she remained a Christian and her children and parents were Muslim. She went to Dar al-Fatwa, bought a headscarf (a white one, she remembered) from a store underneath the mosque, and went to meet the sheikh. Zahra told him that she wanted to become a Muslim again, explaining that she had only recently converted to Christianity to facilitate her divorce. The sheikh was not amused and stipulated that she take religious classes at Dar al-Fatwa before he "accepted her" back into Islam. This request infuriated an already exhausted Zahra, who angrily told the sheikh that she probably knew more about Islam than he did and that she came from one of the oldest Muslim families in Lebanon. She left that office but vowed not to leave Dar al-Fatwa without a certificate of (re)conversion to Islam.

Zahra returned to the store under the main building of Dar al-Fatwa; she bought and wore a blue headscarf. She went back into the main building and ducked into the first sheikh's office that she saw. She spoke in more detail to this younger man about her abusive marriage and how she would have done anything to leave her marriage, knowing all along that her conversion on paper did not change anything "*really*." She was still, and always was, a Muslim, Zahra said emphatically. The sheikh understood her predicament, asked her to profess her faith in Islam, and welcomed her back. "The whole thing," she said, "took five minutes." Carrying a certificate that confirmed that she had converted from Greek Orthodox Christianity to Sunni Islam, Zahra left Dar al-Fatwa content. She took her certificate to the state census registry to file the paperwork. The clerk sternly preached that religion was not a joke and that it was odd to convert from Muslim to Christian to Muslim in less than a month. An exasperated Zahra shouted at the clerk to stop pontificating and do his job. The price of Zahra's "final" divorce was staggering. Throughout this story Zahra was paying money to her lawyers and, via them, to the priests, to the sheikhs, to the witnesses, to court and census employees. By 1990, she had paid more than $6,000, an exorbitant amount of money in the 1980s, a decade marked by civil war and bracketed by the rapid devaluation of the Lebanese pound. Zahra's conversion and reconversion from Islam to Christianity and back, as well as her interactions with priests, sheikhs, and state bureaucrats, all occurred during the final two years of the war.

Zahra considered her foray into Christianity and back again to Islam as nothing but misguided legal advice. "It was a paper," she said, referring to her conversion to Christianity, "when I was done with it I threw it away." When pressed as to why, if these changes in religion did nothing to affect who she is "on the inside," she made sure that she changed her paperwork again to be known as a Sunni Muslim, she spoke of the legal problems that could arise after her passing: She was a Christian and her children were Muslim, and they would not be able to inherit her estate, nor would *she* inherit from *her* parents. Custody was also an issue as long her children remained minors because Lebanese civil law stipulates that children follow the personal status of their father, who had remained Muslim. Muslim courts discriminate against non-Muslims in custody decisions. If she was not a Muslim on paper, her family would not be legally safe. She had not considered converting to Shi'i Islam (which her children were) because her sense of self was tied to being a Sunni Beiruti and because "it doesn't really matter, we are all Muslims anyways." The economic and legal registers of sectarianism conditioned the stakes of Zahra's conversion, divorce, and money.

A comparison of Husayn's and Zahra's stories highlights a tension within what I have so far been illustrating as an *intersection* between liberalism, secularism, and governmentality. At the time of our meeting, Husayn was in his early thirties, had a PhD in sociology, and was on the academic job market in Lebanon. He was a self-described "secularist." Husayn was one of the first to remove his personal status from his government records when the Ministry of the Interior made the necessary paperwork available. He was pleased that his new status aligned with how he viewed himself—a citizen—and not, as he put it, a *sectarian* citizen. Three years prior to removing his sect, Husayn had converted from Shiʿi to Sunni Islam because he wanted to move his census registration from a city in southern Lebanon, to Beirut, where he resided. Unfortunately, a senior politician was making it difficult for Lebanese Shiʿa to move their census registry out of that city because it was an election cycle and the politician wanted to concentrate voters from that sect. To circumvent this hurdle, Husayn first converted from Shiʿi to Sunni Islam. Once he was a Sunni, the process of moving his registration from southern Lebanon to Beirut was smooth. Afterwards, he went to the Shiʿi Higher Council[59] and converted *back*, a process that he says was more difficult because he had "left" the community at a height of Sunni-Shiʿa tensions. I asked him why he reconverted given his anti-sectarian atheism and since there were no inheritance complications for men. Husayn responded that had he remained a Sunni, it would have been a "choice." Returning to Shiʿism, however, was an inheritance imposed on him. "I didn't want to be Sunni, and I didn't want to be Shiʿi. But I never had a choice about being a Shiʿa, and I didn't want to choose or have agency [in this system], so I went back [to Shiʿi Islam]."

Husayn described his act of conversion in markedly different terms than his act of removing his personal status altogether (*shatb*) years later. His conversion was a *necessity*, a *strategy* to pull the levers of a sectarian census regime. Removing his sect, however, represented a cathartic announcement of his "true self." It was an act that, in his words, made his "outside personal status match his inside: nothing."[60] For Husayn, both his atheism and his achievement in transcending sectarianism (unlike others, he stated several times) inflected his choice to remove his personal status from state registries. He had recently gotten married, and one of the perks of his new nonstatus was that he and his wife were allowed to register their Cypriot civil marriage certificate, a right they had been denied when they were both officially Muslim.

Husayn believed in a clear distinction between "inheriting" a religious personal status and/or converting between them, and making a "choice" to opt out of the system of personal status as a whole. This "choice" was productive of the autonomous individual, a project that Husayn believed we should all, as Lebanese citizens, be invested in. The exercise of "choice" builds the architecture of the self within, and contained by, the body.[61] Despite his emphasis on the importance of personal choice, Husayn did not believe that when his future children inherited his status, they would experience it as an injury, or as a misrecognition, or even as an "inheritance" in his pejorative use of the word. "Why should they?" Husayn said during one of our interviews. "It's not the same thing at all. They won't be born as Shi'a Lebanese. They will be *just* Lebanese."[62] In our interview, he did not question the fact that his children could only inherit his status, and not that of his wife, who was still a Sunni Muslim in conviction and on paper.

Zahra strongly believed and *felt* that her bureaucratic categorization had little to say about her own sense of self and religious sensibility. It was the always-present potential of *mis-recognition* that allowed her to experience her brief foray into Christianity as "nothing more than a piece of paper" that she could "throw away" when it was no longer useful. She was clear that her conversions from Sunni Islam to Greek Orthodox Christianity and then back to Sunni Islam were built on three factors: her right as a citizen to convert, the fact that she is a woman, and her ability to "sign papers and pay money." She had the absolute right to convert, but had she been a man, she never would have thought to. Instead, she could have initiated a divorce at the time and place of her choosing. Without money, she would have still been able to convert and convert again, but not on her terms. Zahra was finally able to divorce her abusive husband only because of her ability to speak within a particular personal status framework (gambling, drinking) that is deeply gendered, and because she had the financial resources, social standing, and force of personality to persevere and insist that her civil right to convert was "stronger" than any claims that religious or civil institutions may lay on her. Conversely, Husayn and others like him who removed their personal status from government registries wanted to erase the gap between the government's recognition of their personal status and religions and their own identification of their true selves as "only citizens." They sought a more sincere form of self in removing their personal status. The effects of this removal were complex and contradictory, and because all of this is occurring in a sectarian system, they are gendered. Husayn's reproductivity as a sect-less citizen, the fact that he became a progenitor of a new inheritable status of Lebanese citizens, was not because his relation to the state or religion is sincere, banal, or massaged by financial resources. Rather, it was because he was assigned male at birth. It was due to his structural position in a sectarian system.

If one of the core tenets of liberalism is the right to keep your "internal" distinguishing mark protected from the practices of governmentality,[63] then how shall we read Husayn's sense of accomplishment at having his government ID accurately diagnose, represent, and announce his "internal" self to the state? In Husayn's mind, by removing his personal status he broke out of the state's sectarian misrecognition of his identity and announced who *he* believed he was and who he wanted to be: a sectless, "real" Lebanese citizen. The sincerity and publicity of nationalism, after all, is not a tension within liberalism. Instead, this tension is constitutive of liberalism. Converts such as Zahra, and even Husayn when describing his conversion to Sunni Islam to move his census records, have a different reading of the relationship between what they are recognized as legally and who they understand themselves to be. Zahra, for example, emphasized that her official identity did *not* map onto her internal private self and that, in fact, it was not the business of the state or of any authority (such as Dar al-Fatwa) to tell her what she could and could not *be*. Thus the convert recognized her personal status *as* nothing more than a bureaucratic category of recognition separated from how she defined herself *and* how she was recognized socially, as a Sunni Beiruti from an old and respected family. However, the citizen who removed his personal status *desired* the state to recognize him as who he really was: a universal and unmarked citizen. Husayn's life history demonstrates how the universality of citizenship and the sovereign space of the state is built through gendered management of sexual difference, through the differently gendered stakes of sextarianism. Universalism is another word for the *authority* to decide—to lay claim—on the content of the universal, often through raced, classed, and gendered elisions.[64]

The Speaking Subject/The Subject and Truths

The practice, management, and experience of religious conversion indexes an opacity, and a right to opacity, that the state protects and that converts insist on.[65] In cases concerning converts, the Assembly refused repeatedly to interrogate the sincerity of the convert subject. The only truth that mattered was the truth of bureaucracy—and bureaucracy represents the promise of equal access to the state through anonymization and serialization. To the Assembly, often to the consternation of personal status courts, religious conversion is as banal as the bureaucracy that defines it and gives it a legal life. Religious freedom *is* the right to shield one's beliefs from state interrogation; indeed, it is the right to an always present potential misalignment between identitarian categories of governmentality and how individuals actually define themselves. However, while access to bureaucracy may be equal, the bureaucratic effects of conversion are starkly different for men and for women.

Secular sovereignty is built on and builds the architecture of the private, the public, the religious, and of sexual difference. Secular sovereignty is the ability to disarticulate the categories of religion, sect, sex, and personal status—just as it is the ability to define the public order. Public order necessitates treating all personal status courts equally, as well as facilitating and surrounding the jurisdiction of personal status courts with that of the sovereign secular state—the space that allows citizens to convert in and out of personal status jurisdiction. The equality between personal status systems rests on their equal right to determine and juridically practice regimes of sexual difference. Thus claims of fraud and discrimination based on gender are almost always routed through the state's mandate to grant equal status to personal status courts and thus ensure public order. State sovereignty is enacted as that which resolves conflicts between individual and "community" rights.

We are all constituted by and pressed into regulatory categories assigned to us by bureaucratic regimes at birth, and we all press into and against these regulatory categories at different points in our lives. Religion and sect may not be any different. Instead, they are hypervisible modes of structural difference that, like citizenship, are patrilineal inheritances that determine how and which laws apply to you. Rather than assuming that religious conversion is always a shift in subjectivity, I have sought to present religious conversions as they are presented to, understood by, and ruled on by the Assembly and converts themselves. Thinking about religious conversion from the standpoint of Lebanon allows us to consider how secular power and sovereignty are practiced and amplified at the intersections of governmental categories that are born of disciplining the messiness of life. These census categories are the afterlives of colonial and postcolonial knowledge production that centers hypervisibility, demography, statistics, and anonymization as key technologies of biopolitical power. The state's regulation of religious conversion performs its secular sovereignty and its nesting and overwhelming of religious personal status jurisdiction within its own. Academic literature has thus far not addressed the banality of Islam, and of religion more generally, as a category of secular governmentality. Instead of banality, opacity, and contradiction, sincerity and coherence anchor a multidisciplinary academic archive on conversion, religion, and sectarianism. And yet, banality and sincerity are terms that intensify, anticipate, and attenuate each other. They operate as avatars—as projections of how people understand their relationship to the state, and of how the state understands and articulates its relationship to religious pluralism. The Assembly, as we have seen, regularly massages claims anchored in religious sincerity and coherence, and the intentionality behind religious conversion, into a legislative record that stresses the bureaucratic banality and opacity of religious difference and conversion. Meanwhile, converts and secular activists stress both banality *and* sincerity in their narrations of religious conversion and the removal of their sectarian affiliation altogether from census registries. Citizenship, secularism, and religion are not only ethical, authorizing, affective, and embodied practices or epistemes. They are also biopolitical modes of governance. Thus while religious conversion may be the site of my research and analysis, this chapter also traces the contours of how people and states try to manage what Mayanthi Fernando calls the constitutive contradictions of liberal secularism.[66] If liberal, secular state power can be understood as formal equal *access* to equality, this should not be confused with structural and informal equality itself.[67] The legal and bureaucratic effects of religious conversion highlight that *access to* equality is managed through articulating and reproducing structural forms of *inequality*.[68] The Lebanese state, both liberal and secular, produces itself as equally dispassionate about and distant from, yet sovereign over, religious communities, in part through granting each sect equal right to a personal status law grounded in sexual difference and gendered inequality. However, the state insists that the Assembly—a body composed of first-rank justices—has the sole right to decide and transcend conflicts that emerge *between* regimes of sexual difference.

Key to this sovereign transcendence is the marking of religious difference as the right to specific regimes of sexual difference.[69] This knot of sect and sex is precisely what is retied during a religious conversion. The lesson, perhaps, that religious conversion in Lebanon teaches us is that Islam and Christianity may be no different, no more sincere or enchanted or visceral, than any other governmental category. Rather than expressing a shift in subjectivity or speaking the truth of a shift in subjectivity, religious conversion may speak the truth of the state—the power to define, arrange, and rearrange religion and rights through legal and bureaucratic procedures.

There is no necessary alignment between a state's classification of a citizen and a citizen's experience of that classification. For their part, converts such as Zahra demonstrate how the assumed truth of sectarian and/or religious subjectivity are exercises in what Chela Sandoval calls oppositional consciousness. Religious conversion may be no more or less than subjectivity as a masquerade: turning, turning again, or refusing to turn, based on a sober reading of one's structural position within a sectarian system.[70] Citizenship, religion, gender, and sect, all categories that claim a form of universalism,[71] are not coherent or unitary categories of practice or experience. They should not be considered coherent or unitary categories of analysis either.

CHAPTER 4

Are You Going to Pride?

Evangelical Secularism and the Politics of Law

"My daughter is the first true Lebanese citizen ever born."
—Khaled
"Neither French nor Turkish secularism,
[we want] a Lebanese secularism!"
—Chant, Laique Pride March

IN THE SUMMER OF 2010, more than 5,000 people walked from the seaside corniche to Parliament—a distance of approximately one kilometer. Despite refusing many offers of sponsorship from political parties, the number and diversity of the people who attended the inaugural 2010 Laique Pride march greatly exceeded organizers' expectations. A broad coalition of people and groups marched to the tune of a short track written and performed by a leading Lebanese rapper that had been recently and regularly featured on the radio. Some held up their identification papers with "/" as their personal status and/or their civil/secular marriage certificates issued in foreign countries. These documents functioned as badges of pride in heterosexual, civil unions conducted abroad. Others stated their intention to marry in Cyprus. Still others demanded a Lebanese secular personal status law as part of a broader set of reforms that sought to ensure Lebanon's tolerance and secularity. Young children held signs proclaiming themselves as the offspring of a secular union. English language banners reading "Queers for Secularism," "Say Yes to Civil Marriage and No to Civil War" and "Secularism? I Laique It" were waved in the air. Marchers wore t-shirts branded with the Laique Pride logo and carried messages like "What is my sect? None of your business!" and "I want to be President of the Republic. Should I convert to

FIGURE 6. Laique Pride poster, march for secularism.

FIGURE 7. Poster for march for secularism during the uprising in
Lebanon, 2019. The hashtags read Lebanon Rises Up, and All of
Them Means All of Them, in reference to the political class.

Christianity?" Local celebrities, musicians, actors, and public intellectuals were among the marchers. State security officers had placed barriers
blocking the marchers' route from downtown Beirut to Parliament. As
they approached the armed men, the marchers stopped. Some began to
dance the *dabke*, a dance performed throughout the Eastern Mediterranean, to the percussion of their fellow marchers' drums. Others sat in
front of the officers chanting about women's rights to give citizenship
to their husbands and children. At the center of this cavalcade of imag-
ery and sound, billed as a manifestation of the "culture of secularism,"
two gay men staged a "kiss in." One group shouted a chant that had
been heard throughout the day: "Neither Turkish nor French secularism, a Lebanese secularism!" Almost ten years after the first Laique Pride
march, during the 2019 October uprising, a group of organizers planned
a "march for secularism," citing the Laique Pride marches of 2010–2013
as inspiration.[1]

Kafa, an NGO centered on combatting domestic violence, introduced
a draft comprehensive and compulsory civil personal status law to Parliament for debate in 2019. The draft law proposed removing legal ju-
risdiction/power of civil enforcement from religious and sectarian infrastructures. Under Kafa's vision, one law would govern marriage, divorce,
custody, adoption, and inheritance for all residents in Lebanon. Religious
institutions and courts would stop being spaces of compulsory contact. A
main revenue stream of religious organizations, those court and bureaucratic fees, would be cut off. A few days after they introduced their draft
law, on October 17, 2019, the Lebanese uprising ignited and effectively
neutralized Parliament for months. Kafa's members were thrilled by the
uprising and quickly joined the movement. They sponsored an "open discussion session"—one of many that became an important feature of the
uprising—in martyr's square in downtown Beirut. I was invited to attend
the discussion session and help in answering questions that might arise.
Many people came, and once the presentation of the law was complete,
the floor was opened to debate. The compulsory nature of the law was
its most controversial aspect.[2] The lawyer for Kafa reiterated a point she
often made: Optional civil marriage and/or personal status laws only created further discrimination and inequality between citizens, particularly

FIGURE 8. Photograph of Laique Pride march, 2010.
Image from les mouvement des jeunes.

between women citizens. Both proponents and opponents were invested in maintaining what they understood as Lebanon's regional and global exceptionalism as a haven of religious freedom, sectarian co-existence, and commitment to pluralism. They disagreed over how to interpret and guarantee religious freedom and religious pluralism.

A few weeks later, in December 2019, and under protestors' pressure to resign, the president of Lebanon, Michel Aoun, gave a televised speech calling for the end of political sectarianism. While giving lip service to protestor demands' of ending political sectarianism in parliamentary representation, Aoun added a caveat that had *not* been adopted by the protest movement: Only the adoption and implementation of a unified civil personal status law, Aoun suggested, could end political sectarian representation. Such a move, he continued, would change people's cultures and attitudes. Otherwise, what would ending political sectarianism look like if voters were still sectarian? The motivations inspiring Aoun's and Kafa's calls for a secular personal status could not have differed more. Kafa had done the work of submitting a law to Parliament and grounded their project in the language of equal rights for all citizens, particularly for women citizens. President Aoun, on the other hand, used the idea of a unified personal status law as a cudgel, a tactic meant to delay the uprising's growing demand for the immediate end of political sectarianism and the cronyism it fostered.

The centrality of mass protest to the post–civil war politics of the country arguably began in 2005 after the assassination of Prime Minister Rafik Al Hariri, when dueling political camps mobilized hundreds of thousands of people over the question of Syria's power over Lebanese politics and politicians.[3] In the decade between 2010 and 2020, political sectarianism, the Arab uprisings, corruption, economic inequality, and the lack of basic public goods and services inspired the 2011 *hirak*,[4] the 2015 You Stink protests,[5] and the October 2019 uprising.[6] Of these three, the 2011 and 2019 movements explicitly called for the removal of political sectarianism and the establishment of a democratic civil state. The October uprising of 2019 inspired hundreds of thousands of people—some estimate as high as two million, almost half of the country's resident citizens—to take over and proclaim public squares and spaces throughout the country.[7] It was a clear break in the politics and history of Lebanon, unprecedented in the postwar era. The demand for a civil, anti-sectarian, capable, and meritocratic state echoed across decades in Lebanon.[8] But as the demands echoed, so did the reverb: The demand for a secular and anti-sectarian state inspired sexual, sectarian, and national panics. To be more precise, the demand to end political sectarianism inspires sextarian panics. The political dissonance between Kafa and the president in their advocacy for a unified personal status law had historical precedent. If we return to earlier moments of activism, we see that the subject of a civil personal status or marriage law has long fostered strange bedfellows.

A fluorescence of secular activism coalesced in 2010—activist campaigns to reform the personal status system, change the sextarian census regime, and organize the first Laique Pride march. Many prominent organizers and participants of these campaigns became key members of subsequent protest movements, including the 2019 uprising. Activist coalitions formed through Laique Pride continue to work together, underscoring a key success—the synergy made between individual and activist groups. There were notable differences between 2019 and 2009, most importantly the fact that the secular activism that I engage with in this chapter was purposely not directed at politicians or political camps, nor did it seek regime change or early elections. Secular activism did not frame itself as, and nor was it, an uprising or a revolution. Instead, it sought to pass bureaucratic and legal reform, on the one hand, and to practice a politics of secular visibility—through a pride march focused on coming out as secular—on the other.

What might secular activism in Lebanon teach us about how people live, imagine, and stage secularism as both a system of rule and as a way of being in the world? How might we think of secular multiplicities, of the differences between the dispassionate, managerial secularism of the state and the "culture of secularism" that many activists embodied and advocated for? What can the concept of evangelical secularism teach us about the missionary, transformative aspects of secularism, as driven either by the colonial mission, the nationalist state project, or contemporary civil society activists?

We can learn more from studying the articulations and contradictions of secularism and secularity in any given context than from asserting that any given context is or is not (sufficiently) secular.[9] A primary way that secularism is articulated in contemporary Lebanon, for example, is the equivalence that people make between "being secular" and being "anti- or non-sectarian." The form of secular activism outlined in this chapter intends to reform the type of secularism that the state practices and reform Lebanese citizens so that they transcend sectarian communities and commitments. The state produces its secularism and its unitary sovereignty through the dispassionate and banal disambiguation and management of religious, sectarian, and sexual difference. But activists believed that secularism in Lebanon should be both a managerial state practice *and* a culture that individual citizens should embody and aspire toward. It is perhaps not surprising that activists in countries with high volumes of civil violence, often singularly coded as sectarian, desire secularism as an antidote to sectarianism, even when they acknowledge that political sectarianism is a form of secular governance. Secular activists and the Lebanese state were both invested in a national discourse that emphasized tolerance, pluralism, and freedom of religion as quintessentially

"Lebanese" principles. After all, Lebanese exceptionalism is evidence of the success of nationalism in Lebanon—the idea that something is distinct about Lebanese culture, history, and "way of life" that sets it apart from the rest of the region. The contradictions and articulations of secularism vary across the Middle East, just as the role of religion in public and legal life varies. Because articulations of secularism and secularity are historically specific, I take seriously what activists in Lebanon are *doing* when they make statements such as "I have only secular friends."

Secular activists were calling for a secularism that had no functional role for political sectarianism, or sectarian difference more broadly. In this secularism, sectarian difference was to be relegated to the "cultural" or "private" realm. More often than not, activists assumed that once a "culture of secularism" was hegemonic in Lebanon, the regulation of sexual difference would become more liberal and progressive. Women's rights, and the rights of sexual and religious minorities were posed as the natural accouterments of "true" secularism,[10] despite the fact that, as Joan Scott has shown, secularism historically facilitated the exclusion of women from the public realm of politics.[11] Secular activists called for an optional civil marriage law and/or an optional secular personal status law, relying on a mandate-era law that forms the grounds for recognition of a secular community. However, 60 LR does not apply to Muslims, a majority of the population of Lebanon.[12] An optional secular personal status is different from a civil marriage law because it, like current sectarian personal status laws, would contain inheritance, custody, and burial clauses. This legal and bureaucratic infrastructure, in effect, would produce a secular sect, one with its own sextarian infrastructure.[13] Many prominent feminists in Lebanon, including the legal scholar, professor, and activist Marie Rose Zalzal, did not agree.[14] She thought the idea of an "optional" and "additional" personal status law or civil marriage law would only further normalize gender inequality at personal status courts[15] through creating an optional, more liberal law open to the select few—those with financial, social, and educational capital. Women's rights should not be "optional."[16] Zalzal, prefiguring Kafa's argument ten years later, believed that only a unitary and compulsory law regulating all aspects of a citizen's personal status would ensure that women in

Lebanon have equal personal status rights. She thought that both an optional civil marriage law and an optional personal status law would compound, rather than transform, the centrality of sextarian difference to Lebanese citizenship as well as state practices of sovereignty and power. The result would be yet another optional sextarian personal status law, albeit this time a secular one.

The management of sexual and racial difference is at the heart of imperial and nation-state power, authority, and legitimacy.[17] Much of this power derives from the ability to disambiguate the assemblage that is race/sex into discrete categories of governmentality and management, such as "race" and "sex." Discrete categories of management are achievements of structural power's ability to fracture what Avery Gordon calls "complex personhood"[18] into categories of rule such as "citizen," "refugee," "sex," "race," or "religion." As theorists of intersectionality have taught us, the intersections between these categories are sites that amplify both state management and activist interventions.[19] Legal archives, at least the archive of Lebanon's highest court, the Plenary Assembly at the Court of Cassation, are filled with conflict between the categories of sex and sect despite—or perhaps because—citizens are ideologically and legally constituted as the vanishing point of difference between them.[20]

Sexual difference is key to ordering the world according to civilizational hierarchies. Moreover, sexual difference—both in terms of sexual dimorphism and as structurally reinforced forms of intimacy such as the heteropatriarchal family—is itself constituted and deployed as a technology of global whiteness and white supremacy.[21] Contemporary imperial power grounds much of its authority in its superior, or more liberal, regulation of intimacy, just as former imperial powers did.[22] The international war on terror, for example, was highly invested in the moral power of discourses on the rights of sexual minorities and women, and circulated war as a public good for women in Afghanistan.[23] Sexual difference, in this respect, is not only a system of sexual dimorphism or a question of sexualities. Sexual difference is national, imperial, religious and, as we shall see, *secular* difference; it produces hierarchies of civilizations and hierarchies of people and peoples. Sexual difference is also increasingly deployed to produce and mark a racialized border between the citizen and the citizen's condition of possibility, the refugee, in Euro-American and Middle Eastern states.

Evangelical Secularism

Academics have explored *da'wa* to study the strategies of Islamic reformers and activists who want to produce a life world that is saturated with Islamic morality and practices.[24] In turn, this life world is meant to help produce the ethical Muslim subject.[25] In Lebanon, *da'wa*, or evangelical, secularists, wanted to produce a public sphere saturated with a culture of secularism, a moral universe that would help produce secular subjects. As Charles Hirschkind has written in the context of Cairo, "the practice of *da'wa* does not map onto the constitutionally demarcated separation of public and private but rather traverses this distinction in a way that is sometimes uncomfortable to those with secular liberal sensibilities."[26] I use *da'wa*, or *evangelical*, to highlight the pedagogical aspect of a type of secular activism that believes that cultural and ethical change must precede political change. In 2009–2011, evangelical secularists in Lebanon were the ones with comfortable liberal secular sensibilities; and they were the ones undertaking "*da'wa* on the streets."[27] They saw themselves as belonging to a minority community that identified as secular/liberal, one that was disrupting normative sectarian space while expanding the existing community of secular liberals through acts of *da'wa*. Their motive was to shape a counterpublic that would disrupt what they saw as a hegemonic sectarian space. Laique Pride organizers linked *da'wa* secularism with Islamic *da'wa*. During the 2010 march, the catchphrase "secularism is the answer" was ubiquitous, and it was in part an appropriation and an upending of the transnational Islamist slogan "Islam is the answer." Evangelical secularism drew on Islamic practices and models of religious activism; was steeped in the global, missionary character of state modernity; and was informed by the structural, historical, and ideological resonance of Christianity in Lebanon. While the overwhelming majority of Christians in Lebanon are Catholic and Orthodox, global evangelical protestant ascendancy and its role in US empire in the Middle East[28] informs global perceptions of and investments in Lebanese exceptionalism. In its Laique Pride iteration, evangelical secularism was also informed by a queer politics of visibility. Evangelical secularism had Muslim, Christian, statist, leftist, and queer genealogies.

Evangelical secularism relied on the belief that individuals could and should transcend sectarian attachments to become modern secular citizens—it was an aspirational discourse. The emphasis on personal attainment and transcendence into communities of choice was capacious and by design cross- and anti-sectarian. The failure to transcend sectarian affiliation into a national one was personalized, thus open to the call of *da'wa*. The notion of evangelical secularism helps us think critically about how secularism can operate and circulate as a set of cultural and ethical practices and values in any given locale, in addition to serving as a marker of identity that separates those who have achieved secular status from others who have not. Evangelical secularism was a mode of intervention into both public spaces and ethical subjectivities—it assumed and produced the everlasting, ever differed, and perfectible futurity of its project. Importantly, the temporality of *da'wa*, both for transnational Islamist movements and for the secular activists I engage with here, was always the future. Evangelical secularism operated within the liberal temporality of redemption and was thus anchored in the futurity of the nation-states—it partook in statist discourse that the majority of Lebanese citizens were not yet "ready" for the end of political sectarianism but they *could be*, in the future.

In 2009–2010, evangelical secularists were active in three campaigns: the fight for an optional civil marriage law and/or secular personal status law, the removal of religious and sectarian identification from individual census documents, and the Laique Pride march. These campaigns, while intertwined and overlapping, also had important differences and potential ramifications. The fight to remove religious and personal status identification aimed to pressure the state into producing a secular personal status, a new category that would be inheritable patrilineally via the census regime. An optional civil marriage law, however, did not necessarily engender the legal and bureaucratic infrastructure of a separate sect precisely because it would *not* include provisions for inheritance and other aspects of kinship that are adjudicated under personal status law. With an optional civil marriage law, religious and sectarian institutions are still sovereign over particular aspects of life and death. A secular or civil personal status would be sovereign over all aspects of life that religious personal status laws are currently sovereign over.

The Laique Pride marches that began in 2010 were the most public manifestation of evangelical secularism. The marches brought together a plurality of causes and activist groups—including those fighting for a secular civil marriage and/or personal status law and those who had removed their sect from government records—under the banner of secularism. A desire for national attachment and a stronger, reformed, and more efficient state animated evangelical secularism across these three sites. Evangelical secularism in Lebanon helps us think about the relationship between secularism and biopolitics, and the ways that secularism is increasingly practiced as an identitarian category, one that can be posed against and alongside other identitarian categories. It was an affect as much as it was a political system, a statement of identity that said something about who you were in the world. When people said they were secularists, they were expressing not only a desired political or legal system but also a desired self. "Secularism" was understood to have a superior (more just, more liberal) regime of sexual difference, posed against other sectarian regimes of sexual difference that were framed as backwards and in need of reform. What made evangelical secularism distinct was that it produced a hierarchy of sectarian difference with secular sectarian difference at its apex.

I Have Surrendered to the State

The first campaign to pass a civil marriage law in Lebanon culminated with a six-month strike by the Lebanese Bar Association in 1951. Since then attempts to introduce a civil marriage law occurred in 1957, 1972, 1976, and 1977. In 1998 the president of Lebanon, Elias al Hrawi (who converted from Maronite Christianity to Greek Orthodox Christianity to divorce his first wife) introduced legislation to the cabinet headed by then Prime Minister Rafik al Hariri.[29] In 2011 the Chaml organization, an important node in the network of evangelical secularists, introduced a draft bill to Parliament. Two years later, in 2013, two Lebanese citizens who had removed their sect from individual census registries performed and registered a civil marriage in Lebanon, following French law.[30] The couple relied on article 17 of decree 60 LR, which states that "Syrians and Lebanese . . . not belonging to one of these [enumerated in decree] sects" are subject to civil personal status laws. Finally, in 2014 Minister of Justice Shakib Qortbawi introduced a bill to Cabinet that would allow Lebanese citizens the rights to conduct civil marriages without removing their personal status from census documents. Feminists critiqued the bill—it did not become law—due to the stipulation that a couple's civil marriage registration in Lebanon required a fee paid to the husband's personal status court.[31] This stipulation underlined the economic investments and interests of the religious personal status court system. All nine different attempts to introduce a Lebanese civil marriage law have all been additive in nature: an optional civil marriage law would be the sixteenth Lebanese marriage law. Only Kafa's 2019 draft law was clearly compulsory in nature and included stipulations on inheritance. Yet inheritance is a key reason why many Lebanese citizens in interreligious marriages continue to convert, especially when they have children, even if they were married under the civil law of Cyprus, for example. Because children are assigned the personal status of their father, such conversions are gendered female. Moreover, none of the bills introduced to Cabinet or Parliament have addressed the fact that while Lebanese judges are obligated to adjudicate marriages by Lebanese citizens according to the law under which they were married (most commonly Cypriot and Turkish)— Muslim Lebanese do *not* have this right. If both members of married couple are Muslim, it is the Muslim personal status courts that have jurisdiction over the marriage—even if the couple in question were married in Dekalb County, Georgia.[32]

Activism for both an optional civil marriage law and an optional secular personal status argued that the state had failed to uphold equality between citizens and to protect the freedom of religion. They pointed to the state's negligence in fulfilling its obligation, outlined in the French Mandate–era directive 60 LR to "recognize" a community that does not belong to a religion or sect. Further, activists thought the Lebanese state had an ethical duty to recognize a secular/civil personal status law, if it was truly committed to pluralism and coexistence.[33] They believed there was a direct link between the ever-present threat of a sectarian civil war in Lebanon and the absence of a civil marriage law. For them, the presence of a civil marriage law would demonstrate the freedom to love whomever you choose, regardless of religious sect, and the need for a strong state that can guarantee the freedom to make those choices. The freedom to love and marry someone from another sect or religion not only was a political demand but, in this discourse, also demonstrated a redemptive quality in a society perpetually dancing on the edge of a civil war. Here, love was emphasized as that which would save us from ourselves. This sentiment can be clearly demonstrated by the popular tagline used by activists at demonstrations: Say Yes to Civil Marriage and No to Civil War.[34] The redemptive and reformatory functions of love were heterosexual, reproductive, and progressive—the goal was to raise new generations of citizens born into secular and civil unions.[35]

The link of secularism to the absence of civil violence ignored the fact that much of the most destructive violence unleashed in the world has been secular, state violence.[36] However, many feared civil sectarian violence so much that they actively and consciously ignored this contradiction. Looking back on this moment from the vantage point of a decade of further instability, financial collapse, uprising, and decay, it may be tempting to dismiss the existential danger that evangelical secularists, and indeed everyone in Lebanon, felt they were living. After all, this feeling of despair was before the war in Syria and Hizballah's involvement there; before the arrival of more than one million refugees; before the Islamic State in the Levant; before the Arab uprisings; before a presidential vacancy that paralyzed the country for two years; before the rapid decay of already dilapidated state institutions under a regime of negligence, corruption, and politicization; before one of the largest nonnuclear explosion in the world. It is useful to remember that desperation and feelings of existential crisis are recursive temporalities even if each moment feels exceptional. Moreover, desperation can be a creative political force—it propels people to demand change precisely because the stakes are so high. The other side of desperation, however, is paralysis.

Secular activists had lived through the liberation of South Lebanon from Israeli occupation in 2000, the securitization of rule in Lebanon under Syrian regime tutelage, the assassination of Prime Minister Rafik al Hariri, the polarization of the country into two camps, and a devastating 2006 war with Israel. They were also living in a landscape of political assassinations and acts of terrorism. Many cited the events of May 2008[37] as a radicalizing moment in their secularism and framed those events as a "mini–civil war" that foreshadowed a coming Sunni-Shi'a civil war. The coming war between Shi'is and Sunnis was imagined to be catastrophic and "worse" than any previous Lebanese civil war due to the fact that the two communities were "brothers," and war between brothers has always been framed as apocryphal.[38] In this context evangelical secularists understood their work as an urgent attempt to intervene into a future civil war that required the deferral of other deeply held political and ideological beliefs, such as communism, resistance to Israeli occupation of Palestine and Lebanon, or forms of regional nationalism. For many, this translated into a nationalism and an investment in the Lebanese state that would be anathema in less existential times. For example, in 2010 Leila was a twenty-something activist who had studied marketing at the Lebanese University and was working in the private sector as a sales associate. She had been an anti-state and anti-corruption activist before 2008, but after that year she started to worry more about her co-citizens and politicians than "the state."[39] The displacement of her political anxiety from the state to her co-citizens resulted in her "surrender" to the idea of the Lebanese state. She viewed this surrender as violent because she was an Arab nationalist. The seeming permanence of refugee status among Palestinians in Lebanon informed her attachment to citizenship. The Palestinian experience in Lebanon was "foundational" to her politics and illustrated that "nobody is coming to save us." The stakes of citizenship could not be higher in a country where almost 30 percent of residents are refugees who routinely experience violence, abjection, and xenophobia at the hands of both the Lebanese state and citizens.

> LEILA: Look Maya, here, on the ground, what are we supposed to do? Give up our citizenship because we have read books and don't believe in this state and how it came to be? We know what

happens to people who don't have a state, look at how Palestinians here live. We have to be realistic.

MAYA: So what do we do?

LEILA: I have surrendered (*istaslamit*) to this state. Khalas, it is here.
It is not going anywhere. So now we have to make it stronger.[40]

Issam, an atheist who came from a Sunni family and lived in the
Hizballah-dominated southern suburbs of Beirut, highlighted nationalism as the antidote to civil strife. Like Leila, he believed that one could
choose to cultivate a sense of nationalism and a sense of attachment to
the state and one's fellow citizens. Issam, who had removed his personal
status from his identification papers and was recognized by the Lebanese
state as not following any particular personal status, was convinced that
peace would come to Lebanon only once citizens stopped prioritizing
political issues that are "not Lebanese." Issam used what he told me he
knew was a controversial and, he said, "extreme" example.

If at some point it becomes clear that we could benefit from a strong
relationship with Israel, we should do it and not have to worry about
Palestine or Syria or anyone else . . . [W]e have to start thinking like
this, about ourselves first, if we are ever going to be a strong and
unified country and stop killing each other. Even if I hate Israel, and
I think they are a state built on racism and dispossession, and even if
my family has a long and proud history of resistance and I consider
myself a resistor, I want to become someone who just wants what is
best for Lebanon as a whole—whatever that is—even if I have to deal
with the devil to get it. I want to be able to put Lebanon first. I work
towards this, and it is very difficult, trust me, every day.[41]

Evangelical secularism entailed ethical practices that were supposed
to produce a different order of political affect and attachment for both Issam and Leila. For Leila, this meant abandoning an intellectual, affective,
and ideological opposition to the Lebanese state and instead "surrender-
ing" to the state, indeed working to strengthen it, to avert a civil war. She
operated in the shadow of statelessness, a condition akin to being cast

out of the legal infrastructure of humanity-as-citizenship itself.[42] The fact that refugees and displaced people in Lebanon were mostly Palestinian (and now, Syrian and Palestinian) made her dilemma only worse because to Leila, Palestinians, Syrians, and Lebanese formed one coherent people within a larger Arab nation living in artificial states crafted by and in service of European imperial powers. She had come to the conclusion that if anything, a stronger Lebanese state would allow her intellectual, affective, and political commitments to Arab nationalism to flourish because, at least, she would be living and working in peace. If Leila focused on the state, Issam was more concerned with nation building. For Issam, the ethical practices of evangelical secularism were intended to engender a national political community powerful enough to transcend even the most divisive and deeply felt political commitments in Lebanon. He used the example of peace with Israel, which made him "nauseous"[43] to illustrate the difficulty of an ethical project of citizenship—a sincere, nationalist attachment to the state. He considered the right to anti-colonial armed resistance in Palestine and in Lebanon "sacred." Producing the nation, however, required sacrilege, a reordering of political affect, action, and practices of community. Both Leila and Issam were children when the Lebanese Civil War ended. These interviews were conducted in 2009, only one year after armed clashes in 2008. They were haunted by the idea that civil war could erupt like a whirlwind at any moment, swallowing their lives just as it had their parents' lives.[44]

Ethical practices reorder one's notion of "community" and who counts within a nation. These practices rely in part on a politics of disposition[45] as well as a politics of public space. In contemporary Lebanon, people are formed by war, political and economic stagnation and collapse, and perhaps most importantly, a *fear* of war and displacement in unquantifiable ways.[46] Evangelical secularism was an attempt, most broadly, to intervene in the realm of political dispositions and orientations in Lebanon. It sought to engender a reordering of affective investments in political projects, placing nationalism and forming a strong state, both of which were understood to be corrosive to sectarianism, above all others. The personal and individual removal of personal status from state registries was one of the ethical practices that emerged from and challenged citizens' political dispositions. Issam explained that removing his personal status served two aims. One was to sever institutional ties with his sect and thus proclaim his desire to belong to the state alone. The second was to demonstrate to his fellow Lebanese citizens that we could build a new nation based on commonality not difference. He wanted to prove to *other* citizens that "we don't have to be trapped." However, one year later he "returned" to his sect to ensure that both his marriage and his inheritance were legally secure.[47]

The Reorder of Things: Religion, Sect, Citizenship, and Authority

In 2007 the Ministry of the Interior sought legal advice from the Department of Legislation and Consultation at the Ministry of Justice, after four citizens requested to have their sects removed from their census registration and all states IDs.[48] In response the Department of Consultation and Legislation issued a nonbinding legal opinion that citizens have the right to remove their sect from their documents on the basis of the freedom of religion. The ability to remove your sectarian identification from your government ID was won through tactical and protracted lawfare.[49] The campaign was spearheaded by attorney, public intellectual, and civil rights activist Talal Husseini.[50] In 2009 the Ministry of Interior issued a binding memorandum facilitating the process. A number of Lebanon's public intellectuals and civil society leaders joined the effort. They removed their personal status identification, and with it what they perceived as an unjust and dangerous mechanism of sectarian recognition, from state records. Their fear was that the state's recognition of its citizens through the category of sect had a performative effect on people's self-identification as sectarian citizens, and vice versa. In this argument, the state's recognition of people as "sectarian citizens" imprisoned them in an atrophied version of themselves, denying Lebanese the opportunity to be "true citizens." Unable to or prohibited from being "true citizens" in turn made them more prone to inflict and be subject to sectarian violence. Gregoire Haddad, the former Melkite Greek Catholic Bishop of Beirut and Tyre, was one of the first to remove his sect from census documents. Since resigning from his bishopry in 1975, he had been a bishop emeritus and civil society activist, and was an integral and inspiring figure for generations of people, including myself. When he received his new government census record at the age of 83, it listed his name as "Bishop Gregoire Haddad" but his personal status as "/".[51]

By removing their personal status affiliations, activists effectively removed themselves from the jurisdiction of personal status courts and intentionally placed themselves in a legal vacuum. The campaign's motivation was to create a bureaucratic logjam large enough to force the government to pass an additional, sextarian secular personal status law.[52] Throughout the removal campaign, bureaucracy emerged as a strategic site to challenge and subvert the state and its institutions. Bureaucracy was a primary conduit for citizens to contest state power at national and municipal levels. After all, bureaucracy was the quilting point between national and municipal practices that entwine biopolitical, governmental, and disciplinary state power. As such the "removal" campaign relied on persuading large numbers of Lebanese citizens to strike out their personal status and stressed that citizens were sovereign in their decision to identify as a member of a particular sect or religion, or not. The state, however, should not use that self-identification as the bureaucratic and legal architecture of citizenship. For many, the gap between self-identification and sociolegal recognition was an injury to their autonomy. They considered the patrilineal inheritance of personal status a coercive assignation, not reflective of who they actually were or desired to be. Through the removal of their personal status from government registries, they believed they were breaking free of the sect they were coercively assigned at birth[53] and paving the way to realize a true self that was bound ever tighter to Lebanese nationalism and state power. In 2009 the State Shura Council ruled that it did not have jurisdiction to hear a case brought by a citizen who had requested it to order the Ministry of Interior to remove his personal status. The decision stated that "religious freedom requires that every Lebanese citizen belong[s] to one of the 18 officially recognized religious sects."[54] The president of the State Shura Council in 2009 had been the president of the Department of Legislation and Consultations in 2007, and had then advised the Ministry of Interior that citizens had the right to remove their sect based on the principle of the freedom of religion. The high-ranking judge in question was Youssef, the person who facilitated my access to the Cassation Court archives. At lunch one day I asked Youssef why he had changed his mind so dramatically about the relationship between the freedom of religion and the removal of personal status from the census registry offices. During my conversations with activists, they alleged that Youssef had bowed to political pressure. He responded that he had not changed his mind, but that the rules, competencies, and powers of the Department of Legislation and Consultations were so different from those of the State Shura Council that they could lead to contradictory opinions. Furthermore, he added, between the years 2007 and 2009, it had become clear that when citizens removed their personal status they entered into a bureaucratic void and lost access to certain rights, an outcome that he said troubled him deeply. Not many activists were persuaded by Youssef's explanation.

Beginning in 2010, the "removal" initiative stalled in part due to the legal complications of not having a personal status and thus being "outside the law," literally cut off from the possibility of legal kinship. Many citizens who removed their personal status identification starting in 2007 found themselves unable to inherit, unable to run for public office, and unable to register their marriage certificate or their newborn children in government registries. The state's responses to this campaign led to unexpected transformations in the relationship between religious figures, state bureaucracy, and individual citizens. The state did not acknowledge the desired aim of the campaign. Instead, it issued a series of problem-solving directives indicating that citizens who had removed their personal status from government registries had to obtain a certificate of belonging from religious establishments such as the Maronite Patriarchate. Bureaucratic successes and failures, as previously discussed, often lead to more bureaucracy. This certificate would allow them to engage in legal practices such as marriage, divorce, or inheritance, or to run for parliamentary elections, all practices that required the identification of a citizen's personal status. Citizens would thus need the approval of religious leaders in Lebanon, who may consider those who removed personal status as "apostates," a position that some Sunni and Shi'a clerics have taken.[55] A citizen who had not removed his or her personal status, paradoxically, did not need to prove anything to religious figures to access the bureaucratic and legal applications of functional citizenship. A Muslim who publicly professes atheism is still a Muslim by law because personal status and sect are, according to the state, governmental and biopolitical statuses inherited patrilineally through blood-based kinship. They are not necessarily markers of faith or religious practice.[56] An atheist Maronite thus can both be a candidate for political offices reserved for Christians and can (or must) marry under canon law. I debated a sheikh at the Sunni personal status courts on this issue. "Sheikh, if I were an atheist why would I come here to be married or inherit?" Bemused, he responded "*ya binti* (my daughter) I am not asking about your soul or your heart or your mind. I am just asking you to follow the law."

Following the state's response, activists who had removed their personal status affiliation found themselves in a new relationship to religious institutions. The attempt by secular activists to force the state into passing a civil secular personal status had an unlikely result; it reconstituted and reentrenched religion as a separate, measurable category of faith that could be interrogated by religious leaders.[57] This scenario, where religious practice becomes an evidentiary terrain for the legal determination of personal status, would have been unthinkable prior to the campaign to remove one's personal status.[58] It empowered religious leaders to mount public and defamatory campaigns against prominent activists who had removed their personal status from state registries.[59] Many who had removed their sect ended up recovering them. In some instances, religious leaders required religious conversion.[60] In other instances, religious leaders and institutions welcomed people returning to their sect, seeing it as evidence of the folly of youth and of secular activism. The October uprising of 2019 reinvigorated the removal campaign, with activists removing their sect, conducting civil marriages, and trying to register these marriages with the Ministry of Interior. The logic in 2019 mirrored that of 2009; civil marriage and a nonsectarian census option were key to reforming and bolstering state institutions away from the corrosion and corruption of sectarianism.

Evangelical Secularism and the Making of Modern Lebanese Citizens

Evangelical secularists understood sectarianism as a corrosive agent eating away at the possibility of a cohesive national body. In this understanding, sectarianism was the articulation and symptom of group bias, fragmented political allegiances, corruption, and a system of patronage that kept citizens tied to their sect rather than the state. For these evangelical secularists, political sectarianism was the result of the "reality" of sectarianism. In this reading of sectarianism and nationalism, political sectarianism could not be changed until Lebanese citizens were no longer sectarian. If political sectarianism changed before people were "ready," one sect and/or one religion would dominate the state at the expense of others. This future dominating religion was always implied to be Islam, given that a majority of Lebanese citizens are Muslim. For many, such a result would ensure the end of Lebanese pluralism and usher in a more conservative state. Thus instead of calling for the immediate end of political sectarianism, evangelical secularists wanted to saturate the public sphere with the "culture of secularism" to change the hearts and minds of their co-citizens. Only when the reign of the "culture of sectarianism"[61] was over could the Lebanese state be safely moved away from a system of political sectarianism.

Political sectarianism is framed as temporary in the Lebanese constitution, a broader kind of temporality that marks much of the politics of Lebanon and of imperial mandates in the region more broadly.[62] Despite this, there has never been a sustained program for the formation of a nonconfessional state, a goal that has always been projected by politicians and many public intellectuals into the undefined future. The idea that political sectarianism must continue until people are "ready" positions the state as a reformatory structure that makes citizenry capable of secular liberal democracy. Many evangelical secularists believed that if political sectarianism were abolished tomorrow, the country would cease to be safe for minorities, including themselves. The investment in the temporary enabled the everlasting delay of arrival at the better self, the better state, all the while ensuring and assuring a hierarchy of citizens defined by the attainment of that better self. Kamal Salibi, the late prominent historian of Lebanon, put in stark terms the difference between those who are activists for a secular, nonsectarian political identity and those who are sectarian. "It is a choice," he told me as he showed me his framed census document that listed his personal status as "/", "between civilization and barbarism."

Secular activists wanted to create a legal infrastructure that they believed would enable free choice. In this framework, personal status was an inheritance not from the biological father but from a broken and dangerous history riddled with sectarian violence. The inheritance of religious personal status oppressed one's ability to *choose* their faith, their community, and their right to the freedom of religion. They often used what they considered the "absurdity" of religious conversion to evidence how sectarianism not only corrupts the state and the citizenry but also religion itself. Their marking of "insincere" conversion pointed to an understanding of religion as a faith that requires the believer's continuous consent and commitment. In this logic, creating an optional secular sect would preserve and protect religious personal status courts by ensuring that only citizens who truly believed in and practiced their religions remained within their jurisdiction. Many secular activists believed that an optional secular personal status or civil marriage law would free religion from sectarianism. This conceptualization of religion as first and foremost a sincere individual choice resonates with what scholars have described as a defining characteristics of secularism as it emerges from a largely Euro-Christian genealogy: the personalization and internationalization of religion as a choice that is anchored by and anchors an autonomous individual.[63] Secularism defines and regulates the "proper" place of religion in society. When religious difference is managed through its relegation to the ostensible private sphere, both family law and individual choice become defining features.[64] The evangelical secularism practiced by activists in Lebanon produced secularism as one such *sincere* choice among many (other) religions.

Absense as Announcement

Khaled,[65] a corporate lawyer and evangelical secularist in Beirut, believed that Lebanon's sects were cultural communities, a definition that allowed him to be both an atheist and a Shi'i, he explained. Each and every sectarian cultural community needed to be protected and have a say in the direction the country takes. "If political sectarianism were abolished to-morrow, the entire government would be run by Shiʻis (the largest sect) because people are not yet politically educated enough to be trusted with a 'one citizen-one vote' system," Khaled explained.[66] In years of field-work, this explanation for the continued need for a system of political sectarianism was often offered as the self-evident dangers of a Shiʻa-majority government: more religion, less secularism, the oppression of women and minorities, more censorship, a crackdown on nightlife, and a rollback of human rights across the board. This sentiment was linked to but not subsumed by the fact that the strongest political and military power in Lebanon then and now is Hizballah, an explicitly and specifi-cally Islamic and Shiʻi. Religious sects, after all, are never just religious sects, they are assemblages that contain and erupt religious, legal, class, gendered, transnational, and racial archives of knowledge. The deploy-ment of the threat of a Shiʻa-majority constituted a public that would view this possibility as dangerous. Khaled, himself born into a Shiʻi fam-ily, understood himself as transcending its trappings. When I asked him to explain why he feared a government where the majority of democrati-cally elected officials might be Shiʻa, or more likely Muslim (Sunna and Shiʻa), he looked at me incredulously. He had assumed, based on his read-ing of my own location in Lebanese society, that I shared the self-evident truth of his statement.

Khaled had removed his personal status from his census documents and recently become a father. His daughter had inherited his status per the sextarian system, and her birth certificate and census document did not list her personal status or sect. At first, Khaled encountered resistance from bureaucrats when registering his daughter's birth in the Lebanese census. However, he "made a few phone calls," and the matter was set-tled. Others who removed their personal status did not have the financial resources or the social networks that Khaled had mobilized to overcome the bureaucratic resistance he encountered. A different man, Nadim, who had removed his personal status also ran into complications when he tried to register his newborn son. Like Khaled, the employees at the cen-sus registry refused his application at first. Unlike Khaled, he reconverted to his original personal status to register his son as a Lebanese citizen.

Another man also had to reconvert to his original personal status for the Internal Security Forces (ISF) to accept his application for employment. Despite the fact that this refusal was illegal, the man in question did not have the resources to fight the case in court. More pressingly, he could not afford to be unemployed. During our interview I asked Khaled whether his daughter was the first Lebanese citizen to be born "sect-less." He smiled and corrected me: "My daughter is the first Lebanese citizen ever born."[67] Generations of Lebanese citizens were erased because they were (and are) coercively assigned a sext at birth and had not been able to break out of this assignment. The claim that only those who chose to remove their personal status achieved "true" citizenship must be read against the reality that "choice" is available to only those who can mobilize the necessary legal, financial, and social capital.

Activists who removed their personal status saw themselves as achieving citizenship because they placed themselves fully, and solely, within the jurisdiction of the state. Like other religious groups in Lebanon that do not have an officially recognized personal status, evangelical secularists sought recognition of their difference from the state and its institutions. However, they saw *their* difference as more modern and capacious. Anyone could join them and be welcome. In fact, they viewed their minority status as transitional because they were working toward reorienting the public toward a different form of secular modernity. Their aspirational commitment envisioned a public that would ultimately affiliate with them.

For secularists, removing one's personal status was, at its core, an act that expressed an internalized intent or desire. They saw it as at once an enunciative and performative action that constituted them as modern and secular Lebanese citizens. For the Assembly, however, one can practice the full rights and duties of citizenship only when all branches of law converge to form the juridical body of the citizen. While Khaled and others who had removed their sect saw themselves as having achieved citizenship through their actions, the legal system viewed them as vulnerable citizens because they did not fall under the jurisdiction of a particular personal status and were thus foreclosed from the practice of various rights. The divergences and convergences between activist and state practices and discourses of secularism and citizenship were on display during the 2010 Laique Pride march in Beirut.

The Logic of Pride

Laique Pride began on Facebook. One night in the winter of 2009, five friends traded status messages and comments between Paris and Beirut, decrying a recent increase in censorship of the arts. That previous August, the Lebanese government had banned a Brazilian Carnival troupe from performing in the conservative city of Sidon after senior religious leaders complained about the performers' scant clothing. A few months later in October, a heavy metal concert was canceled by a town municipality after Catholic priests issued statements warning of the links between heavy metal music and devil worship. On Facebook, the conversation expanded to a more generalized concern about the threat public religiosity could pose to Lebanese civil society and pluralism.

Laique Pride was intended to show that Lebanese could take part in the performance of a joyful civic, like any other secular modern nation. Organizers emphasized that they were organizing a march, and not a protest. One of the organizers explained: "Pride is peaceful, it is positive. It is going to be different. We are not going to burn tires or garbage." Here, she revealed not only her faith in the relationship between secularism and nonviolence but also how class inflected the discourse of evangelical secularism. Young men burning tires and garbage during protests is a common sight in Lebanon, but they are always discursively framed by the media as poor, uneducated, and dangerously angry.[68] The five friends who started Laique Pride were from Lebanon's middle- and upper-middle classes. At the time, two lived in Paris and the other three resided in Beirut. They were all French-educated and knew each other through Lebanon's extensive network of artists, activists, and the LGBTQ community. One of these friends, Jean, was emphatic about the similarities between a "gay pride" event and Laique Pride: "Of course, Laique Pride is inspired by the San Francisco gay pride marches of the 1970s, which were all about the announcement of presence and of demanding rights." Jean continued, "*Our* pride is about declaring our presence and telling everyone that secular people exist in Lebanon and their needs are not being met.

We are proud of who we are, of our secular identity. We are not going to hide in the closet."[69]

A politics of queer visibility informed Laique Pride and was deployed for political and social demands that were explicitly heterosexual—a civil marriage law.[70] The Laique Pride march was in effect a public and mass coming out party—not of the initiative's LGBTQ members but for a community of people who identify as members of a secular counter-public. Planners insisted that the primary goal of the march was to give *others* the confidence to come out as seculars who claimed a different, secular, kind of heterosexual love and were "true citizens." In fact, one of the founders of Laique Pride encouraged marchers to "shed all identities other than the secular one" while marching. During organizing meetings, she equated and banned both the LGBTQ rainbow flag and that of Hizballah, a group that was widely supported for its role in liberating South Lebanon from Israeli occupation and for successfully fending off Israel during the 2006 war, but a group that was also growing increasingly divisive.[71] Of course, members of the LGBTQ community and members of Hizballah could attend, Rima said, but only if they agreed to circulate publicly as "seculars" and forgo the signs and symbols of their divisive politics. She was both Shi'i and queer and proud of both "traditions," as she called them. She hoped that if people could focus on what they shared, a desire for a better life, they could overcome what they represented to each other in a polarized society, if only for one day. Rima explained this divergence: "Jean says it openly, that he is queer and that this is an important part of our work. But I don't agree, I don't think it's a priority. We have so many bigger issues than gay rights right now."

Evangelical secularists framed secularism in contrast to sectarianism, not in contrast to religion. This distinction was important. It demonstrated that articulations of secularism, secularity, and religion are always historically specific. Moreover, *within* Muslim majority countries, secularism, secularity, and religion are historically specific. The secularity of the Lebanese, Turkish, and Egyptian states, all Middle Eastern Muslim majority states, are distinct, and so is the secularism that activists call for in these contexts.[72] In Lebanon, activists sought to institutionalize a culture of secularism, defined by tolerance, open-mindedness, and freedom of choice. Thus, reforms such as decriminalizing homosexuality, changing the nationality law to include women, and promoting the freedom of artistic expression were all associated with evangelical secularism. In this way, *evangelical* secularism was contingent on transforming the *type* of secularism that the state practiced. This desired transition was one from of secularism as a classically liberal political and legal praxis to a secularism that joins disparate practices, dispositions, values, embodiments, and affect. In many ways, this distinction *between* secularisms mimics a distinction between liberalism as a structural and ideological state practice and the ways it is mobilized politically to signify a center left political agenda and identity.

During the Laique Pride march, organizers cynically highlighted practices of religious conversion that they believed were "strategic" rather than faith based. They printed signs for the march that read "I want to be President of the Republic. Should I convert to Christianity?" and "I want to marry you, shall I become Muslim?" For Jean, the fact that "sect can be used like this is an absurd idea that insults religion." In our conversations about religious conversion, Rima was more blunt. "This kind of conversion is a farce. Religion is something that you really believe in, it is so important. So you have to change it to get married or to get divorced or to inherit? And this is secularism? What a joke." A belief in sincerity as both a political and religious affect and an emphasis on tolerance constituted much of what evangelical secularists considered the culture of secularism. This vision of secular sincerity was mediated through calls that urge others to identify with the Lebanese state above all other identifications and warns of dire consequences—a sectarian civil war—if people continued not to do so. Talal Asad has written that citizenship is the medium of secularism in an era of nation-states.[73] For evangelical secularists, the relationship between citizenship and secularism was structural but also ideological. One could be a "sincere citizen" only if one was secular. "True secularism" could flourish only when citizens became sincere in their singular attachment to the state and relinquished all other sociopolitical attachments. Thus Laique Pride was open to everyone as long as they demonstrated that they identified, or *desired to identify*, as secular citizens, above all other political identifications.

The secularism that Laique Pride planners envisioned operated through a series of binaries—beginning and emerging from the primary binary between secularism and sectarianism. Just as secularism connoted liberal values and practices, for evangelical secularists, sectarianism connoted repressive and negative practices. Secularism was projected as a "safe space" that would allow generations of women, sexual minorities, and intersectarian families to flourish and be protected from the discriminations inherent to patriarchal religions. Meanwhile religion, in their view, needed to be saved and protected from sectarianism.

Controversy: Political Sectarianism, Queers, and Pluralism

Weeks before the March 2010 Laique Pride, the president of Parliament and leader of the political party and ex–civil war militia Amal, announced that he supported the end of political sectarianism. To be more precise, he suggested that the time was right to form a committee to study the end of political sectarianism, one of the conditions of the Ta'if Accord, the peace deal that had ended the Lebanese Civil War. Nabih Berri's statement was met with both support and distrust. Many understood it as a veiled threat aimed at his political rivals. The Shi'i sect, which Berri claimed to represent, was one of the largest in Lebanon. If they voted as one bloc, which evangelical secularists believed they would, they would dominate elections in Lebanon if they ceased to be based on region and sect.[74] Thus, rather than being lauded for offering a plan to fully implement the decades-old peace agreement that ended the Lebanese Civil War, Berri was accused of inciting sectarianism. The logic of evangelism was evident in politicians' statements, op-ed columns, and newscasts critiquing Berri: Political sectarianism could not be removed until sectarianism was ended, and ending political sectarianism before the citizenry was reformed was akin to a sectarian power grab cloaked in the logic of democratization. Ten years later, facing down a political uprising, the president of Lebanon would repeat this logic and call for a civil, nonreligious personal status law to precede any discussion of ending the system of political sectarianism.

Berri's statement surprised and disturbed Laique Pride planners. Berri was a notoriously corrupt wartime militia leader turned postwar political leader. He inspired so much distrust that a goal he ostensibly shared with many Lebanese activists—ending political sectarianism—immediately became suspect. The planners distanced themselves from his statements in public meetings and press interviews. However, Laique Pride could not avoid the controversy that Berri's statement engendered. Planning meetings broke down over the question of how much of a priority ending political sectarianism should be on Laique Pride's platform. In 2010, in fact, people could not agree on what "ending political sectarianism" meant, in ways that foreshadowed debates that occurred among activists during the October 2019 uprising. Did ending political sectarianism mean strictly following the constitution, which called for a nonsectarian Parliament? This first interpretation was adopted by most. Did it also imply ending the practice whereby the office of the presidency is reserved for Christians, the office of the prime minister for Sunnis, and the office of the speaker of Parliament for Shi'is? This interpretation of ending political sectarianism was more controversial. Some members of the coalition, particularly socialist, communist, and radical feminist activists, argued that the logic of sectarian power sharing had to be rooted out at all levels and replaced with direct liberal democracy. Others argued that this would clear the way for the tyranny of majority rule and the further disenfranchisement of Lebanon's minorities. Even a woman's right to grant citizenship to her children and spouse, a principle crucial to the founders of Laique Pride and most of its participants, became a source of contention after Berri's announcement. During a Laique Pride planning meeting, a trio of men who were college students representing a university secular club suggested "granting" women the right to pass on their citizenship could alter the already fragile sectarian demographics of the country. They repeated the well-worn sextarian argument that posed the regulation of women's sexuality and marriage choices as key to the country's demographic balance and its pluralism. As soon as the college students made their intervention, they were accused of sexism, anti-Palestinian bigotry, and sectarianism by many in the meeting. In turn, they and their supporters accused others of sectarianism, radicalism, and purism. The meeting grew volatile, and organizers almost stopped it. An appeal to the common desire for an optional civil marriage law, yet another sextarian law, was all that ensured that the meeting continued. A member of the Laique Pride planning committee suggested that instead of ending political sectarianism, the focus of activism should be on developing secularism and meritocracy, and ending government corruption, causes everyone in the room could get behind.[75] As the October 2019 uprising proved a decade later, ending endemic corruption among the political class and their clientelist allies is *still* the most unifying of political platforms.

Some participants of Laique Pride worried that the abrupt end of political sectarianism was synonymous with the further marginalization of Christians in the Middle East. At a meeting of LGBTQ activists who planned to attend Laique Pride, one young woman said that she would be afraid and might leave the country if Maronite Christians were no longer guaranteed the post of president of the republic. Another participant asked her how she could march in Laique Pride but oppose the end of political sectarianism. She responded that she was just saying out loud what many people felt. Indeed, many citizens of all sects agreed that the prospect of a majority Muslim Lebanese government would endanger Lebanese diversity, women's rights, and Lebanon's burgeoning LGBTQ and "secular" communities. If political sectarianism did end abruptly, a leading evangelical secularist explained, "They will make us wear chadors, like in Iran."[76] The assumption that a Muslim-dominated government would be *less* secular, *more* conservative than today's state draws on familiar Lebanese nationalist narratives as well as transnational discourses on Islam, democracy, and secularism. In fact, there is a sectarian logic to evangelical secularism, one that partakes in and amplifies suspicions as to the modernity (read class, education) and secularity (culture, attachment) of all Lebanese citizens who are not "free" of sectarianism. However, this suspicion is unevenly distributed toward Lebanese Muslim citizens, particularly toward Lebanese Shiʿa citizens.[77] No such fears over the loss of pluralism, cosmopolitanism, or the Lebanese "way of life" were articulated when Parliament, executive power, and judicial and administrative power were dominated by Christians, as they were from the founding of Lebanon in 1943 to 1990, the end of the civil war. "If we remove political sectarianism today," Rima (herself Shiʿi) said, "then everyone [in the government] will be Shiʿa, and nobody wants that. We need to spread awareness first." This unequal weighing of the "danger" of sectarian and religious domination mimicked the founding logic of the state in important ways, and was also expressed through sextarian discourse. It reproduced the logic of securitizing women's sexuality by centering demographic anxiety in conversations about reforming the nationality law. Much of the "danger" that a Muslim majority government was assumed to pose—about women's rights, queer rights, and religious freedom and bodily autonomy—was steeped in sextarian discourse.

Lebanese political leaders have spoken publicly about the role that Lebanon plays in a region where Christian communities are under increasing pressures. The disastrous effects of the 2003 American-led invasion of Iraq on Iraqi Christian communities; Israeli aggression that Palestinian Christians face, most notably in Jerusalem; and the regional rise of ISIL—all were rendered evidence of Lebanon's exceptionalism and the need to maintain Christian political power in at least one state in the Middle East. Many evangelical secularists deferred to and shared the political emotions and vulnerabilities of Lebanese Christians. They saw their own presence as a secular minority vulnerable in a state that did not actively avert the possibility of a Muslim majority state. Ending political sectarianism was subject to the successes of *da'wa*, and organizers disinvested from public calls for a new political system precisely because it became too controversial. Another controversy that emerged among the Laique Pride coalition was the place LGBTQ activism should play in the march

Jean, introduced earlier as one of the leaders of the Laique Pride movement, was openly queer—a fact that caused controversy within the coalition of activist groups that came together for Laique Pride. One night, a leader of a well-established civil society group and an evangelical secularist called me. He was blunt: "This is not how *I* feel, but a femme gay man should not be the public face of our movement, it sends the wrong message to everyone. Only the girls should be on TV and giving interviews. That would be much better for all of us." When we hung up, I turned to one of the queer women founders of Laique Pride, who was at my house, and relayed the message that only *she* should be on the news because Jean was apparently too gay. We laughed. In fact, despite the fact that a majority of Laique Pride organizers were queer, evangelical secularists took measures to ensure that their cause was not explicitly associated with that of LGBTQ rights. Days before the march an activist from a prominent secular group informed Rima that the group would not attend without a guarantee that there would be no obvious queer signage, such as rainbow flags, or demands at the march. The activist explained that a public association between the first secular march and queer rights would be a disservice to the larger cause and discredit it in the minds of the public. The woman on the phone assured Rima that she and her group personally did "not have any problems" with LGBTQ activists and their struggle, but that society at large did. This disassociation from queer politics and bodies could be read as an articulation of the temporality of evangelism, or *da 'wa*. Many evangelical secularists contended that they, personally, were not homophobic. They argued that they needed to cater to the larger trend of homophobia until people became secular enough to extend tolerance toward LGBTQ people in Lebanon. Evangelical secularists used similar arguments when confronted about their positions on women's rights. In 2011 a prominent secular activist group submitted a draft secular personal status the Lebanese Parliament. The draft law upheld different ages of consent for men and women, and did not address the question of inheritance. When I asked why inheritance was excluded, lawyers and activists who drafted the law replied that Lebanese Muslims (by which he mainly meant men) would never accept a secular inheritance law. Rather than include Muslim citizens in a current civil law that regulates inheritance for Christians and Jews in Lebanon, they excluded it, anticipating that it would be too controversial. These activists displaced sexism and religious patriarchy onto others who needed to be reformed. This was similar to how they performed homophobia while displacing it onto others.[78] However, while the idyllic temporality of evangelism is the future, that future is an ever delayed (im)possibility.[79]

Tolerance is a central aspect of the culture of secularism.[80] Beginning with the principle that a secular Lebanese is one who tolerates all other sects, evangelical secularism extends this imperative to groups that are assumed intolerable in a culture of sectarianism—LGBTQ bodies and secular bodies themselves. The denial of homophobia and sexism, even as one engages or deploys sexist and homophobic sentiment, is evidence that we are always acting in future-oriented liberal time.[81] In this framework, some evangelical secularists knew that even if they found LGBTQ people intolerable, they *should* tolerate them to claim association with internationally articulated secular modernity.[82] For their part, LGBTQ activists chafed under what they considered homophobia at the first Laique Pride march. Because the majority of Laique Pride's founders were openly queer, at first many in the LGBTQ community did not take the ban on markers of queer visibility seriously. When it became clear that the founders had agreed on avoiding forms of visibility that some in their coalition viewed as divisive, many LGBTQ activists were angry and felt betrayed. They brought in transnational markers of queer identity to the march. In turn, and perhaps not surprisingly, these smuggled rainbow flags became some of the most photographed signs by international press.

A fear for Christians in the Middle East informed the very creation of the Lebanese state and its system of sectarian power sharing. A fear for LGBTQ and "seculars" is a newer articulation of the stakes of secularism and sectarianism in Lebanon. This discourse positions LGBTQ bodies and Christian bodies in the Middle East as in need of protection from a religion and culture uniquely mired in a backwards regime of sexual difference—Islam. In reality, Christian Churches are just as invested in sextarianism as any other religious institution and is an active, loud proponent of homophobia in Lebanon. As Lara Deeb has written, Christianity operates as an unmarked category in Muslim-majority Lebanon to the extent that the danger of religiosity is always assumed to emanate from Islam. In this framework, Christianity in Lebanon is more modern, less oppressively "religious," and more secular than Islam. Islamophobia can operate as an affect of internationally articulated secular modernity, even in Muslim majority countries.[83]

Evangelical secularism helps us understand the multiple itineraries and practices of secularism, pluralism, sexual difference, and tolerance. These itineraries may resonate with aspects of the war on terror and/or with itineraries of cultural imperialism, but they are neither subsumed nor determined by them. They also emerge from Lebanese history and French colonialism in Lebanon—to the very founding of the state as a haven for Christians in the Middle East. They indicate the ideological durability of the Lebanese state and of the capaciousness of sextarianism. Secular activists in Lebanon articulated a version of secularism different from that of the state on one level, and similar to it on another. Their vision of secularism was still highly invested in the creation and regulation of sextarian difference, and framed secularism's moral authority as the protection religious pluralism. To religious pluralism, however, they added sexual pluralism.

A Politics of Deferral: Liberal Time, Redemptive Time

Evangelical secularism engaged in a politics of deferral. It invested in the ostensibly "temporary" character of political sectarianism and in a temporary solution of a "secular sect" *until* people were ready for direct liberal democracy. At that point, the secular sect was supposed to dissolve into a secular nation. The investment in the temporary enabled the everlasting delay of arrival at the better self, the better state. Both the Lebanese state and evangelical secularists believed that they should be the impartial arbiter between religions and/or sectarian groups, and that they should be committed to pluralism and the continued flourishing of minorities. In fact, evangelical secularists perhaps represented the success of the Lebanese national project in that they struggle for *their difference* to be recognized and protected through the presence of a secular personal status. The demand for an optional civil marriage law and/or a personal status law amplified the sextarian biopolitical and ideological power of the state. Secular communal difference was best expressed and through a legal and bureaucratic project that pivoted on retrenching the centrality of sexual difference. Finally, evangelical secularism took part in the ideological foundations of the Lebanese republic, a republic that was designed to assure the structural impossibility of a Muslim-dominated state. The vision of evangelical secularism was one of political containment. It reached for the security and peace that activists believed a highly structured and efficient state offered. Secularism emerged not as a potential space of emancipation but as an alternative space of sextarian regulation.

The politics of deferral are evident in the three scenes of evangelical secularism discussed in this chapter: activism for a secular personal status and/or civil marriage law, campaigns and strategies that aim to pressure the Lebanese state into legal recognition through the removal of personal status from census records, and public protests and marches such as Laique Pride. These scenes of secular evangelism relied on the state and its bureaucratic legal apparatuses for meaning and the felicity of practice. The nation-state is a highly regulated genealogical structure that engenders subject positions that are inflected with an impossible desire to be, in the words of an activist I worked with, "just citizens."[84] A desire to be "just a citizen" neglects the fact that the "citizenry" itself is a highly regulated population that is hyperconnected through various political, legal, and bureaucratic technologies. The citizen, quite literally, cannot exist alone. The price of such imagined autonomy is attachment and reattachment to the state through practices that reproduce both the stability of state structures and a practice of state sovereignty. It is perhaps the thick layer of scar tissue that emerges from such necessary attachment and reattachment to the state that we call "the citizen."

The politics of deferral is linked to a progressivist understanding of history and an investment in the futurity of liberal time,[85] and it achieves two goals. First, it performs a temporality of equality that is deferred eternally and secures the futurity of nation-states and of biopolitical securitization. Second, the politics of deferral produces a hierarchy of modern subjects—for example, between those who have achieved "true citizenship" through transcending sectarianism and those that have not (yet). Civilizational logic is the heart of liberalism—a logic that power shields at the same time that it promises equality and tolerance (in the future)—through the redemptive and reformatory structures of nation-states. Civilizational hierarchy, in Lebanon and in the world, is produced through regimes of sexual, religious, sectarian, and racial difference, their amalgamation, and their disambiguation. The nation-state's burden, as it were, is to make modern citizens out of divided and polarized communities—a burden that evangelical secularists wanted to shoulder.

CHAPTER 5

The Epidermal State

Violence and the Materiality of Power

THE LEBANESE STATE DOES not—and has never—had a monopoly, legitimate or otherwise, on the use of force or violence. Academics, politicians, and political organizers have called for the intensification of state power and sovereignty, linking systemic political instability, corruption, and threat of war to Lebanon's status as a "weak state."[1] The 2019 uprising in Lebanon definitively showed the stakes of unmitigated calls for an intensification of state power. Across the country protestors were shot, tear gassed, and brutally oppressed by different branches of the Lebanese security state. Here was, finally, the state everybody had been asking for, but rather than protecting citizens, it was protecting the political regime from them. To members of vulnerable populations and their allies, this was not surprising. After all, the same security officers beating protestors with batons had been beating people for years in interrogation rooms and detention centers. From the standpoint of migrant workers, refugees, sex workers, people living with drug addictions, the incarcerated, and people who have and enjoy "unnatural" sex, the state was always already violent and sovereign. How do calls for state power sound when we hear them from the site of sexual difference? How might asking from the site of sexual difference modulate the question and stakes of state power and sovereignty?

Anthropologists have theorized the state as a form whose content and practice is both specific and modular, a form that can be perceived, felt, and understood through the experience of its power.[2] States appear bounded—discrete, identifiable, and coherent, even if only as a chimera, through their performance of boundary making.[3] Feminist theories of the state have drawn attention to the work that the private/public does in framing and measuring the state as a space of protection, representation, and redistribution for women, queers, and vulnerable populations.[4] The public/private, and its corollaries political/society/economy/family, are amalgamated and disambiguated, bordered and crossed, as techniques of sextarian power. The relationship between violence and sovereignty should center everyday relations between citizen, noncitizens, and the states that purport to protect them and represent them.[5]

The structure and coherence of religious "sects," of secularism, of sovereignty, and indeed of the nation-state—emerges from the regulation of sex and sexuality across a wide set of institutions, actors, and moments of encounter with law and bureaucracy. Thinking hymen and anal exams together rather than as separate moments of sexism, racism, classism, or homophobia reveals biopolitical power's polyvalent production of sexual difference, as well as how sexual difference mediates and amplifies state power. Sometimes the exams themselves—the brutal performance of power—are the point. Sexes and sexualities are cohered, stabilized, and arranged as always in relation to each other legally, bureaucratically, ideologically, and through violence.

Hymen and anal exams may perform the "truth" of sex and sexuality, but they also perform a truth of state power.[6] Both exams purportedly test for penetrative sex constructed as illicit, whether that be premarital penetrative vaginal sex for women or sex between men. The exams are conducted by doctors and rely on being able to "see" an impression, or mark, of penetrative sex on, and in, a body. Depending on what kind of sex is being tested for, they are conducted in both legal and extra-legal settings. Regardless of what the exams find, however, they materialize and perform the body as available for state interrogation[7] and simultaneously perform sovereignty as the ability to materialize and regulate bodies and sexualities.[8] These exams and their sextarian deployment shed light on the epidermal state, a state that performs its sovereignty by materializing bodies and their gendered stakes through securitization, violence, and law. The term "epidermal state" evokes the role of state power in materializing and regulating the materiality of the body as a contained, felt, and visible evidentiary terrain of sex and sexuality.[9] It shows how this process materializes the state as a bounded, contained, and sovereign entity as it turns inwards, exerting violence against people positioned differently, and at various levels of precarity, in a sextarian system. We follow the counters of the epidermal state in criminal law and public discourse, the Plenary Assembly and personal status courts, and the interrogation rooms of Internal Security.[10] A line can be traced between the state's impunity in handling vulnerable people and the impunity with which it turned on millions of protestors in 2019. The epidermal state had long shaped, mediated, and intervened in refugee, migrant laborer, women, and queer bodies through violence, law, and bureaucracy. Every time a protestor lost an eye, was detained, or was beaten during the 2019 political uprising, the epidermal state was in view. For these reasons it was not surprising that members of vulnerable groups, including queer, feminist, and migrant labor activists, were prominent in the 2019 uprising. They, more than others, had been living, fighting, and *feeling* the epidermal state for decades.

It Gets Better, Sometimes

In 2012 the ISF raided a cinema house that screened pornographic films in a diverse, working-class neighborhood of metro Beirut. There are many such cinemas in and around the city. The ISF arrested thirty-six people for violating public decency and engaging in unnatural sex under article 534 of the penal code, a French Mandate–era law. At the police station, the public prosecutor ordered anal examinations on the detainees to determine whether they had been anally penetrated during sex with another man. The following year, 2013, in another diverse and working-class neighborhood close to Beirut, a queer bar was raided by municipal police, and five Syrians—four men and one woman—were arrested. The police abused them in detention and forced the woman, who was trans, to strip. They then took pictures of her and distributed them on social media. All five were released the next day without being charged, but the police hung a copy of their report on the door of the gay bar where they had been arrested. The police report contained their full names. The mayor appeared on TV and justified his actions as necessary to preserve the moral character of his neighborhood.[11] LGBTQ and civil rights groups in Lebanon sued him. The contexts of the raids in 2012 and 2013 were increasing xenophobia, racism, and classism in Lebanon against migrant workers, refugees, and displaced persons. The neighborhoods where both raids occurred were working class and multinational, affordable neighborhoods where Syrian refugees, migrant laborers, and Lebanese lived together. The state had conducted sweeps in both areas amid xenophobic and racist crackdowns on migrants and refugees, arresting hundreds of people at a time. The raids on the cinema house and the bar articulated the securitization of migrant, refugee, and queer life. Accusing people of "unnatural sex" or "violating public morality" and abusing them in detention were part of "security-sector struggles to discipline dangers and desires"[12] of vulnerable communities in Lebanon.

Local and transnational LGBTQ and human rights activists and groups launched a campaign against the use of forced anal examinations as tests for homosexual sex. The exams, often coupled with compulsory HIV tests, were framed as a form of torture conducted on men suspected of engaging in sex with other men—though it was unclear that all the people in question identified as men. The campaign highlighted sexuality and, to a lesser extent, race, class, gender, or nationality status. Yet these were the very intersections that made some bodies more available for these tests and more susceptible to public and/or police violence.[13] According to Rasha Moumneh, the criminalization of unnatural sex, including the use of forced anal examinations in detention, is a tactic the security state deploys to demarcate and police the boundaries of citizenship in a country where one in three residents is not a citizen. In her words, the "focus on the gay rights claim serves to obfuscate a larger narrative of gendered and racialized sexual regulation in Lebanon."[14] Activists, journalists, and human rights workers framed anal exams as "barbaric," but not the xenophobic and violent raids on migrant, poor, and refugee communities that made people available for these forced exams in the first place. Framing anal examinations as torture against men suspected of being gay[15] resonated locally and transnationally. Perhaps framing them as forms of torture against refugees and migrants via the deployment of sexuality-as-racialized and classed securitization would have resonated less.

In the decades of LGBTQ activism and advocacy in Lebanon, the outcry against anal examinations was unprecedented. Mainstream Lebanese media renamed the Republic of Lebanon "the Republic of Shame" and called the state's use of anal exams scandalous and barbaric.[16] Human Rights Watch issued a report and video called *Dignity Debased* on the practice of anal examinations in different locations across the global south, including Lebanon. The campaign to end the practice of anal examinations in Lebanon convinced the Lebanese Order of Physicians to issue a directive in 2012 calling for the exams to end and stating that the exams are not medically sound and are "a humiliating practice that violates [human] dignity, and it is torture according to the definition of Convention Against Torture."[17] The minister of justice and the public prosecutor's office also called for an end to anal exams. The public prosecutor's office, however, did not issue new compulsory guidelines banning the practice outright.[18] Despite promised changes in Lebanese institutional policy, anal examinations were conducted on men suspected of having had "unnatural sex" with other men as late as 2019. Recent controversies over anal exams in 2014 and 2016[19] concerned migrant or refugee men accused of engaging in sex work or accused of public indecency. Raids that target racialized and classed outsiders continue, and people caught in these raids continue to be detained on suspicions of "unnatural sex." Anal exams are still sometimes used as a threat during interrogation to coerce a confession.[20] The exams continue to be used as technologies of securitization, despite legal victories that suggest the decriminalization of sex between men.

In 2016 a Lebanese misdemeanors court issued a ruling that article 534 of the criminal code does not apply to gay sex because gay sex is not unnatural. While this was a victory for gay rights and activism, it is unclear if all of the defendants were men. The court decision mentioned that one of them "is a man dressed as a woman due to his feminine disposition." The ruling relied on the fact that this defendant's legal sex was male, then stated that article 534 of the Lebanese criminal code should not be applied because sex between men was not unnatural. Thus the success of this and other rulings that weakened the applicability of article 534 to men who have sex with men also potentially denied transwomen their very ability to love and have sex and define and live their lives *as* women.[21] Furthermore, the same ruling that found sex between men "not unnatural" found the defendant guilty of overstaying their visa and re-siding in Lebanon illegally. Migrant and refugee communities are par-ticularly vulnerable to the definition and criminalization of "unnatural sex." In 2014 a different criminal court decided that a defendant, a trans-woman, had not engaged in "unnatural sex"; she was a woman engag-ing in heterosexual sex with men. The same ruling stated that the court *would have* found it "unnatural" if the defendant had been having sex with other women. The defendant in the 2014 case, just as in the 2016 case, was not a Lebanese citizen. Instead, she was stateless and did not have a registration number or a civil status (*maktoum al-qayd*). She had been living in a chalet (owned by somebody else) in a crowded and rela-tively cheap beach complex when her neighbors accused her of engag-ing in unnatural sex, by which they meant sex between men and group sex. Both the 2014 and 2016 cases highlight how access to a private home, and thus to privacy itself, is classed, gendered, and raced.[22] Many refugees, migrants, stateless people, and transwomen live in shared and sometimes informal housing. In 2018 a ruling from the Criminal Court of Appeals in Mount Lebanon asserted that homosexual[23] sexual acts were unnatural only if they occurred "in view or in earshot of another person or in a public space or whenever they involve a minor who must be pro-tected."[24] This ruling both sanctified a right to privacy and reinterpreted it. The soundscape of some queer sex acts, even if they occurred inside private homes, was unnatural and corrupting if loud enough to be heard by others. Public sex—or sex outside of private property—and even loud queer sex in private homes continued to be "unnatural." Both relate to public morality and its violation—a charge often added to the dockets of people accused of having "unnatural" sex. "Public morality" and "pub-lic order" are two sides of the same sextarian coin. As we saw from the Assembly's rulings, public order is central to how the state manages reli-gious difference and coexistence as the right to unequal regimes of sexual difference. Public morality, on the other hand, regulates sexual difference through criminal law. The state maintains the sovereign right to define both the content and practice of both public morality and public order.

The criminalization and decriminalization of homosexuality never happens in a void. Instead, state regulation of sexual difference is intersectional[25] and happens across a hierarchy of control that is articulated across sex, nationality, legal status,[26] gender, race, and class.[27] This hierarchy is at work when the violation of men's bodies can constitute "torture" and be a cause of "shame" for Lebanon, while hymen exams, practiced and endured often, have yet to be interrogated as forms of state and state-adjacent violence. As a researcher, writer, and woman, I have lived for years with the specter of hymen testing. In high school a friend had undergone hymen testing at the insistence of her parents, who feared she was sexually active. When I was in college hymenal reconstruction surgery—a twin of hymen exams—was popular. A decade later, another friend was sexually assaulted. The investigation into her accusation included a hymen exam, in part to determine whether she had been a virgin at the time of the assault, a difference that mattered legally. In the 1990s and early 2000s, many women feared what could happen if they were ever detained by vice police during raids at queer parties and nightclubs. Hymen exams were part of those fears, even as we knew that men were more likely to be detained and more likely to be violently abused under detention. Those fears came true for a friend in 2010 when she was threatened in an interrogation room with a forced hymen exam. As a writer and editor, I had reviewed and published articles on the use of hymen testing as part of a counter-uprising strategy in Egypt.[28] As a researcher, I had seen investigative reports and copies of doctor's testimonies on hymens in archival files from personal status courts and the Court of Cassation.

Informed by this lived experience, during queer, feminist, and legal advocacy meetings, as well in private conversations, I asked why hymen exams were not included in the campaign against anal exams. A leading activist and a lawyer associated with LGBTQ legal victories explained that hymen testing was a more difficult, if not an impossible, fight. First, it was hard to get access to cases that involved hymen exams, in part because plaintiffs, victims, and court systems themselves found the subject too sensitive to share.[29] Second, the difficulty of mounting a campaign against hymen exams stemmed in part from their more widespread use. Women sometimes consent to hymen examinations and indeed sometimes request them to prove their sexual status, family members sometimes demand the exams, and the state uses them as evidence in cases of alleged rape, sex work, and abuse. The practice is both more widespread and less visible than anal exams, more experienced and less talked about, more diffuse and less confined to criminal law.[30] There was no clear culprit from which to seek redress or an end to hymen exams, as there was with anal exams—the state.[31] The imagined zone of "privacy" offered no protection, given the deep implication of "the family" as a sextarian, parastatal actor in ordering, sanctioning, and regulating women's sexuality, including through the practice of hymen exams.

Queer and straight sexualities are not separate spheres of regulation or of securitization. Instead, they are constituted and regulated in relation to each other,[32] a relation that is grounded in and grounds gender dimorphism. A comprehensive approach makes clear the nation-states' investment in sexual difference itself, and emphasizes the ways that sexual difference is materialized as a regime of sexualities and as sexual dimorphism, all of which are the effects of biopolitical power and not (only) its concerns. The legal and epistemological separations made between majoritarian and minoritarian, natural and unnatural, legal and illegal, normative and nonnormative, or straight and queer sexualities and genders are not the starting point of our analysis. Nor are the taken-for-granted differences between religious and secular courts. As we have seen in previous chapters, the regulation of sextarian difference integrates religious and secular courts into one national, sovereign legal system. As such, we have much to learn about state power and sovereignty from thinking about the regulation of sexuality and gender holistically. Heterosexuality has been taken for granted, has been normalized as that which regulates others, that which is natural. Thinking about sexual difference as a system of *relation* makes visible a grid of power that produces, materializes, and regulates sexes and sexualities as part of a larger field. This approach allows us to hold, for example, the tensions between women's sexuality and men's sexuality—whether queer or straight or neither—as grounded within the making of "man" and "woman" legally, medically, and in moments of encounter within the state. It also helps clarify that the stakes of sexuality are multiple[33] and that state power is invested and expressed as the maintenance and regulation of an entire sex-gender system.[34] National and international regulation of this system in part stabilizes discrete and measurable sexualities and genders. The states' role in defining sexuality as modulations of licit and illicit sex is precisely why for both queer and feminist activists "the state emerges as the central locus and guarantor through which non-normative sexual identities it once criminalized are now protected, liberated, and reconfigured."[35] Straight sex, particularly for unmarried women, can be just as, and sometimes more, risky as sex between men.

The violence and violation of anal exams became a public conversation in Lebanon due to the important work of activists, legal researchers, and human rights organizations. The violence and violation of hymen exams have not been addressed in a concerted away.[36] Hymen exams have not been framed as shameful or scandalous, nor have they led to changes or proclamations on behalf of state offices, officials, or doctors' syndicates. Yet as a case decided by Muslim personal status courts and in the Plenary Assembly in the late 2000s demonstrates, hymen exams are productive technologies of state and state-adjacent violence and sovereignty. This case, like many I found in the Assembly archives, was transnational—the series of events that brought Hana and Ramzi together, as well as the evidence presented in their divorce case, came from the United States, a country in the Arab Gulf, European countries where they had honeymooned, and Lebanon. The case traversed civil, religious, and criminal branches of law and demonstrated their imbrication in a sextarian system.

Violence, Sex, and Money: Hymen Exams as Evidence

In 2009 the Plenary Assembly decided the case of a young couple divorced by a Muslim personal status court.[37] The trouble began even before they were married. Ramzi alleged to the court that he had almost ended their engagement because his fiancée had persisted in wearing what his lawyers called "revealing" clothing. He presented himself as a graduate of a US university who was well traveled and cultured. He presented Hana as someone primarily concerned with meeting and marrying a man with access to transnational mobility, capital, and status: a man like himself. Hana's side of the story, unsurprisingly, was different. She recounted that on their wedding night Ramzi had made her wait in her wedding dress in the lobby of a chic hotel for three hours because he did not want to pay for an extra night's stay. "His cheapness was revealed," she said, pointing to this as a failed moment of masculinity. On that same night, Ramzi could not perform sexually and became violent. They then traveled to several European capitals for a honeymoon. They did not consummate their marriage for weeks after their wedding night because Hana was experiencing pain. After weeks of waiting, Ramzi forced himself on Hana and engaged in "unnatural acts"—a legal term that usually refers to sodomy but, in this case, referred to Ramzi using his fingers to try to penetrate Hana.[38] Hana and her lawyers called what happened rape. The day after, Hana asked Ramzi to make an appointment with a female gynecologist to help her with the pain she was experiencing both after the assault and while trying to have "natural" heterosexual sex with him.

On the day of the hymen exam appointment, the woman doctor was away and her male colleague was seeing her patients. At first, Hana refused to allow him to examine her. After struggling for over an hour, she finally agreed to the fifteen-minute hymen exam. In his report the doctor stated that there was a tear of unknown origin on her hymen. He added, however, that a woman's hymen is partially intact until childbirth, and hymens can be torn in a variety of nonsexual activities. As such there was no medical evidence that could certify without doubt that a woman is or is not a virgin, despite the fact that the hymen in question *was* perforated. He used the French term "pas de defloration" to denote that the test did not show a lack of virginity. Ramzi later framed Hana's resistance to the exam as evidence that she was not a virgin and suggested that the doctor had conducted a visual exam because Hana would not allow him to touch her. In response, Hana provided expert testimony from a forensic doctor in Europe stating that hymen exams are visual by nature.[39] After the hymen exam, the couple began to have what they both describe as a "normal" sex life. After they first had penetrative sex, however, he was further convinced that Hana had not been a virgin. There was not even "a little" blood. He shouted that "he might as well have married an American girl," in reference to the fact that he had been living in the United States for years when they met.

Afterwards, Ramzi traveled to a country in the Arabian Peninsula where he worked. Hana joined him weeks later. Their marital problems escalated, and the domestic violence Hana was subjected to by Ramzi intensified. Finally, after family, police, court, and community intervention in both their country of residence and in Lebanon, Ramzi agreed to allow Hana to return home. A week after Hana landed, Ramzi began a court case demanding that she live in their house, a strategy sometimes deployed by husbands to receive divorce settlements in their favor when their wives "refuse" to live with them. In such cases, the wife is usually declared "nashiza" or "discordant" and loses her rights to spousal support. Hana and her lawyer countersued for a divorce.

Instead of ordering Hana to live with Ramzi, the judge at the Personal Status Court of First Instance divorced the couple and found Ramzi at fault. The judge reasoned that Hana had presented convincing evidence of physical abuse and hateful behavior. He explained that Hana's injuries were so extensive and well documented that it was impossible to believe anything other than what Hana had said: Ramzi was an abusive husband. Furthermore, he didn't find Ramzi's allegation against Hana's virginity "serious" because he brought it up only late in the case and more than a year after the marriage was consummated. The judge rhetorically asked, why would Ramzi wait so long to present this evidence if he was truly, as he said, from a traditional and conservative family and social environment? Why didn't he bring up Hana's virginity the first or second time the court met instead of waiting until it was clear that a decision was close? The judge was angry about the physical and emotional abuse that Hana had suffered. Ramzi was ordered to pay Hana spousal allowance for the time they had been married and damages, in addition to the remainder of her dowry.[40]

Ramzi turned to the Personal Status Court of Appeals and asked that it overturn the divorce decision and reopen it as an annulment case because he had been deceived regarding an issue fundamental to marriage—his wife's virginity. He wanted the financial terms—the damages, spousal allowance, and dowry[41]—of the divorce revoked. He explained that his delay in bringing up Hana's virginity at the lower court was because of his desire to protect her reputation. He repeated that he thought to himself the night they consummated their marriage that he may as well have married an American girl, and that this thought grew over time in his head until it was all he could think about. Ramzi and his lawyers identified two more reasons why the ruling from the Court of First Instance should be overturned. First, they said it had relied on fabricated records of spousal abuse. Second, the lower court did not take into consideration a statement from a dean at a university in Lebanon about a friendship Hana had while in college.[42] In response, Hana countersued him at the Court of Appeals and again requested to be divorced from Ramzi. She asked that the spousal allowance granted to her by the lower court be quadrupled and the damages be more than doubled.

Unlike the Court of First Instance, the judges at the Personal Status Court of Appeals focused on Hana's virginity. Despite the multiple narratives threaded through hundreds of pages of legal argumentation, the court fixated on the hymen exam and on Hana's refusal to engage in sexual intercourse for the first month of their marriage. In its telling, her allegation that Ramzi had assaulted her with his fingers became her forcing *him* to use his finger to penetrate her. According to all religious traditions, the judges wrote, any man who discovered that his wife had engaged in premarital sex and had lied about it had the right to pursue a legal resolution. While the Personal Status Court of First Instance found it suspicious that Ramzi had not mentioned his wife's virginity until very late in the case, the Personal Status Court of Appeals rendered that same delay evidence of his desire to protect her reputation, a testament to his performance of protective patriarchal masculinity. The judges twice repeated Ramzi's statement that because Hana had allegedly engaged in premarital penetrative heterosexual vaginal sex, he might as well had married, or would have been better off marrying, a foreign woman. The judges clarified that at the time of marriage Hana's sextarian census registry identified her as a single woman. Being recorded as "single" in the census bureaucratically means never having been married and is thus distinct from "divorced" or "widowed." "Single" status is often collapsed with virginity, as women's sexuality is connected to and confined to heterosexual marriage.

The Court of Appeals turned to the subject of physical abuse but did not focus on it as the lower court had. It brought up Ramzi's previous history of violence, including against a girlfriend in the United States. Based on the medical reports and photographs that Hana had furnished to the court, the judges agreed that Ramzi had been violent toward Hana. Despite its sympathy, the Court of Appeals ruled against her. It noted that it had offered to solve the issue amicably and issue a mutually agreed-upon divorce, but Hana had insisted on being declared innocent of all allegations—which had meant reopening the entire case. The judges wrote that marriages can be annulled if there is a mistake in the identity of the person or deception regarding their essential characteristics, especially if that deception was key to the marriage itself. All religions, they wrote, agreed that the virginity of the wife was an essential characteristic.[43] While virginity is an essential characteristic of both spouses, Ramzi had never claimed to be a virgin, nor had Hana expected expect him to be. The fact that Ramzi expected Hana to be a virgin while she had not expected him to be pointed to the gendered economy of virginity both socially and legally. As Judith Surkis has demonstrated, virginity articulates legal and social histories and anxieties.[44] The Muslim appeals court decided, two to one, that Hana had married Ramzi under false pretenses and that the divorce from the lower court had infringed on Ramzi's rights. The appeals court found both Ramzi and Hana responsible for the failure of their marriage, but judged that Ramzi's actions came in reaction to Hana's. Ramzi was provoked, and as such Hana was not entitled to damages. The court also revoked her spousal allowance because she left the marital home, and indeed their country of residence, without Ramzi's consent. She had also refused to return to the marital home when asked.[45] Hana was, however, entitled to all gifts given during the marriage and the entirety of dowry. The financial settlement given to Hana by the Personal Status Court of First Instance was revoked.

Personal status appeals court decisions issued from all religions and sects usually definitely end cases, but not this one. The case was not unanimously decided. One of the three judges at the Personal Status Court of Appeals wrote a powerful dissent to his colleagues' decision. He argued that they had taken what Ramzi and his lawyers said at face value and as such had relied on unverifiable evidence. Additionally, they had not clarified the *ijtihad*, or the specific Islamic legal interpretation, they had used to reach their decision. Their omission meant that Hana could not fully defend herself. Hana was forced to leave her home because it was unsafe, not because she had left or abandoned her husband. Because it was impossible for Hana to live with Ramzi given the nature of their relationship, she should not have been faulted for refusing to return to the marital home. As such she should be entitled to damages and spousal support. Hana had lived through inhumane treatment, the judge wrote, and what could be described as rape. She was hurt and harmed in ways not accepted or allowed in Islamic law. By issuing a contradictory ruling, the judge wrote that his colleagues had acted as if "the rights of Muslim women could be meted out in parts." He even at times seemed exasperated by their legal reasoning and their decisions. The judge drew on a tactic of dissenting judges globally: he clarified a series of legal avenues an appeal could take and stressed procedural and substantive issues with the ruling. There was only one place left for Hana to appeal, the Plenary Assembly at the Court of Cassation. And that is exactly what she did.

The Plenary Assembly can and does hear cases stemming from personal status court decisions when they concern a substantive issue and/or procedural violations that may impact public order.[46] In their arguments to the Assembly, Hana and her lawyers alleged judicial misconduct at the personal status courts and substantive violations of procedural laws and norms.[47] Ramzi's family was politically connected, a fact that illegally affected court proceedings. They echoed the dissenting judge and wrote that by relying on a vague, unspecified category of Islamic jurisprudence, the Court of Appeals had denied Hana her right to defend herself by studying and responding to the ijtihad in question. Hana and her lawyers also alleged that the Personal Status Court of Appeals had violated civil law by neither taking the opinion of the public prosecutor's office at the sharia courts nor keeping it up to date with court proceedings.

They drew the Plenary Assembly's attention to the fact that the clerk at the Personal Status Court of Appeals had changed or misspelled words in his transcription of court proceedings. The term "pas de defloration," which in context meant no evidence of nonvirginity, was changed to "paste defloration," a typo that means nothing. While Hana testified that she had been experiencing a "severity of pain" related to sex, the clerk changed it to "because of pain." Hana and her lawyer returned to the hymen exam, arguing that the Personal Status Court of Appeals had misused the doctor's testimony. The doctor had testified that there was a scratch on Hana's hymen but did not give a reason or date as to how or when that might have happened, implying that it also could have happened while they were married. In fact, the primary reason for going to the hospital was because of the pain Hana was experiencing after Ramzi had assaulted her. The Personal Status Court of Appeals, however, assumed that the primary reason for the visit was a hymen test, which itself could only be, in its mind, a virginity test. The decision thus relied on the judges' own beliefs on the issue of virginity and hymen exams, despite the fact, Hana's lawyers wrote, that the judges were not experts on the matter of hymen exams. The Personal Status Court of Appeals *wanted* to reach this ruling, to side with Ramzi and to find Hana at fault for the divorce.

Let's pause here and review some facts. First, the Assembly practices a conservative interpretation of its own rights vis-a-vis personal status courts. For example, the Assembly rarely overturns personal status court decisions on substantive grounds, and it is even rarer for the court to overturn a personal status court decision because of judicial misconduct, which is a criminal offense. For example, the Assembly is sometimes asked by women plaintiffs to rule based on substantive differences between the constitution (the highest law of the land), which states that all citizens are equal before the law, and personal status laws that place women at a disadvantage when it comes to divorce or custody. Instead of ruling on such substantive grounds, the Assembly often overturns rulings from personal status courts on procedural grounds. Examples of that standard include a party not being represented by a lawyer, a party not being informed of scheduled court sessions, and the fabrication of evidence.[48] Second, very few cases reach the Plenary Assembly at the Court of Cassation, but each case that does is entered into the archive and is public record. It takes resources and perseverance to pursue a legal case to its fullest, to appeal to the highest court in Lebanon, the Plenary Assembly. If Hana was anything, she was resolute in her conviction that Ramzi should be held accountable for their divorce. She and her lawyers repeatedly, clearly, and forcefully underscored the sexual, physical, emotional, and psychological violence she had endured throughout her marriage. Hana did not accept to resolve the divorce "amicably," nor did she cower when Ramzi and his lawyers tried to shame her by alleging she had had premarital sex. They responded to every allegation and made it clear that some—such as the "evidence" that she had had a romantic relationship in college—were absurd. She stressed that Ramzi's father had occupied an important post in one of the security branches of the state,[49] making it clear that they believed his presence during court proceedings and his position in the state apparatus influenced the outcome of the case.

Third, there was no mention of Ramzi's premarital sex life at all. Although we perhaps expect the sexist focus on women's virginity as opposed to men's, we should not normalize it to the point that it escapes analytic notice.[50] When Ramzi's previous romantic relationship in the United States was brought up, it was in the context of his alleged violence. The relationship itself was uncontroversial. On the other hand, Hana's research project with a male classmate from college was enough to raise doubts and suspicions as to her premarital sex life.[51] Finally, it is crucial to stress that Hana and Ramzi's case was, fundamentally, about money. Like everywhere in the world, divorce cases in Lebanon that end up in court usually involve disagreements about financial settlements, regardless of whether the couple has children. In many legal systems, women too often barter their right to financial settlements to (finally) divorce their husbands and/or to receive or maintain custody over minor children. Hana, like many women featured in the Plenary Assembly archive, refused to do so. Like many of them, she lost her case.

The Assembly rejected Hana's appeal and let the Personal Status Court of Appeals ruling stand. The judges reasoned that the procedural mistakes that Hana and her lawyers outlined had either not happened, were subsequently rectified, or had not been substantive enough to effect the ruling itself.[52] The Assembly's decision was dry, perfunctory, and sanitized—a tone that set it apart from the Personal Status Court rulings that preceded it.[53] The judge at the Personal Status Court of First Instance was clear that Ramzi had crossed all acceptable boundaries within a marriage—physically, sexually, and emotionally. The decision he wrote was progressive and primarily concerned with Hana's welfare and safety. Even as the Personal Status Court of Appeals ruled against Hana, it was careful to stress that she had been a victim of domestic violence.[54] One out of three judges at the Court of Appeals disagreed with colleagues to the extent that he entered into the public record a dissenting opinion. In the Plenary Assembly decision, however, there was no mention of domestic violence or assault, and the word "hymen"—so central to the case—was missing. I asked Cassation Court archivists about this discrepancy, and they speculated that the jurists may have been uncomfortable with the facts of the case, uncomfortable with some of the details becoming public record.[55] While the Assembly often relays facts in its decisions that concern allegations of domestic violence and sexual misconduct, the explicit nature of Hana and Ramzi's case may have given it pause. The fact that Ramzi's father occupied an important post in the state apparatus could also have influenced their decision to censor specific details of the narrative. At the end of its decision was a strange detail. It did not require her to pay for the court fees, as is usual when someone loses a case. Instead the Assembly wrote that the Treasury would pay all relevant court fees because Hana's appeal was in good faith. Of course, all appeals to the Assembly are, on the surface, in good faith. The Assembly somehow set Hana apart even while ruling against her, ordering the Treasury to pay her court fees in a case while deciding that she was not entitled to a financial settlement from Ramzi. Perhaps this detail was a confession that the Assembly knew its decision was unjust, the price of consensus, or an admission that while it could or would not decide the case in Hana's favor, it was willing to perform this small gesture.

Seeing Truth

Hana and Ramzi's divorce case demonstrated the articulation of a medical-legal-security apparatus at the site of the vagina and at the sight of a hymen. The ability to see the hymen and its tears was affirmed by the plaintiffs, the doctor who had administered the test, and the expert testimony from a doctor in Europe who Hana furnished to the courts. However, what exactly were they seeing? Were they seeing evidence that

Hana was a virgin or evidence that she had had vaginal, penetrative sex? Were they seeing the effects of sexual assault, of previous sexual activity, or of the myriad other, nonsexual reasons a hymen could be torn or stretched?[56] Regardless of what they saw, legal and medical expertise had already materialized the hymen as a "test" in the high-stakes game of women's sexuality. The hymen could be seen, could be measured, and could be legally deployed. The exam materialized the hymen as the truth of sexual difference in at least two ways. First, the presence of a hymen produced the materiality of the bureaucratic and legal category of a single woman, a woman who had never been married, divorced, or widowed. Such women should be virgins, and as such should have untorn hymens, according to the Personal Status Court of Appeals. Second, the hymen exam materialized vaginal penetration as the truth of licit and illicit heterosexual activity for women. In fact, the ability to "see" the hymen, to make it bleed, and to produce it as an evidentiary terrain for sexuality is part of a multimillion-dollar industry called hymen reconstruction. The aim of hymen reconstruction is to ensure that there is a hymen to be lost to penetrative sex with a legitimate partner, a male husband with a penis. Private economic interest is also invested in the public and shared regulation of women's sexuality, and the public fiction of the virgin, via hymen exams and surgeries.

In similar ways, the penetrated male anus was materialized by legal and medical expertise as evidence in the high-stakes game of male homosexuality. Anal exams relied on examining the anus visually, and also articulated a medical-legal-security apparatus at the site and sight of the anus. Depending on the doctor, anal exams could also be physical and invasive.[57] A forensic doctor who conducted anal exams relayed to Human Rights Watch that "I only do an external examination. Some doctors put their finger in to see if the sphincter is tight or loose. I have also heard of the older generation using objects. This [anal exams] is a bullshit thing. You can find nothing. There are false positives and false negatives. If you find a funnel shape, it can be from some disease, or from other anal sphincter issues. Or you can have a real homosexual with a normal anus. You cannot conclude anything, medically."[58] The president of the Forensic Medicine Society of Lebanon also told Human Rights Watch, "It's impossible to find any signs to say this is definitely homosexuality,"[59] a statement that echoes Hana's doctor when he relayed that hymen exams were not conclusive evidence of female sexual activity. And yet, the exams continue, even though some of the doctors conducting them are clear that they are inconclusive. Why? Because rather than passively viewing, testing, or measuring bodily tissue, anal and hymen exams actively construct the body as a site for sexual truth and intervention by an epidermal state. They amplify and perform the state as that which can both command an exam and give that exam legal force.[60] Anal exams materialize the anal cavity and what it should and should not look like, and materialize scientific expertise as key to state power, even when the exam is inconclusive. They test for sex that the state considers "unnatural"—penetrative anal sex between men. As such the tests themselves construct the bodies being examined *as* male. When the state conducts anal exams on transwomen, it is resignifying and fixing their bodies as male. The stakes of anal exams include arrest, detention, and assault while in detention. Even when used as a threat, hymen and anal exams reproduce the power of the epidermal state to lay claim on a body and to materialize it as an evidentiary terrain for legal procedures.

"I Am the Law"

In 2010 my friend Yasmine was threatened with a hymen test by a security officer in an army barracks in Beirut. She had not been arrested or detained. Instead, Yasmine was there with another friend, Rula, to check on Basel, a client. They were both queer women and feminist activists who worked in human rights organizations. Yasmine worked for a well-known global human rights organization, and Rula worked for a local NGO focused on sexual rights in Lebanon and in the region. Basel was a young Syrian man who had been arrested and detained during a sweep on a poor and multinational neighborhood in Beirut. He was accused of engaging in unnatural sex and violating public morality. Yasmine and Rula were there to speak with him on behalf of the organizations they worked for. When they were called in by Internal Security officers to visit Basel, Yasmine and Rula were subject to interrogation. The officer was fixated on whether they were sexually active, if they were "girls or married." When they refused to be cowed by his aggressive behavior or answer his questions about their sex lives, he threatened them with a forced hymen exam "to find out." That night, Yasmine told me what had happened.

First we were asked if we were married, or rather, if we were "girls or married" . . . he was talking about sex. When we refused to answer he got more belligerent. He separated us into different rooms and kept interrogating us about our sexual activity and our connection to Basel. Why was I his contact? To me he tried to play good cop, telling me that I looked like I was from a good family and was respectable, a "daughter of a family" (*bint ʿayli*) unlike the person I was with. I wasn't sure if this was because Rula was more masculine in appearance, because my last name is recognizable, or because I worked for an international human rights organization and she worked for a local one. It was probably a combination of all three plus just an interrogation strategy. He implied that because we were both Muslims we surely both found effeminate gay men intolerable—or we *should*. He also said "I am with Hizballah (*ana maʿ Hizballah*),"[61] and I interrupted him and said "so what? (*eh wiʾza yaʿani?*) When I cut him off and said "so what" he got angry and pushed me against the wall. It hurt. He threatened to force us—to literally hold us down—to take a virginity test to find out if we were sexually active, which was essentially a threat of medical rape and torture. When I told him he had no legal basis to do so, nor did he have the right to interrogate us without evidence of a crime (again, we were just going to check a client who had been arrested) he lost it and shouted "I am the law (*ana al qanūn*)." It got really tense and confrontational. It was pretty terrifying. And this was *me*, an employee of one of the most well-known international human rights organizations in the world, which he knew, because I told him that, several times. Basel was released a few days later. He said he had not been assaulted while in detention, but really, who knows. I was his contact, and I guess this made me suspicious, like why would I waste my time defending the rights of people like my client? Why would a respectable, "daughter of a family" be in an army barracks to check on a Syrian, potentially queer man who had been arrested by the police?

I lodged a formal complaint for violence and intimidation against the interrogating officer with his superiors at the Internal Security Forces. I was told by the guy's superiors (right in front of this asshole, who was in the room) that I had to understand how the presence of our client and the crimes he had been accused of made the officer angry and disgusted. We had made him angrier by refusing to answer his questions. His superior said I should understand why he might have thought I was a sex worker since I was visiting a gay man in prison, and because of my large back tattoo which peeked out a little from my shirt. Of course, by saying this he insinuated that even him *thinking* that I was a sex worker justified his actions, including his threat of a hymen exam. These were all just excuses, who knows why this guy acted like he did other than he could. Maybe he was bored, or crazy. Maybe he was just a piece of shit. Whatever the reason his supervisor was just protecting him.[62]

Hymen and anal examinations are used as intimidation tactics because they are terrifying and invasive. The threat of a virginity test by the ISF officer to Yasmine and the way he described it—we will hold you down and do it—was intended to terrify her. He performed the impunity with which he—as a representative of an epidermal state—could violate her bodily integrity. When Yasmine, instead of showing fear, informed him that his interrogation and his threats of a hymen exam were illegal, he responded "I am the law," clarifying that he, not her, wielded and represented the power, malleability, and impunity of law. The law of the state becomes manifest—and is materialized—at these points of intimate and violent bodily contact. As a representative of the epidermal state, the security officer had the right to define and shape law's content in practice. If he was the law, how could his intimidation and interrogation without cause be illegal? By announcing his embodiment of law, he wanted Yasmine to feel vulnerable and exposed to the state, to know, and *feel*, that she had no recourse. Sextarianism was key to staging his embodiment of the epidermal state.[63]

Their encounter began with the officer wanting to know whether Yasmine was sexually active, whether she was "married or a girl." The phrase implied that unmarried women are by definition virgins or "girls." It also defined women in relation to the men in their lives—they are either wives or daughters—mirroring state practice and census bureaucracy. The more Yasmine refused to answer his invasive questions and instead invoked her rights to not be interrogated, the more invasive the officer became and the more he violated her rights. His apparent disgust at homosexuals was a performance of his heterosexuality, and throughout the encounter he was pushing Yasmine to publicly distance herself not only from homosexuality but also from the wrong kind of heterosexuality—the kind that would have sex with a man who was not a husband. When he suggested that because they were both Muslims they felt the same way about Basel, the Syrian man, also a Muslim, he was testing her. She failed his test. When she cut him off mid-sentence, or mid-threat, he pushed her against the wall and said he would hold her down for a hymen test. My friend—a queer woman—was asked to both engage in homophobia and claim virginity to be a "daughter of a family" in the eyes of the interrogating officer. The reference to her tattoo was another fleshy, epidermal site—it materialized a woman's skin as evidence of sexual practice and sex work. The officer's continued invocation of the term "daughter of a family" contained an implicit threat of outing Yasmine to her family, either as queer herself or as sexually active with men. The scale and fungibility of law's impunity—the bordering of what was or was not a legal interrogation—was at stake.

Yasmine's status as potentially deserving of respect and integrity, as opposed to Basel's, was not only linked to their sexuality. Homophobia is most viciously deployed against people whose multiple vulnerabilities—legal status, class, nationality, gender performance, and race—make them more available for violence in Lebanon.[64] Yasmine was a Lebanese citizen, was from a recognizably upper-middle-class Beiruti family, was not masculine presenting, was dressed professionally and expensively, and worked for a well-known international human rights organization. This enabled her to push back against the interrogating officer and to submit an official complaint against him to his commanding officers. However, privilege is relative. That night, talking on her couch, we both doubted whether her European or American colleagues would have been subjected to the same treatment.

Yasmine submitted a complaint to the interrogating officer's superiors. The commanding officer used sex work and homophobia to massage his subordinate's intimidating and violent behavior into new, understandable, and legal descriptions. The officer was so angry at the presence of this young Syrian man under detention that he lashed out at anyone coming to see or represent him. Homophobia was a legitimate reason for homophobic and sexist violence and intimidation.[65] Similarly, the superior officer rationalized the interrogating officer's threat of a hymen exam by claiming that he must have suspected Yasmine of sex work. Not only was she visiting a gay, effeminate man in jail, but she had also refused to answer whether she was married and had ignored all of the officer's questions that were linked to sex. She had refused him the right to question her sexuality, and this made him suspicious, angry, and frustrated. The allegation of sex work was itself a threat because sex work without a license is a criminal offense, and suspected sex workers are sometimes subjected to forced hymen exams in detention. Accusing Yasmine of sex work was intended to perform the absolute power the security branches of the epidermal state have over women's bodies that have been coded as potential sex workers.[66] The commanding officer responded to Yasmine's complaint by mentioning her back tattoo and the fact that she was the official contact of a "faggot" in detention (he used the word *liwāt*). Both were signs that Yasmine was in fact not conforming to the patriarchal codes of gender and sexuality, they were evidence that she was in fact not a good girl, a *"bint 'ayli."* The threatened deployment of hymen exams, of "medical rape and torture" in Yasmine's words, was rendered by his commanding officer a legitimate[67] way to collect evidence to prove or disprove a crime. Or at least, this was the narrative he used to protect his subordinate officer and explain away Yasmine's complaint.

Torture is violence that has been legally framed *as* torture.[68] The judiciary in Lebanon and the state's security apparatus have regularly been accused of brutality against political activists, sexual minorities, suspected Islamists, and people who are detained and/or incarcerated more generally.[69] Within this background picture of state violence, two years after Yasmine and Rula were threatened with hymen exams, the Lebanese Ministry of Justice and the public prosecutor's office were cowed by public pressure on the practice of anal examinations, described them as violations that rose to the level of torture, and pledged to stop them.[70] There is a transnational political economy at play in the withholding and deployment of "torture" as a threshold at which point violence becomes a *violation* of human rights. In prison cells and in interrogation rooms all over the world, people are violated physically, psychologically, and sexually.[71] The Lebanese state, however, has to date admitted to torture and pledged to combat it only in the case of anal exams on men suspected of having sex with men. In this context, the treatment of suspected queer bodies served as a barometer of a country's modernity, an indictment that Lebanon was "a Republic of Shame."[72] In Lebanon, many of these men and boys are Syrian refugees.[73] Refugees, displaced persons, and migrants are vulnerable to the law regardless of whether they are accused of homosexual sex or terrorism; they are more likely to be targeted for arrest, more likely to be violated in detention, and less likely to have the financial resources or social networks to help ameliorate their circumstances both predetention and postdetention.

Parastatal actors are also licensed to commit violence and to violate bodily integrity, particularly against women. Agencies that import foreign women who work as domestic labor under the Kafala system in Lebanon regularly conduct pregnancy tests on them with or without their consent.[74] To date, a handful of Lebanese citizens have been found legally accountable for violence against migrant domestic laborers despite hundreds of documented cases, including some that amount to torture and murder. In a similar vein, Hana's description of Ramzi as her captor and of living with him as "torture" could only be metaphorical: married men freely exercise state sanctioned rights of violence and control over their wives and children. They have the right to rape their wives and to demand cohabitation from them, and the ability to divorce them according to a different set of sextarian criteria, such as virginity. These rights are enshrined and regulated in personal status, criminal and civil law, and crucially, in the structures that knit them together such as the Plenary Assembly at the Court of Cassation.

Both anal and hymen exams emphasize and express confidence in *seeing* as medical expertise. Both exams articulate state sovereignty as a power that has the right to materialize, examine, and handle bodies. But there are also important differences between the exams, the most prominent being who can demand the test. Anal exams can be compelled only by the state, while hymen exams can be compelled by a more diffuse set of actors and institutions that *include* the state. This discrepancy in part emerges from the different and overlapping ways that anal and hymen exams are given legal force. Anal exams operate squarely within the framework of criminal law, while hymen exams enter into criminal law and personal status law. They can serve as evidence in a divorce case; in cases of suspected sex work, rape, sexual assault, child abuse; and in cases across the legal system where "honor" is invoked and equated with women's sexuality. The test can be commanded or solicited not only by the state but also by a wide range of individual actors, such as husbands, parents, and the persons themselves.[75] Anal exams, however, are used only to prosecute suspected cases of rape or child abuse or in prosecuting men for suspected "unnatural sex acts." As such the state—through its official institutions—is the only actor that can command an anal examine and give it legal felicity. The state alone has the right to examine and constitute the legal stakes of men's sexuality.[76] Only the state can violate the bodies it constitutes as male through the violation of an anal exam. When it comes to hymen exams, the state shares and distributes its right to examine and produce the stakes of women's sexuality to parastatal actors such as the heteropatriarchal family or a migrant domestic workers' sponsor—who could be a woman—in the Kafala system. Moreover, hymen exams can be done to "protect" or to "prove" a woman's virginity—in such cases, they are framed as being in service of the person in question.

Finally, anal and hymen tests circulate differently in public national space. While anal exams have justifiably caused public outcry and national and transnational campaigns aimed at ending the practice, hymen exams have not yet triggered the same response, despite the wider framework within which hymen exams circulate. This wider framework troubles the idea, articulated to me in advocacy meetings related to anal examinations, that women's consent to these exams, and sometimes their demand of them, make them difficult to organize around.[77] Indeed the wider legal, social, and economic frameworks that hymen exams circulate in troubles the notion of consent itself. Even if Hana consented to the test, her consent was conditioned by physical and emotional coercion. Consent and "force" are highly gendered, raced, and classed practices. It is more difficult to frame hymen exams as a "human rights violation"[78] because they implicate families as well as states. It is also more difficult to frame hymen exams as "shameful" precisely because women's sexuality is more highly regulated, and women's premarital sexuality is constructed as illicit no matter the kind of sex being had. The multiple stakes of hymen and anal exams are clearer when they are thought across sextarian difference. Thinking these exams together allows us to reapproach sexual difference and its relation to sovereignty, citizenship, and how sexed and gendered bodies are constituted within a hierarchy of violability. The body in pain is sovereignty's ability to violate without committing the legal definition of violence.[79]

Sovereignty, Sex, and National Coherence

State and transnational sovereignty are built and articulated through the regulation of sexuality, gender, and the family.[80] State power is inflected with the unique ability to demand and submit the body to forms of touch, inspection, and intrusion under the rhetoric of protection of society and the body public. These forms of bodily "touching," as Asli Zengin has theorized, and particularly the violation of bodily integrity, are key to sovereignty.[81] In the interrogation room, Yasmine was pushed against a wall and threatened with a forced hymen exam because she had refused to answer questions about her sexuality and had refused to perform homophobia to cement her status as a good Lebanese girl. When she continued to refuse and instead insisted that she had the right to bodily integrity, the security officer threatened to hold her down and conduct the exam himself. When she filed an official complaint, the commanding officer explained his subordinate's actions through the logic of law and its brutal enforcement against women suspected of being sex workers. He did so in front of the officer who had assaulted Yasmine—performing yet another layer of impunity. Though the narrative was flawed according to the standards of evidence set by Lebanese law, to say nothing of the violations of women's bodies that it rendered "logical," it didn't matter. Law was not the legal articles themselves. Law was the ability to speak and act as a representative of the epidermal state, and Yasmine had lost that fight.

Scientific, legal, and medical expertise materialize the body and its components as available for capture by state[82] and state-adjacent actors.[83] Sexual difference, understood as a mutually reinforcing relationship between sexuality and sexual dimorphism, is not merely regulated by state power. It is produced through governmental, disciplinary, and biopolitical techniques. A hymen exam does not only examine the body for traces of sexual contact, it (re)produces bodily material as *the* evidentiary terrain for both sex and for sexuality—a woman has a hymen, that hymen is the surface upon and through which sexuality can be read. In Hana's divorce case, the hymen test demonstrated the ways that medical and legal expertise shuttle through and unite secular and religious institutions in their regulation of licit and illicit female sexuality. The hymen exam even produced the terms of sex: as long as a hymen can be "seen," that *woman* has not engaged in sex, or at least, not in sex that counts *as* sex. Anal exams, meanwhile, produced the anus as an abundant surface upon which men's gender, men's sexuality, and state power are produced.[84] Biopolitical logic constructs normative and disciplinary categories of gender and sexuality in part through visualizing, securitizing, and personalizing the failure to perform them.[85] Normative categories such as heterosexuality require bodies that fail, and that fail in different ways. A woman who fails a hymen exam and a man who fails an anal exam have both failed to embody and practice normative heterosexuality. Anal and hymen exams serve as "gender checkpoints"[86] as much as they serve as "sexuality checkpoints." They aim to fix gender into binaries and sexuality into defined legitimate and illegitimate couplings of those binaries. Yet what these exams actually test *for*, what makes sex *sex* and what make sex licit or not, is penetration by a penis. In this way, both hymen and anal exams stage the authorial power of the phallus. This authorial power penetrates irrevocably, shapes flesh, and leaves material traces that can be seen, measured, interpreted, and given legal force by the epidermal state.

Sextarian difference is both built by and builds hierarchies within a biopolitical grid, across intersections of race, sect, legal status, class, and sex.[87] This hierarchy has as much to do with who *can* violate as it does with who is being violated and is upheld by how, when, and what forms of state violence are understood as violations.[88] The epidermal state maintains its right to materialize men's gender and sexualities through anal exams in the arena of criminal law, but distributes and licenses its sovereign right to materialize women's bodies via hymen exams to a set of actors within a shared sociopolitical space, one that includes natal families, civil and personal status courts, and husbands.[89] The different ways that sexuality is regulated emerges from the different ways that sexes are produced as always already within a relational and hierarchical sextarian system. In this way, sexuality exams serve to test for more than the truth of sex—they are used to determine whether a citizen or resident has upheld the sexual architecture of the very nation as a distinct and coherent category. After all, Hana had allegedly failed not only a hymen exam but all that a hymen exam implies. Because she had a tear on her hymen, and because she may have had illicit, premarital heterosexual sex, she "might as well have been an American." Because Yasmine refused to engage in homophobia or answer questions about her sexual practices, she lost the ability to claim the position of a "daughter of a family." She was instead threatened with a hymen exam.

The Epidermal State

The legal, medical, secular, religious, and securitized materialization and treatment of bodies—the structure of violability—are key to understanding how sovereignty is expressed, produced, and *felt*.[90] Sovereignty is the demand and command to produce a body and/or a population, the power to decide which bodies and populations matter and how and when, but it is *also* the power to produce and signify and modulate the *matter* of bodies.[91] Sovereignty is expressed as the ability to intervene, to touch,[92] and to violate without committing a violation. Nation-states have the power to define violence that is legally actionable, and transnational bodies have power to set standards for thresholds of acceptable and unacceptable violence by individual states.[93] However, states are rarely accountable when they exceed these thresholds, including when they commit torture against political opponents, incarcerated people, or people in police or migrant detention facilities. When the body being tortured is considered "dangerous" enough to warrant such treatment, torture can and has been promoted as a public good, a form of state violence in service of public security.[94] However, not all forms of state intervention into bodies are understood as torture, or even as violence. The deployment of terms such as torture or violence to describe forms of state intervention into individual or groups of bodies marks how and when such intervention is viewed as excessive, as an unwarranted intervention into bodily integrity. Anal exams were framed as a form of "torture" conducted by the state onto suspected queer male bodies. Yet they continue—particularly on bodies that are discursively produced as less deserving of integrity by nationalist ideology, bodies more vulnerable to state violence and deployment of sex-as-securitization.[95] Hymen exams have yet to be framed by Lebanese state as torture, and the state has yet to recognize them as a form of violence. The discrepancy between exams that by and large rely on similar forms of medical expertise and test for the same presence—that of a penetrative phallus—emerges from legal, bureaucratic, and ideological differences between women and men and their sexualities in a sextarian system.

Bringing together the production and regulation of sexualities and binary gender subject positions allows us to study the circulation of power as it stages, arranges, and rearranges a hierarchical and always already relational system of subjectification, securitization, and violence. When we define our categories of analysis differently from the achievements of biopolitical power, such as homosexuality and heterosexuality, male and female binary genders, citizen and noncitizen, or religious sectarian categories of analysis, we can see state power's investment in materializing political and sexual difference as a staging ground for sovereignty. We see the state's investment in violence and in directing that violence internally, performing itself as a bounded entity. That violent turning inwards also materializes a sextarian, intersectional body politic that is not synonymous with citizenship. When we think state violence against protestors in 2019 together with decades-long state violence against vulnerable people and groups, we find ourselves—all of us—surrounded by, embedded in, and pushing against a sextarian, epidermal state.

Epilogue

FOUR MONTHS INTO THE 2019 uprising, in January 2020, I visited the Ministry of Justice, the Beirut Courthouse, and the lawyer's syndicate. I wanted to check whether the Cassation Court archives had been digitized and to see how government employees were faring. The uprising had the law squarely in its crosshairs: People were accusing the judiciary of political and economic corruption and demanding that it be empowered, independent, and fair. Almost two years later the Plenary Assembly was asked to intervene in the Beirut explosion investigation by politicians who had been identified as persons of interest and defendants by the special investigator. The Assembly was asked to recuse that special investigator and to give up the judiciary's jurisdiction into the investigation. It refused, and yet as of this writing the legal destiny of the investigation is unclear. Back in 2019, I visited the judiciary complex to see old friends and learn what *they* thought about, and whether they were participating in, the uprising.

I was not surprised that the Beirut Courthouse and in particular the Cassation Court archives were, as always, as busy as a blur.[1] Mona had retired, but many of the people I had worked with years earlier were still employed. The head archivist, Evelyn, was there, her employees still called her "bash," and she still walked too quickly for me. Since I met her in 2009, she had been committed to organizing, digitizing, and professionally preserving the Cassation Court archives. Beginning in 2018, she finally had gotten her way, but she had had to fight for it. Evelyn and a powerful, well-respected lawyer had acquired the permissions and resources to consolidate the archive. She started by sending the pre-1943 independence archive, which had been a pile in an attic when I first conducted research, to the Council of Ministers archive, where they had organized the Cassation

FIGURE 9. Photograph of door to Cassation Court archive in parking lot depot, 2020. Name of NGO helping archival preservation listed.

Court files according to date, file number, and plaintiff names. The correct file could now be found through a digital search. An NGO connected to the lawyer helping Evelyn had been brought in to help.

The files from the 1960s to the year of the fire in 1985 were still in a depot in the parking garage, but there were no longer "a mountain of files," as Evelyn and Mona had described them in 2011. Instead, they were being organized, refiled, and catalogued. Old metal lockers lined the walls, each had been painted with a Cassation Court chamber and the years it contained. Files that had not yet been re-archived sat in stacks on tables, and one table supported the gloves, masks, and brushes that had been used to remove as much dust and debris as possible from the archive of the country's Cassation Courts, including that of the Plenary Assembly.

Many of the papers and files and ledgers were frail and brittle, damaged by water, smoke, the cold and humidity of attics and cupboards, and the mundane and irreversible ravages of time. I was afraid to touch anything. The effort to conserve the courts' archive had been on the news lately, and the Lebanese body politic had seen, literally, the making of this archive. There they were, public sector employees and members of an NGO, sorting, refiling, and preserving files—almost forty years after they had burned. There was no forthcoming budget from the government, no international funds had ever materialized, but finally the work had started. There were hundreds of thousands of documents and files to sort.

I felt afraid of history fraying at the pressure of my touch—I was intimidated by the files' fragility. While I was all jumbled up in my feelings, employees at the courthouse were organizing files around me, stacking and restacking and reshelving them. They were experiencing the need for a legal archive to be functional, to be able to search for and within files and court orders and decisions and to be able to know what could and could not be found. There is practical, methodological, and theoretical utility to know and accept what you could *not* know. Not everything can be saved, and some documents, like victims of a war or an explosion, are just gone. Many files and papers were sequestered to a table that housed documents too damaged to work with. But documents damaged beyond repair were not discarded. Wars destroy and create without mercy. After all—archival files that a war's fire destroyed become an archive of that

FIGURE 10. Archival files on table, metal cabinets containing organized files lining walls.

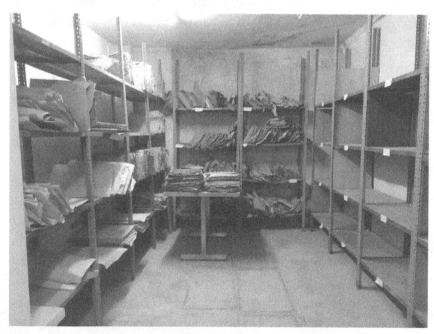

FIGURE 11. Table with files and documents too burnt to salvage.

war, become an archive of workers trying to put out a fire and recovering—a day, year, decade, and forty years later—what they could *and* what they could not. Moreover, the material history of the court contains the materiality of its own destruction; archival files are littered with the burned debris of other files, marked with smoke and filled with pages curling upwards for air during a fire, and waterlogged—damaged irrevocably by efforts to save them.

There are multiple histories—material, national, legal, individual—in that underground parking lot depot that holds the archive of Lebanon's highest court. This tangle of history impresses on your body. One can read, smell, squint at, and be dirtied by the history of the Lebanese judiciary's transition from French to Arabic. The imprint of courts belonging to empires that no longer exist, but whose existence continues to forge futures, make you think about power and temporality, but they also make you sneeze because there is so much dust on these old papers. The archive holds and arrests the lives and careers of jurists and archivists and lawyers and Ministry employees, an altogether different history of Lebanon. These jurists and archivists heard, curated, and tended to case files concerning divorce, custody, property, bigamy, murder, embezzlement, violence, war crimes, sexuality, voting, judicial misconduct, rent disputes, and taxation. The Cassation Court's work performs the state's regulation and investment in all arenas of life. Nothing is personal or private. Nothing is outside the purview of the state and its highest court. Sex was a seam that held the archive together, stitching together hymens and property, voting and marriage, murder and honor, sexuality and public space, violence and intimacy, corrupt judges and politicians, rape and war, citizenship, guardianship, and bank accounts. The state's neglect of the archive of its own Cassation Court also told a story. It was only when Evelyn got help, and made it clear to the Ministry that she did not need much from them, that the work began in earnest. While the epidermal security state was deployed to quell protests sometimes only hundreds of meters away, the bureaucratic, organizational, archival state had continued its work at the Ministry of Justice and the Beirut Courthouse. Sectarianism was the logic and system that articulated these different facets of state power into one, seemingly immovable, object

FIGURE 12. Photograph of case file from 1944.

FIGURE 13. Close-up of 1944 file and fire debris.

FIGURE 14. Photograph of 2019 Intro October uprising
in Lebanon. Image from Nabil Ismail.

FIGURE 15. Photograph of security forces and protestors at
Ring Bridge, Beirut. Image by Ahmad Gharbieh, 2019.

Outside, on the streets, many of the lawyers, activists, and intellectuals whom I had spent much of my fieldwork with were protesting, demanding, screaming, running, and choking on tear gas. Some were holding daily teach-ins on the intricacies of law, including civil marriage and personal status law, in downtown Beirut. Some were detained by different branches of the security state, while others rallied outside their spaces of detention. They were interviewed on television, they were writing in local and transnational media platforms, and they were planning and organizing events for and of the uprising. They were marching, strategizing, and setting up mutual aid networks. The downtown areas of several cities, most notably Beirut and Tripoli, had become a grand experiment in public pedagogy and claiming public space—just as they had been in Egypt and in Tunisia and elsewhere. Groups and individuals who for years had been building social movements related to public accountability, a transparent judiciary, secularism, women's rights, and an end to political sectarianism found new audiences and collaborators to join their movements. Secularism, or anti-sectarianism, was again centered as a political demand. Women's citizenship rights, custody rights, and sexual rights were central to anti-sectarianism. That is, they were framed as sextarian rights. However, unlike when I had conduced fieldwork, these protests were aimed squarely at the regime of economic, political, and sectarian power relations that had controlled the state for decades. There was an urgency and a break in the politics of deferral. But there was still a belief in and an almost desperate desire for, as a friend put it, "a state. Any kind of fucking state, as long as it works." Protestors lauded and called for the Lebanese constitution to be implemented fully and impartially, as well as for early parliamentary elections. The precarity of everyday life locally, nationally, regionally, and internationally pushed, compelled, and incited people into the embrace—the promise—the fantasy—of the republic. Many were convinced, again, that there was a civil war coming. But in some ways, the war against ordinary people has never ended. Thirty years earlier, the peace deal that ended the Lebanese Civil War was heralded not with faith or hope but with the kind of desperation that can only be felt, not understood. Through that desperation new weapons were acquired: the state, the judiciary, the Central Bank. The

2019 uprising was and is, in many ways, an attempt to save the state and its promise from the politicians who had degraded and ransacked it. There was a generational discourse to that saving; postwar generations argued that unlike their predecessors they were not easily swayed by the promises and threats of wartime militia leaders/postwar politicians. This time things were different. This was a breaking point, a new horizon. It was exhilarating. But even in that moment, it felt like nostalgia. Like I could already see us, shaking our heads, remembering this feeling, turning it into a moment, an event, in time. Two years later, years filled with unimaginable scenes of violence and despair, with countless events that have yet to become a narrative, a friend and I talked about the elasticity of suffering. Walking home in a Beirut without electricity, a darkness that was not new to either of us—instead, the kind of familiarity that is full of dread—he asked, "What is worse, the stretching or the breaking?" The conversation felt like déjà vu, and in some ways, so does this writing.

So many endings, and not an end in sight.

Acknowledgments

HAVING TOO MANY PEOPLE to thank is a good problem to have, and it is an accurate description of the generosity and support I have enjoyed while writing this book. Researching and writing *Sextarianism* allowed me to split my time between the United States and Lebanon. In Beirut, I am grateful for Nayla Geagea and our continuing coffee dates and the gift of friendship; Marie Rose Zalzal and Talal Husseini for opening many doors; Mona for always keeping it real; Nizar Saghieh, Karim Nammour, and Lama Karame for advice; Basil Abdullah and Vartan Avakian, Joelle Hatem for their generosity; and Alexandre Paulikevich and Kinda Hassan for bringing me along for some wild and beautiful rides.

This project would not have been possible without the love and support of Rasha Moumneh, Ahmad Gharbieh, and Leila Kobeissi. They have been my family, my bedrock, my sounding board, and my buoy since I was a teenager. It has been a great privilege to grow up with them, and *Sextarianism* has been greatly influenced by conversations with and provocations from them. Sherene Seikaly, Nadya Sbaiti, Bassam Haddad, John Warner, Elizabeth Gelber, Jasbir Puar, Noura Erekat, Dima Abi Saab, Amar Shabandar, Ziad Abu Rish, and Rasha Khoury have each shaped and shared my life in innumerable ways. I do not know when, or where, or whom I would be without my friends. For friendship, generosity, conversation, card games, and impromptu phone calls, emails, questions, and texts I also thank Zahra Ali, Nadje al Ali, Andrew Arsan, Anjali Arondekar, Paul Amar, Elizabeth Ault, Dima Ayoub, Morgan Clarke, Bassem Chit, Lara Deeb, Mayanthi Fernando, Jo Hammoud, Jowe Harfoush, Sami Hermez, Laleh Khalili, Ghassan Makarem, Ilham Khouri-Makdisi, Ussama Makdisi, Georgina Manok, Carlos Motta, Lina Mounzer, Adnan Moussa, Ghassan Moussawi, Edwin Nasr, Laila Shereen

Sakr, Kyla Schuller, Myriam Sfeir, Sima Shakhsari, Hamed Sinno, Judith Surkis, and Neha Vora. I am always somehow thinking and learning with my colleagues at Jadaliyya and the Arab Studies Institute—I am so proud to be in their company. Sometimes the smallest gestures from strangers can mean everything to a junior scholar—the emails, comments after a presentation, and words of support. Thank you

At Columbia University's Anthropology Department, Nadia Abu El-Haj and Elizabeth Povinelli modeled for me the stakes, importance, and joy of politically engaged anthropology; Brinkley Messick a love of research; and Rashid Khalidi the grace of humility and of action, of being in multiple worlds. Lila Abu Lughod has been the best mentor one could ask for. She shared with me the knowledge and the confidence to focus on the craft of writing, to build theory, and to do both with generosity. Saba Mahmood and Suad Joseph also modeled mentorship outside of formal institutional ties. Suad Joseph has been a consistent, and fun, interlocuter. Saba Mahmood was an early supporter and provocateur.

Sextarianism began to take shape as a concept at NYU's Kevorkian Center for Near Eastern Studies, and I thank my students and my colleagues at NYU for a rich and stimulating environment. In particular, thank you to Michael Gilsenan, Zach Lockman, Asli Igsiz, Lisa Duggan, Benoit Challand, Dima Abi Saab, Adnan Moussa, and Elif Sari. At the department of Women's Gender and Sexuality Studies at Rutgers University I learned that making a *difference* can be just as important as making an *intervention*. I am inspired by my colleagues and students. I am lucky to work with Sylvia Chan-Malik, Brittney Cooper, Marisa Fuentes, and Kyla Schuller (the OG junior faculty crew); Rhadika Balakrishnan, Ethel Brooks, Charlotte Bunch, Abena Busia, Ed Cohen, Carlos Decena, Nicole Fleetwood, Judith Gerson, Toby Jones, Dana Luciano, Rebecca Mark, Jasbir Puar, Zakia Salime, Louisa Schein, Sarah Tobias, Mary Trigg, Deb Vargas, and Asli Zengin. A. Haziz-Ginsburg, Amir Mohammad Aziz, and Zandi Sherman have also been important interlocutors.

I have presented parts of *Sextarianism* at the University of Chicago, Brown University, Berkeley, UCLA, Columbia University, NYU, George Washington University, Georgetown University, Yale University, Oxford University, Rutgers University, the American University of Cairo, the

American University of Beirut, and the Lebanese American University. I am thankful for the opportunity to share my work and for the feedback of colleagues.

Lila Abu Lughod, Sherene Seikaly, Jasbir Puar, Lara Deeb, Paul Amar, Anjali Arondekar, Ziad Abu-Rish, Nadya Sbaiti, Judith Surkis, Asli Zengin, Ghiwa Sayegh, Lama Karame, and Andrew Arsan each have read and commented on the manuscript, or on big chunks of it. Their engagement enriched *Sextarianism* beyond measure. I am also grateful to my writing partners Lara Deeb, Ghiwa Sayegh, Sherene Seikaly, and, too briefly, Hamed Sinno. Thank you for keeping me on task! I cannot put into words the care and love that Sherene Seikaly has held me and this book with. Our partnership is a gift that only grows with time, and I can't wait for what comes next. Kate Wahl has been an early and consistent supporter of this book, and her keen editorial eye is evident on every page. The work of Caroline McKusick and Gigi Mark on *Sextarianism* was also critical to its final shape.

I thank the Caland family for the rights to use Huguette Caland's piece "Untitled 1973" for the book cover. I have been a fan of Caland's work for years, and am proud that her art adorns this book. When I first saw this particular sketch, it stopped me in my tracks. Kaelen Wilson-Goldie and Shiva Balaghi helped me understand why. I also thank Zaven Kouyoumdjian for his generosity in letting me reproduce images from his book, *Lebanon Shot Twice*.

The material conditions of our research directly impress on our research itself. I offer myself as an example of the need to be transparent about the political economy of academic research, particularly as tenure-stream positions, research funds, sabbaticals, PhD funding, and *time* are increasingly diminishing goods in the US academy. In addition to being written during a pandemic and as Lebanon imploded, it is important to note the generous funding that enabled me to dwell for years on this project. My research has been supported by grants from the Social Science Research Council, the Wenner-Gren Foundation, and the Middle East Research Commission. These grants were supplemented by research funds from Columbia University, NYU, and Rutgers University. The generosity of this funding coupled with my dual Lebanese and American citizenship allowed me to conduct two and a half years of uninterrupted research, more than five subsequent, months' long research trips, and a year and a half of paid sabbatical writing time. If research and writing take time, we have only the time we are, literally, unequally afforded.[1] I thank Oxford University Press, Cambridge University Press, and Duke University Press for the rights to repurpose previously published material.

Charlene, Tarik, Nadya, and Ziad Mikdashi have supported me in all my endeavors for as long as I can remember. My mother taught me to love reading and talking about books, my Baba the art of a good and fiery argument. Both inspire me with their relentless curiosity about our worlds. I will miss talking about *Sextarianism* with them. My brother remains the most incisive person I know, and my sister is the best cut-througher of bullshit out there. My siblings ground me. My nephew Zayn is my joy, my motivation, and my superhero. I miss my grandparents every day. Asli Zengin's brilliance, love, and care animate the pages of *Sextarianism* as they do my daily life. Karim and Zaara lived this book with me, and have walked, and slept, over almost every page.

Lebanon, of course, is not only a research site. It is my home, where the most of me makes sense, and the space that shapes my being in the world. Writing this book has been measured in time away from home, time away from the sea (the sea). It has been difficult, and I have felt ambivalent about writing and publishing this book as Lebanon, and much of the world, is pulled apart. Many people have helped me navigate this particular, painful, contradictory space with care and love. This book is for anyone and everyone, in Lebanon and elsewhere, fighting to make better, more capacious, and more just worlds. You inspire me. You give me strength.

Thank you.

Notes

Preface

1. The term "Middle East and North Africa" has an imperial genealogy that centers Europe as the geographic location from which other locations are measured. Middle, or East, of whom? However, in the context of my usage, MENA is a more apt descriptor than some of the terms often used instead, including SWANA—Southwest Asia and North Africa—and "Arab world"—a term that discursively erases the multiplicity of people, nationalities, and identities in Arab majority states and territories.

2. Saudi Arabia is enabled by its allies in the war against Iran, the United States, the UAE, and Israel. Iran's allies include Syria, Hizballah, Yemen and, in a different capacity, Russia.

3. In fact, two protest movements were launched in 2019—an uprising against the economic and political, and social disenfranchisement of Palestinian refugees in Lebanon, and an uprising against the political order as a whole, months later.

4. Applications like WhatsApp are critical because they serve as a buffer against the corrupt, ineffectual, and hyperexpensive telecom industry. In 2019 there was a sense that the Lebanese government had chosen to push the costs of their own corruption onto ordinary people.

5. Mikdashi, "Lebanon"; Arsan, *Lebanon*.

6. For a historical overview of the relationship between the banking sector, the Central Bank, and the state, see Safieddine, *Banking on the State*.

7. Ghassan Hage has written about "crisis" and "stuckedness" as everyday temporalities. He writes, "Crisis today is no longer felt as an unusual state of affairs which invites the citizen to question the given order. Rather, it is perceived more as a normalcy, or to use what is becoming perhaps an over-used concept, crisis is a kind of permanent state of exception." I am taken by Hage's theorization of the temporality of being stuck, but with a caveat: The phrase "is no longer" assumes an earlier time not defined by the recursively of crises. I am less sure of a "before" as it constructs a temporality of stability that was only possible by producing and ensuring the recursively of crisis for racialized, colonized, and indigenous subjects. For example, from the standpoint of a Palestinian in Lebanon, the only "before" crisis in Lebanon was the crisis of ethnic cleaning and settler colonialism in Palestine—itself a temporality that culminated, but neither began nor ended, with the Nakba of 1948. Hage, *Alter-politics*, 8.

8. Braidotti, *Nomadic Subjects*; Alexander and Mohanty, "Cartographies."

9. I resist collapsing analytic categories with governmental categories. That is, if the aim of power is to make visible, regulate, and surveil categories of difference, that power is amplified when we uncritically reproduce the effects of power, such as sect, sexuality, and sex, as untroubled and untroubling analytic categories.

Introduction: Sextarianism

1. The civil personal status courts adjudicate the 1958 inheritance law for non-Muslims in Lebanon. Judges from the judiciary populate this court system, which also adjudicates civil marriages conducted outside of Lebanon and administrative issues related to the census regime. For an overview and analysis of the civil personal status system, see Bakkar, *'abed al Mun 'im. qadāyā al al- ahwāl al-shakhsīyya wa al jinsīyya fī lubnan.*

2. The years 2005–2008 witnessed major historical events in Lebanon: the assassination of former prime minister Rafik al Hariri, the formation of March 14 and 18 political parties, another Israeli invasion and war in 2006, a two-year campaign of political assassinations, a year without an official government in place, and a military campaign against an armed Islamist group taking refuge in the Palestine refugee camp Nahr el Bared.

3. Stoler, *Duress*; Hull, *Government of Paper*; Merry, "From Law and Colonialism."

4. "Sextarianism" has also been written about in the context of Northern Ireland, where Maginn and Elisson have unpacked the relationships between power sharing, heteronormative patriarchy, sexual minorities, rights, and sex work. See Maginn and Ellison. "'Ulster Says No.'" Comparative work between "sextarianism" in Northern Ireland and Lebanon is needed to elucidate its contours in practice. It is noteworthy that two very distinct contexts inspired the term "sextarianism."

5. Harris, "Whiteness as Property."

6. J. W. Scott, "Sexularism"; Mahmood, *Religious Difference*. Scott's formulation of "sexularism" inspired the term "sextarianism."

7. Cady and Fessenden, *Religion*. For a generative and critical conversation on the concept of sexual difference, see Cheah et al., "Future of Sexual Difference." For an overview of how sexual difference has evolved in feminist theory, see Stone, "Sexual Difference"; Hird, "Feminist Matters." My own use of the term explicitly ties it to biopolitical power and the generation and stabilization of sexual difference as a category of power, meaning, desire, and securitization.

8. Pateman, *Sexual Contract*.

9. Pateman, *Sexual Contract*, 41.

10. French law, particularly the civil code and its attendant concept of public order, shapes many postcolonial legal systems. For a genealogy of French law grounded in Algeria, see Surkis, *Sex, Law, and Sovereignty*.

11. Alexander, *Pedagogies of Crossing*, chap. 5.

12. In 2012 the Plenary Assembly at the Court of Cassation heard a case also concerning the stakes of sexual difference and international law; a person who is "illegitimate" had sued to inherit equally to his "legitimate" siblings (his father had been married to a different woman at the time of his birth). He used the UN Convention on the Rights of the Child, which Lebanon has signed, as the legal basis for his case. He lost in both the civil personal status courts and at the Assembly. See sāder fī tamyīz, qarārāt al hay'at al 'āmma, 2011, 2012, 2013.

13. James Scott writes that "the categories used by state agents are not merely means to make their environment legible; they are an authoritative tune to which most of the population must dance." J. C. Scott, *Seeing*, 153.

14. While the state has not officially released census data since 1932, they do collect and store sectarian demographic data. In fact, almost every election cycle voter's lists by sect are leaked and illegally available for purchase.

15. Cornell, "Rethinking Legal Ideals," 158, 163. "There are, at least at first glance, two kinds of violence at issue here: the violence of the foundation or the establishment of a legal system and then the law-conserving or jurispathic violence of an actual legal system. . . . The madness of law is law's disappearance of the violence of its conserving power through an appeal to the reality that it has shaped."

16. Makdisi, *Age of Coexistence*.

17. Chanock, *Law, Custom, and Social Order*; Dirks, *Castes of Mind*; Mamdani, *Citizen and Subject*.

18. Lebanon's tradition of legal pluralism is built on the multiplicity of personal status law. As a form, legal pluralism requires an overarching, surrounding, sovereign state. See Merry, "Legal Pluralism"; Moore, "Law and Social Change"; Griffiths, "What Is Legal Pluralism?"; Ghamroun, "Effets d'État," 84–89. Some theories of legal pluralism have rejected the centrality of state law and instead investigate the relationship between different forms of ordering. Theories of "new legal pluralism" suggest that no overarching rule manages the different legal orders but that social groups develop their own legal systems, thus moving away from the centrality of state law. Griffiths also calibrates the relationship between law and the state; he qualifies the situation where there is "some form of law" that differs from state law but that is recognized and validated under state law as "weak" legal pluralism. Reflecting this debate debate, Ghamroun describes the Lebanese legal system as falling into a scientific "no-man's land" since it does not qualify under the "new" theories of legal pluralism nor does it prescribe strictly to a state of legal monism since the state has deliberately delegated its primary regulating function and its authority in the domain of the family, thus offering a particular form of "institutionalized" pluralism.

19. Brown, *States of Injury*; Cornell, *Heart of Freedom*; Das, "Violence, Gender, and Subjectivity"; Pateman, *Disorder of Women*.

20. Halley and Rittich, "Critical Directions"; Seikaly, *Men of Capital*.

21. Pateman, *Sexual Contract*.

22. For the historiography of nationalism in Lebanon and its role in producing a coherent national narrative, see Hakim, *Origins*.

23. Gellner, *Nations and Nationalism*; Koselleck, *Futures Past*; H. White, *Content of the Form*.

24. Azoulay, "Potential History."

25. Abu-Lughod, *Dramas of Nationhood*; Brubaker, *Nationalism Reframed*; Tsing, *Friction*.

26. Joseph, "Public/Private"; Thompson, "Public and Private."

27. Pateman *Sexual Contract*; Cornell, *Beyond Accommodation*.

28. Das, *Life and Words*.

29. Brown, "Finding the Man."

30. Schuller, *Biopolitics of feeling*; Spillers, "Mama's baby"; Wynter, "Unsettling"; McClintock, *Imperial Leather*; Mohanty, *Feminism without Borders*; Pateman, Wade Mills, and Wright Mills, *Contract and Domination*.

31. For the need to move beyond these binaries in our feminist analysis, see Ali, "Feminisms in Iraq."

32. Agamben, *Homo Sacer*; Schmitt, *Political Theology*; Benjamin, "Critique of Violence"; Aretxaga, "Maddening States"; Derrida, "Force of Law."

33. Mbembe, *Necropolitics*; Puar, *Right to Maim*.

34. Povinelli, *Geontologies*.

35. Butler, *Bodies that Matter*.

36. Weheliye, *Habeas Viscus*; Wynter, "Unsettling"; Snorton, *Black on Both Sides*.

37. Braidotti, "Sexual Difference."

38. I. Feldman, *Governing Gaza*.

39. See Zacka, *State Meets the Street*; Kauanui, *Hawaiian Blood*; Barker, *Sovereignty Matters*; Zengin, "Violent Intimacies."

40. Hardt and Negri. *Empire*; Gramsci, *Gramsci Reader*; Gramsci, "State and Civil Society."

41. Simpson, *Mohawk Interruptus*.

42. Povinelli, *Cunning of Recognition*.

43. Deringil, *Conversion and Apostasy*; Makdisi, *Culture of Sectarianism*; Makdisi, *Age of Coexistence*; Mahmood, *Religious Difference*.

44. The use of the term "nested," as opposed to "recognized," is important, and in the context of the history of Lebanon, it may be cunning. The French Mandate had to withdraw its sovereign claim to recognize religious difference due to organized resistance by Sunni Muslim authorities who insisted that no state structure had the power to "recognize" the power of God. But that is precisely what the independent Lebanese state has effectively done, albeit by claiming to have nested, rather than having recognized, a preceding sovereignty within its own. While in theory Muslims were excluded from decree 60 LR in 1939, the law regulating the Sunni and Ja'fari courts was later enacted by the Lebanese Parliament (law of July 16, 1962), following the legislative decree 18 issued on January

13, 1955, regulating the affairs of the Sunni community (amended by the May 28, 1956, law). Also, article 33 of the 1951 law defining the legal jurisdiction of Christian and Jewish groups confirmed this obligation to submit their personal status laws within one year to be approved by the Parliament. Despite having submitted the laws for review, the Parliament never reviewed nor approved the personal status laws of Christian communities. However, the Court of Cassation adopted a "pragmatic" solution, by which it recognized the validity of the said laws and their applicability despite the absence of Parliament's approval. See Gannagé, *Le pluralisme des statuts personnels dans les États multicommunautaires*, 55–63. For a genealogy of the relationship between Islamic law specifically and the Lebanese state, see M. Clarke, *Islam and Law*.

45. On the colonial and postcolonial history of the personal status system, see I. Traboulsi, *al ʾanzima al ahwāl al shakhsīyya fī lubnān*; Rahhāl, *al qawaʾid al ʾāmma lil al- ahwāl al-shakhsīyya. al jiziʾ al thani, ahkām al zawāj al dīnī wa al madanī*.

46. Adrienne Rich theorized heterosexuality as a compulsory framework across different registers historically. See Rich, "Compulsory Heterosexuality."

47. For how recognition is an act of sovereignty that stabilizes, materializes, and amplifies state power, see Markell, *Bound by Recognition*; Povinelli, *Cunning of Recognition*.

48. See Salime, *Between Feminism and Islam*, for more on these suffusions in the context of Morocco. For secularism as state practice with an emphasis on women's rights in Egypt, see Al-Ali, *Secularism*.

49. They also enjoy an equal right to structure religious education.

50. Alexander, *Pedagogies of Crossing*, chap. 5; Canaday, *Straight State*; Puri, *Sexual States*.

51. On heteronormativity and heterosexuality as cultural, institutional, and disciplinary practices, see Sehlikoglu and Karioris, *Everyday Makings of Heteronormativity*. For work that rethinks and theorizes gender and the categories of "man" and "woman" in the Middle East, see Shakhsari, "Killing Me Softly"; Shakhsari, "Queer Time of Death"; Najmabadi, *Professing Selves*; Zengin, "Afterlife of Gender." For an overview of the historiography of sexuality, see Peirce, "Writing Histories of Sexuality." For work that also seeks to allude the conservative ways "gender" has been used in Middle East Studies, see Pursley, *Familiar Futures*.

52. When I use the terms "heterosexuality" and "homosexuality," I am referring to them as regulatory categories, not to sexualities as lived categories (queer, straight).

53. Foucault, *Security, Territory, Population*; Foucault, *Birth of Biopolitics*; Foucault, "Subject and Power."

54. Mikdashi, "Sextarianism." For a history of postwar state institutions and sectarianism in Lebanon, see Salloukh and Barakat, *Politics of Sectarianism*.

55. Irigaray, *Luce Irigaray*. Spivak, "Can the Subaltern Speak?"

56. Derrida, "Force of Law"; Benjamin, "Critique of Violence."

57. For example, they could have cross-referenced answers about marital status with church marriage records had they wanted to.

58. In Arabic, *al hay'at al 'āmma la mahkamit al tamyīz*. For an overview of the legal system, see Mallat, "Lebanese Legal System"; Mansour, Daoud, and EMHRN, "Independence and Impartiality."

59. See Mallat "Lebanese Legal System."

60. For a history of the Assembly and interpretation of the different conditions see I. Traboulsi, *al 'anzima al ahwāl al shakhsīyya fī lubnān*. The decisions of the assembly can be found in a collection regularly published by the premiere legal publishing house in Lebanon, Sader Publishers. See sāder fī tamyīz, qarārāt al hay'at al 'āmma, 1983–1992; 1993; 1994, 1995; 1996, 1997, 1998; 1999, 2000, 2001; 2002, 2003, 2004; 2005, 2006, 2007; 2008, 2009, 2011; 2011, 2012, 2013.

61. In 2021 the Plenary Assembly heard cases against the special investigator in the Beirut port explosion investigation and was asked to decide the jurisdiction in cases in which ministers and parliamentarians are accused of crimes.

62. Article 95 of the Lebanese Code of Civil Procedures outlines the five conditions under which cases can be advanced to the Assembly's chambers.

The Plenary Assembly, which convenes according to the procedures set by the law that organizes the judiciary, has jurisdiction under the following circumstances:

1) In a case against the state regarding its liability for the [illegal] acts of Judges who are part of the Lebanese judiciary.

2) In any case whose resolution requires and rests on vital legal principles or in any case whose resolution has the potential to contradict [jurisprudential] precedents. Under these circumstances, the case is referred to the Court of Cassation by the original court dealing with the case.

3) In requests to decide court jurisdiction when there is a positive or negative conflict of jurisdiction:
   a. Between two *'adliyya* courts [courts where state-appointed judges preside];
   b. Between an *'adliyya* court and a Muslim personal status court and/or a Christian Personal Status Court;
   c. Between a Muslim Personal Status Court and a Christian Personal Status Court;
   d. Between two different Muslim or Christian Personal Status Courts.

4) In an objection to a final decision issued by a Muslim or a Christian personal status court because of the lack of that court's proper jurisdiction [over the case] or because of an infringement of the substantive forms [of legal proceedings] that can impact public order.

5) In the appeal in cassation of judicial decisions submitted in the interest of the law by the Public Prosecutor to the Court of Cassation.

Furthermore, article 30 of the Judicial Organization Law of 1983 stipulates that the Assembly can issue decisions only in the presence of the 1st President of the Cassation Court and at least four other presidents of the different chambers that make up the Courts of Cassation. When there is a split decision, the 1st President of the Cassation Court casts the deciding vote.

63. In 1981, as the plaintiffs complained that the Greek Orthodox patriarchate of Antioch in Damascus should be considered a "foreign" entity, Syria was playing an active role in the Lebanese Civil War.

64. This approach could also be understood as the Assembly's strategy to avoid confrontation with religious groups by limiting its own jurisdiction to the "bureaucratic" compliance of religious courts/jurisdictions. In other words, one could argue that the Assembly uses the bureaucratic and procedural arguments to adopt a restrictive interpretation of "substantive rules relating to the public order" and to not intervene in substantive issues, such as gender inequality, in personal status laws and courts.

65. For these reasons, arguments around political, religious, and secular difference must be historically specific and ethnographically grounded. The secularism of the Lebanese state has more in common than the secularism of the Israeli state than either do with, for example, secularism in Turkey. In both Lebanon and Israel is a regulatory category that confers different sets of rights. Neither state has a national civil marriage law, but both adjudicate civil marriages conducted abroad according to those foreign marriage laws.

66. In Édouard Glissant's words, "How can one point out these limits without lapsing into skepticism or paralysis? How can one reconcile the hard line inherent in any politics and the questioning essential to any relation? Only by understanding that it is impossible to reduce anyone, no matter who, to a truth he would not have generated on his own. That is, within the opacity of his time and place. Plato's city is for Plato, Hegel's vision is for Hegel, the griot's town is for the griot. Nothing prohibits our seeing them in confluence, without confusing them in some magma or reducing them to each other. This same opacity is also the force that drives every community: the thing that would bring us together forever and make us permanently distinctive. Widespread consent to specific opacities is the most straightforward equivalent of nonbarbarism. We clamor for the right to opacity for everyone." Glissant, *Poetics of Relation*.

67. See Agrama, *Questioning Secularism*; Deeb, "Thinking Piety"; Jakobsen, and Pellegrini, *Secularisms*; Mahmood, *Politics of Piety*; J. W. Scott, "Sexularism"; J. W. Scott, *Sex and Secularism*.

68. For how the ever-present possibility of violence shapes everyday life, including the experience of research, see Hermez, *War Is Coming*; Moghnieh, "'Violence We Live In.'"

69. Rubin, "Traffic in Women"; Stevens, *Reproducing the State*.

70. Hartman, *Wayward Lives*.

71. Lowe, "History Hesitant"; Arondekar, "Absence of Reliable Ghosts."

72. The work of Nadia Abu El Haj spans both ethnographic and archival research and has been instructive on the relationship between epistemology, methodology, and ideology. See El-Haj, *Facts on the Ground*; El-Haj, *Genealogical Science*.

73. Sandoval, *Methodology of the Oppressed*. On page 29 Sandoval writes, and here I see Samera, "taking and using whatever is necessary and available in order to negotiate, confront, or speak to power then moving on to new forms, expressions, and ethos when necessary—a method for survival."

74. This process had begun at the civil personal status court.

75. I join the effort of many scholars rethinking state power in the context of Lebanon and in the Middle East, including the groundbreaking work of Lisa Wedeen, Tim Mitchell, Paul Amar, Afsaneh Najmabadi, and Yael-Navarro Yashin. In the context of Lebanon, many colleagues have also revisited the question of the state and critiqued analytic and popular perceptions of the absent state. For more, see the *Arab Studies Journal* special issue on the state in Lebanon, vol. 25, no. 1, Spring 2017.

76. Interview, Husayn, September 2010.

Chapter 1: Afterlives of a Census

1. Mainstream political economy and studies of wealth would benefit from thinking through and incorporating inheritance as adjudicated by personal status and/or religious laws and practices. One of the reasons why men hold more wealth than women is because of Islamic inheritance law. By not incorporating personal status laws, political economists continue to study wealth without inheritance (a framing that would make Marxists flinch) in Lebanon and other contexts.

2. If religious figures acknowledging that religious conversion is tied to marriage, divorce, or inheritance seem surprising to some readers, they would do well to remember the phenomenon of "forum shopping" in the United States, where people choose where to marry, incorporate their business, or register property based on sophisticated understandings of different tax and divorce laws, with an eye toward how and where state and federal laws intersect and part ways. People in the Middle East—plaintiffs, lawyers, judges, and religious officials—are no less sophisticated, no less tactical, and no more or less coherent, sincere, or agnostic in their practice of or attachment to religion.

3. My own identification by the state as "Sunni," an identification that has political, legal, and social ramifications, is based on the fact that my father is Sunni. Given the centrality of conversations about sectarianism in academic literature about Lebanon and on the Middle East, it is curious how little of it addresses how sectarian status is structurally produced.

4. See Clarke, *Islam and New Kinship*; Doumani, *Family Life*; Hatem, "Enduring Alliance"; Joseph, *Gender and Citizenship*; Salime, *Between Feminism and Islam*; Tucker, *House of the Law*.

5. This includes, as Lila Abu-Lughod reminds us, the critical component of international and human rights laws and covenants. See Abu-Lughod, "Active Social Life."

6. While civil courts are competent to rule on the registration of the child, a child's rights within the family (guardianship, custody, etc.) remain under the jurisdiction of religious courts. In contentious custody battles, the civil courts may be asked to intervene if the child is at risk. See Najm, Mehanna, and Karamé, "Lebanon."

7. Mahmood, *Religious Difference.*

8. Shehadeh, "Legal Status."

9. Abu-Lughod, *Do Muslim Women Need Saving?*

10. The arbitrary, reproductive, biopolitical nature of citizenship is important to think about when discussing nationalism or the narratives around citizenship that nationalism engenders.

11. Grafton, *Christians of Lebanon*; Weiss, *Shadow of Sectarianism.*

12. There are currently approximately four and a half million citizen-residents; approximately two million Syrian, Palestinian, Iraqi, Sudanese, and Kurdish refugees; and more than 200,000 migrant laborers residing in Lebanon.

13. Brown, *States of Injury.*

14. See F. Traboulsi, *History of Modern Lebanon*; Salibi, *House of Many Mansions*; Makdisi, *Culture of Sectarianism*; Hanf, *Coexistence in Wartime Lebanon*; El Khazen, *Breakdown of the State*; Picard, *Lebanon.*

15. See Hanf, *Coexistence in Wartime Lebanon*; El Khazen, *Breakdown of the State*; Picard, *Lebanon.*

16. See Khalaf, *Civil and Uncivil Violence*; Hermez, "War Is Going to Ignite'; Hanf, *Coexistence in Wartime Lebanon.*

17. See Khalidi, *Under Siege*; Sayigh, Rosemary. *Too Many Enemies*; Sayigh and Peteet. "Between Two Fires"; Peteet, *Landscape.*

18. See Deeb, *Enchanted Modern*, 201; Joseph, "Public/Private"; Thompson, *Colonial Citizens.* Joanne Nucho has also enriched the analysis of sectarianism by focusing on infrastructure and boundary making. See Nucho, *Everyday Sectarianism.*

19. Najmabadi, *Professing Selves.*

20. Mitchell, "Society."

21. For a sense of the durée of intergenerational feminist activism in Lebanon, see Pratt, *Embodying Geopolitics.*

22. Hacking, *Taming of Chance*; Hacking, *Rewriting the Soul*; Stoler, *Race*; J. C. Scott, *Seeing*; El-Haj, *Genealogical Science.*

23. James Scott writes that "categories that may have begun as the artificial inventions of cadastral surveyors, census takers, judges, or police officers can end by becoming categories that organize people's daily experience precisely because they are embedded in state-created institutions that structure that experience." J. C. Scott, *Seeing*, 148.

24. Maktabi, "Lebanese Census of 1932."

25. Maktabi, "Lebanese Census of 1932."

26. N. Mouawad, "Bigger Struggle."

27. Mukhtars are nodal points in this system.

28. Mikdashi, "Sex and Sectarianism."

29. J. Mouawad, *Unpacking Lebanon's Resilience.*

30. For a generative feminist analysis of elections see Talhouk, "Parliamentary Elections."

31. Mikdashi, "Religious Conversion."

32. Joseph, "Descent of the Nation"; Joseph, *Gender and Citizenship.*

33. Mikdashi, "Sex and Sectarianism."

34. In practice, General Security conducts thorough, invasive, and often long investigations to ensure that the father is unknown to the mother. Many Lebanese mothers have tried to and successfully used this loophole to grant the Lebanese nationality to their children, claiming that their children are illegitimate and that they do not know who the father is.

35. Mansour and Abou Aad (2012).

36. Alexander, "Not Just (Any) Body."

37. Chatterjee, "Anderson's Utopia."

38. Grewal, *Saving the Security State.*

39. Brubaker, *Nationalism Reframed*; Brubaker, "Myths and Misconceptions"; Wedeen, *Ambiguities of Domination*; Wedeen, *Peripheral Visions.*

40. Foucault, *Birth of Biopolitics*; Foucault, *History of Sexuality.*

41. Amar, *Security Archipelago*; Chen, *Animacies*; Puar, *Terrorist Assemblages*; Shakhsari, *Politics of Rightful Killing.*

42. Joseph, *Gender and Citizenship.*

43. There are, however, notable exceptions to this rule. For example, Saudi prince Al-Walīd bin Talāl has Lebanese citizenship through his mother, Mona el-Solḥ, who is the daughter of one of Lebanon's founders and its first prime minister, Riad el-Solḥ. Riad el-Solḥ had the "misfortune" of having only daughters, but they were nevertheless granted citizenship. Yet even in this example, the exception granted to Riad el-Solḥ's daughters stems from his role as "patriarch" of the Lebanese nation.

44. Michel Aoun was eventually elected president by the Parliament in 2016, whose electoral mandate had expired two years earlier. The postponement of both parliamentary and presidential elections contravened the constitution.

45. Law No. 15, promulgated on November 19, 1925, as amended in 1960. The stipulation on "stateless people" is one reason the Lebanese state holds fast to the "Right of Return" for Palestinian refugees.

46. Mansour and Abou Aad (2012).

47. In 2009 a Lebanese court granted a Lebanese woman's children citizenship. Central to her case was the economic hardship she faced in Lebanon raising

children who were considered foreigners. The decision was overturned on appeal, and the head judge who had taken the decision—John Azzi—was reassigned to a lower court. Azzi went on to write a book where he recounted his legal journey and nationality laws. *A Trip of a Lifetime to Nationality* was released in 2012. He had previously written an influential book on his experience as a judge in the civil personal status courts, where he adjudicated the marriage laws of other countries.

48. Artist visas are issued to women who work in nightclubs and cabarets. These women are often trafficked and coerced into sex work.

49. Salloukh et al. (2016).

50. Nationality law allows for granting citizenship for those born on Lebanese soil and at risk of statelessness. There is a large and contentious legal debate over whether Palestinians born in Lebanon fit this criterion for Lebanese citizenship. Similarly, there is a contentious debate over whether Syrian refugees who are unregistered in Syria and born in Lebanon could also eventually be considered stateless and thus eligible for naturalization. The constitution, however, includes a provision that there will be no settlement of "non-Lebanese" people in Lebanon.

51. Many wealthy Muslim Palestinian refugees were also naturalized.

52. Kechichian, "Lebanon Contemplates."

53. Pateman, *Sexual Contract*; Bell and Binnie, *Sexual Citizen*.

54. Gebran Bassil got his own chant during the uprising, one that targeted his mother's bodily integrity as a way to besmirch her son.

55. Pateman, *Sexual Contract*.

56. Joseph, "Public/Private."

57. Abu-Lughod, "Seductions." Article 562 of the criminal code, which mitigated the sentences of people who claim they killed or injured their wife, daughter, or other relative to protect family "honor," was repealed in 2011. However, in the 2016 Manal Assi murder trial the criminal court invoked Article 252 of the penal code to grant mitigating circumstances to the husband, Mohammad al Nhaily, who was found guilty of murdering his wife. He was sentenced to five years in prison, enraging women's rights activists. Article 252 states "a perpetrator benefits from extenuating circumstances if the crime was committed due to severe anger resulting from an unjust act and a degree of seriousness brought on by the victim." The criminal court decision was later revoked by the Court of Cassation, which denied the mitigating excuse and sentenced Mohammad al Nhaily to death. As there has been a moratorium on capital punishment in Lebanon since 2004, he was in effect sentenced to life in prison for murdering his wife. For more, see Saghieh, "Principled Decision."

58. Eng, *Feeling of Kinship*; Kholoussy, *For Better, for Worse*.

59. The public prosecutor in Sunni, Jaʿfari, and Druze courts is a civil judge from the same sect of the court, mandated to perform the duties of public prosecution at the respective appeals courts. Another civil judge is mandated to act as the inspector in each of the said courts. These positions are not full time and are appointed by the Sharia Judicial Council. They are independent of the civil

judiciary's public prosecutor's office and do not report to the general prosecutor. Instead they are civil judges who often hold simultaneous positions at the judicial or administrative courts. Both the inspector and the public prosecutor at the sharia courts are de facto members of the Sharia Judicial Council. Their role is restricted by law and in practice. The public prosecutor in sharia courts can directly file a lawsuit in the cases stipulated by law or related to public order, including matters related to minors. They have the right to appeal the rulings issued in these cases. With the exception of cases related to public order, the role of the public prosecution is limited to expressing an opinion before the Supreme Sharia Court in cases of marriage, lineage, separation, endowment, and so on. However, according to unpublished research by Lama Karame, public prosecutors in sharia courts rarely play this role, and their presence is often considered a formal requirement. The presence of the public prosecutor is mandatory and not contingent on the request of parties. However, interested parties can address letters and requests to the prosecutor.

60. Salloukh et al. (2016).

61. See Human Rights Watch, *Women's Rights*.

62. According to a jurisprudence of the Plenary Assembly of the Court of Cassation, civil courts hold jurisdiction in the divorce of a Druze couple married under civil marriage abroad. The reasoning relied on the fact that Druze marriages, unlike other Muslim sects, are not contract-based, civil marriages. Plenary Assembly decision no. 13, date 9/5/1996.

63. The last time such a law was debated in the Lebanese government the controversies surrounding it were deeply gendered: The main complaints of religious authorities were that it would interrupt religious custody rules (which are deeply discriminatory against women), would allow Muslim women to marry non-Muslim men (a right men enjoy under Sunni and Shi'i personal status law and jurisprudence), would not allow polygamy for Muslim men, and would violate Islamic inheritance laws that are currently determined according to sexual difference.

64. In the presence of a son, the inheritance practices between the two Muslim sects are the same in that a son inherits double the amount of a daughter.

65. There have been many such cases appealed to the Plenary Assembly.

66. Mahmood, *Religious Difference*.

67. Mikdashi, "Sex and Sectarianism"; Joseph, "Public/Private"; Mahmood, *Religious Difference*.

68. Brown, *Regulating Aversion*; Pateman, *Sexual Contract*.

69. Saghieh, "Lebanon's Law."

70. For more on Kafala as a system of laws and practices, see the work of the Anti-Racism Movement (ARM) and Hamill, *Trafficking*. For more on the lives of migrant domestic laborers in Lebanon, see Kassamali, "Migrant Worker Lifeworlds"; Kobaissy, "Organizing the Unorganized"; Pande, "'Paper.'"

71. Another form of migrant labor is sex work and "artists visas," mainly women from eastern Europe.

72. Abu-Lughod, "Seductions."

73. Mounzer, "Going Beyond the Veil."

74. Human Rights Watch, *Women's Rights*.

75. Violence is a crime, sometimes. Technically speaking, the 2014 family violence law does not make an explicit exception for marital rape; however, it does not include an amendment to article 503 of the criminal code, which criminalizes forced intercourse with a person other than the spouse (rape).

76. See chapter 5 on exams to "prove" virginity.

77. Al-Ali, "Reflections"; Das, "Violence, Gender, and Subjectivity."

78. Amar, *Security Archipelago*; Joseph, "Public/Private."

79. In 2014 the Ministry of Justice issued circular 1778 at the request of the General Security. Under this circular, sponsors were obliged to inform the general security of any future act of marriage by a domestic worker, upon which they would be deported. Employers were asked to sign a pledge that the worker did not have any marital or intimate relationship with any other migrant in Lebanon. The circular was later abolished under pressure from an advocacy campaign that framed it as a "love ban."

80. For how law and extra-legal practices construct the categories they surveil, see Volpp, "Citizen and the Terrorist."

81. Human Rights Watch, *Stop Tests of Shame*.

82. Pateman, *Sexual Contract*.

83. Eng, *Feeling of Kinship*; Briggs et al., *Haunted by Empire*; Zengin, "Violent Intimacies."

84. Butler, *Bodies that Matter*.

85. Mahmood, *Religious Difference*; Mikdashi, "Sex and Sectarianism."

Chapter 2: A Fire in the Archive

1. Youssef's decisions were one component of a broad legal framework that grew around Solidere. Law 117/1991 abolished the concept of zoning and thus allowed Solidere to change the urban landscape in the area; and Decree no. 2236, dated February 19, 1992, established Solidere and granted the company ownership rights to all real estate properties in downtown Beirut.

2. The role of judges in how Solidere unfolded, including accusations of corruption, was covered in local press and was subject to a lawsuit. See "Angry Property Owners." Reinoud Leenders has also written about this period in *Spoils of Truce*, 62–64.

3. Sawalha, *Reconstructing Beirut*.

4. "January Start."

5. I don't usually drink alcohol, but several times during my research I felt compelled to drink with my interlocuters in social and professional settings.

Sometimes interlocutors were made uncomfortable by my lack of drinking, and I would have to explain that my not drinking alcohol had nothing to do with the fact that I was Muslim.

6. Without exception, judges, lawyers, and archivists were welcoming, happy to be asked about their work and lives, their jurisprudence and legal opinions and stances, this case or that, and what they thought were the challenges facing the life of law in Lebanon. They were happy to be taken seriously rather than assumed to be corrupt, inefficient, and worst of all, ineffectual.

7. In fact it is a multiclass, multisectarian, and multinational area that neighbors and in some ways mirrors Sabra. It has a top-rated public high school and a university that brings in students from all over the country. It is, however, majority Lebanese, majority Sunni, and majority middle and working class, increasingly so over the years. In 2008 a fight between pro- and anti-government students at Beirut Arab University, in this case designations that mapped onto Sunni and Shi'i political schisms, led to armed clashes in tarīq al jadida that killed at least four people.

8. Cvetkovich, *Archive of Feelings*.

9. The archivists at the Court of Cassation are clerks for their respective courts: ferrying papers; requesting documents; acting as liaisons between judges, lawyers, and the bureaucracy of the courts. In addition, they are in charge of the court archive and access to it. My use of the word "archivist" recognizes that their work, even as clerks, revolves around the maintenance, curation, indexing, and organization of documents, both as they circulate in the temporality of an active court case and in their capacity as archival files. The Arabic word *qalam* traverses the boundaries between what might be called "clerk," "scribe," and "archivist" in English.

10. I am grateful to conversations with Anjali Arondekar for helping sharpen this point.

11. Latour, *Making of Law*. See also Mbembe, "Power of the Archive."

12. In *A Thousand Plateaus*, Deleuze and Guattari conceptualize "lines of flight" as movements or propulsions of thought that may illuminate (if only for a second) or foreclose alternative paths, histories, and futures. Crucially, lines of flight are realized and unrealized when they enmesh with the creative forces of others. They represent the possibility (and only the possibility) of thinking and doing otherwise, even when it may be impossible to do so. See Deleuze and Guattari, *Thousand Plateaus*.

13. Wittgenstein, *Blue and Brown Books*.

14. Trouillot, *Silencing the Past*.

15. Another way to evade sextarian inheritance laws is to "sell" property to your heirs during your lifetime for a symbolic fee and to give your heir access to your bank accounts while you are alive. When I offered this during interviews as an alternative to conversion for Sunni couples, without exception all expressed the prohibitively expensive fees associated with buying and registering property

(as opposed to inheriting) and were wary of losing control over their bank accounts and homes during their lifetimes.

16. Instead of looking for holes, gaps, or ruptures in the archive of Lebanon's highest court, I trace bureaucratic and legal logics, practices, and continuities. I attend to the amplifications, repetitions, and narrations of state power during both war and "peace." I heed Ann Stoler's warning that "the search for 'dramatic reversal,' 'usurpation' and successful 'appropriation' can hide 'events' that are more muted in their consequences, less bellicose in their seizures, less spectacular in how and what they reframe." Stoler, *Along the Archival Grain*, 51.

17. International Center for Transitional Justice, *Failing*.

18. For more on law and its multiple relationships to violence and history, see Mawani, "Law's Archive."

19. Derrida, *Archive Fever*; Steedman, *Dust*; Gordon, *Ghostly Matters*; Hartman, *Lose Your Mother*; Foucault, *History of Sexuality*; Arondekar, *For the Record*.

20. For the inseparability of archival spaces and archival documents, see Mbembe, "Power of the Archive."

21. Haugbolle, *War and Memory*.

22. El Shakry, "'History without Documents.'"

23. Seikaly, "How I Met," 7.

24. See Fuentes, *Dispossessed Lives*; Arondekar; "In the Absence"; Trouillot, *Silencing the Past*; Hartman, *Wayward Lives*; Hartman, "Venus in Two Acts."

25. Stoler, "Colonial Archives."

26. Arondekar, "In the Absence."

27. Cuauhtemoc Vidal-Guzman pointed out to me that most people—including museum workers—did not and could not know everything that was destroyed at the National Museum in 2018. Yet there was a sense of profound loss and a compulsion to mourn what was probably never going to reach the public (nor perhaps even research) domain. I am grateful to him as he alerted me to a disciplinary factor at play within the anthropology of archives: the difference between archeologists and cultural anthropologists in their relationship to archives, publishing, cataloguing, and storing objects.

28. Abu-Lughod, "Romance of Resistance."

29. Weld, *Paper Cadavers*.

30. For the relationship between neoliberalism and public sectors, see Elyachar, "Before (and After) Neoliberalism."

31. By 1985 the country was immersed in a civil war that had pitted Christian militias allied to Israel and the United States against the PLO and their Arab and Lebanese allies, secular and religious Arab parties allied to different Arab regimes against each other, and Christian militias vying for dominance and wartime economic profit against each other. All of these parties were involved with each other in an always-evolving pattern of alliances and counteralliances.

32. United Press International, "Rocket Strikes."

33. United Press International, "Rocket Strikes."

34. Sayigh, *Too Many Enemies*.

35. The UPI characterized it this way: "The Palace of Justice, on the Christian eastern side of the city, was hit twice during militia combat last week. Monday's incident was believed to be the work of Muslim militiamen firing Soviet-made Grad rockets." United Press International, "Rocket Strikes."

36. The terror of war is the knowledge that not only can your death happen randomly but also that your survival. The life you will lead is therefore arbitrary.

37 The terms. 'amti and *khalto* (my aunt) are often used to respectfully refer to strangers who are older and thus could occupy the kinship position of paternal or maternal aunt.

38. There is another formulation of "us" today in Lebanon: everyone who was in the country when an explosion at the Beirut Port, one of the largest non-nuclear explosion in human history, occurred in 2020.

39. Arondekar, *For the Record*.

40. Ann Stoler writes that "the ethnographic space of the archive resides in the disjuncture between prescription and practice, between state mandates and the maneuvers people made in response to them, between rules and how people actually lived their lives." I find this account moving, accurate, and somewhat hopeful. In the context of civil wars and lawfare, the state also moves in response to the maneuvers that people make, including the actions of archivists themselves. Stoler, *Along the Archival Grain*, 32.

41. Shepard, "'Of Sovereignty.'"

42. Freeman, *Time Binds*.

43. Qato, "Forms of Retrieval."

44. The Taif Accord lays out a process through which the practice of sectarian quotas in the public sector is to be ended. More than thirty years after its signing and incorporation into the Constitution, the Taif Accord remains unrealized.

45. See Mauss, *Gift*; Cheal, *Gift Economy*; Rubin, "Traffic in Women."

46. Leenders, *Spoils of Truce*.

47. Ferguson, *Anti-politics Machine*.

48. Office of the Inspector General, *Audit*.

49. Mona was also concerned that my research was funded by any US government money and was adamant in her beliefs that legal reform should not arrive on the wings of imperial power. As a reminder, this encounter was only six years after the US invasion of Iraq and three years after the US-supported Israel-Lebanon war.

50. Haugbolle, *War and Memory*; Arondekar, "In the Absence"; Tsing, *Friction*.

51. For more on how digitization engenders epistemological shifts, see Agostinho, "Archival Encounters."

52. Messick, *Shari'a Scripts*.

53. The transformation from "active" to "passive" files and readers is similar to Ilana Feldman's ruminations on the distinction between archives of governance and archives of history, but with a crucial difference: The legal case files themselves will never be open to the public or housed in a national archive, though court decisions are.

54. Committee on Academic Freedom, "Digitization."

55. Members of the LF, the Phalange, and the SLA have all been implicated.

56. Al-Hout, *Sabra and Shatila*.

57. Plenary Assembly decision 7/92. See all wartime decisions here, beginning in 1983: Sāder fī tamyīz, qarārāt al hay'at al ' āmma, 1983–1992.

58. Brubaker, *Citizenship and Nationhood in France and Germany* and *Nationalism Reframed*; Isin, *Citizens without Frontiers*; Isin and Nielsen, *Acts of Citizenship*. On the performativity of citizenship and of sovereignty, see also Wedeen, *Peripheral Visions*.

59. Hirschkind, *Ethical Soundscape*, 29.

60. I am thinking here of Iraq, Yemen, Syria, and Palestine.

61. See Sayigh, *Too Many Enemies*; Seikaly, "Matter of Time."

62. As Carolyn Steedman writes, "nothing starts in the Archive, nothing, ever at all, though things certainly end up there. You find nothing in the Archive but stories caught half way through: the middle of things; discontinuities." Steedman, *Dust*, 28.

63. Derrida, "Force of Law"; Hull, *Government of Paper*.

64. Interview with ex phalangist militia member, 2013.

65. Human Rights Watch, *Why They Died*.

66. Human Rights Watch, *World Report*.

67. Arsan, *Lebanon*.

68. In *"Society Must Be Defended,"* Foucault wrote of how the specter of war is always already present in dominant understandings of peace. "This does not mean, however, mean that society, the law, or the state are like armistices that put an end to wars, or that they are the product of definitive victories. Law is not pacification, for beneath the law, war continues to rage in all the mechanism of power, eve in the most regular. War is the motor behind institutions and order. In the smallest of its cogs, peace is waging a secret war-peace itself is a coded war." Foucault, *"Society Must Be Defended,"* 50–51.

69. Mikdashi, "Magic of Mutual Coexistence."

70. Akar, *War Yet to Come*.

71. Hacking, *Rewriting the Soul*.

72. Arondekar, "In the Absence."

73. Hana Sleiman has written persuasively about the multiple archives possible within any collection of documents and material objects. In ruminating on the history of the PLO archive and the different curations of it by Israel, the PA, and researchers, she writes, "Here lies the crux of the matter: archives do not

perpetually serve the narrative of their creator. Rather they come to serve the narrative of their captor. Sleiman, "Paper Trail," 49.

74. He was not physically there at the massacre and has denied responsibility for it, although he was a member of the decision-making team of that militia. He has neither denounced nor taken responsibility for the role played by the militia he co-led in the massacre.

75. Rashid Khalidi asked me this question years ago, with the emphasis on the *how* did you not take it. The answer is I still don't, and will probably never know. A few years later my choice was rendered irrelevant when large portions of the case files were leaked online.

76. And yet, what it does it mean to make, or manufacture, a war crime at the scale of Sabra and Chatila? What does it mean to demand equivocation as a precondition to discussing the civil war? At the very least, it produces a postwar order where nobody can be held accountable because everyone is equally guilty, and it makes engaging with sectarian logic the only way to talk about the war and its crimes.

77. Hacking, *Rewriting the Soul*, 238.

78. Despite the many secondary and tertiary explanations Hizballah gave for its intervention (e.g., protecting Shi'i shrines, curbing ISIS and Jihadist activity to prevent infiltration into Lebanon, etc.), it essentially needed to preserve the regime as a point of contact, support, and transportation from Iran.

79. Azouray, "Potential History."

80. Bessner, "House of Cards."

81. See Brim, *Poor Queer Studies*.

Chapter 3: Regulating Conversion

This chapter draws on material originally published in the following article: Maya Mikdashi, "Sex and Sectarianism: The Legal Architecture of Lebanese Citizenship," *Comparative Studies of South Asia, Africa and the Middle East* 34, no. 2 (2014): 279–93. Republished by permission of Duke University Press.

1. Ahmad, *Everyday Conversions*, 8.

2. Conversion to Christianity is dependent on priests who determine whether a convert has satisfied the conditions for joining any given Christian sect. Conversion to Islam does not rely on a clerical intermediary; instead the sheikh is supposed to accept a convert's *shahada*, the sincerity of which is between the convert and God. However, the Druze sect does not accept converts. When I asked a judge who sat on the Druze Court of Appeals how a Muslim sect could not allow converts, he answered that while people could convert into a religion, they could not convert into a history—implying that Druze are as much an ethnic community as they are a religious one. This inability to *become* a Druze, coupled with Druze personal status law's nonacceptance of intersectarian marriage, has led many, including political leaders of the sect, to convert if they wish to marry someone from a different sect. It also means that couples are less likely to convert

to another sect to move the jurisdiction over their marriage because they will not be allowed to convert back in.

3. As Jacqueline Stevens has suggested, "much as legal marriage does not exist without being authorized by the state, one of the principal means that the state can use to prove its existence—to announce its sovereignty and its hold on the populace—is its authority over marriage." Stevens, *Reproducing the State*, 219.

4. Of course, people who are queer, or divorced and remarrying, and in love *do* think about the law quite a bit; they have to. Furthermore, feminist campaigns to inform women about their rights and duties in different marriage laws have invested in public education.

5. Buckser and Glazier, *Anthropology of Religious Conversion*; Van der Veer, *Conversion to Modernities*; Vokes, "Rethinking"; Viswanathan, *Outside the Fold*.

6. Attiya Ahmed writes that "the question of conversion is perhaps most acute in respect to Islam . . . Hegemonic expectations of modernity and secularism produce an incitement to questions about religious conversions, especially Islamic ones, placing the burden of explanation on their occurrence, not on why they are deemed to need an explanation, or the terms through which they are explained." Ahmed, *Everyday Conversions*.

7. Asad, "Comments on Conversion," 263.

8. Keane, *Christian Moderns*.

9. Ahmad, *Everyday Conversions*, 7.

10. Viswanathan, "Religious Conversion," 91; Asad, "Comments on Conversion," 243.

11. The personal status of minor children is automatically changed to match that of their father if and when he converts.

12. Assembly decision 29/2006. See Sāder fī tamyīz, qarārāt al hay'at al 'āmma, 2005, 2006, 2007.

13. The Plenary Assembly has made an exception to this when it comes to two Druze citizens conducting a civil marriage abroad and registering it in Lebanon.

14. Not to be confused with the public prosecutors' office in the judiciary. See footnote 63 in Chapter 1. For a detailed and comprehensive review of the relationship between the offices of the public prosecutors and sharia courts, see Tabbāra, *muṭala'āt al niyāba al 'amma al isti'nāfiyya ladā al mahkama al shar'iyyat al sinyyat al 'lyā*.

15. This is also a way for the state to assert more control over the process and impact of religious conversion.

16. See Butler, *Psychic Life of Power*; Austin, *How to Do Things*; Esmeir, *Juridical Humanity*.

17. Koselleck, *Futures Past*.

18. In 2008 the Ja'fari courts decided not to take an opinion issued by Ayatollah Mohammed Hussein Fadlallah, the leading religious figure in Lebanon, and a global *marja'*, at the time.

19. Halley and Rittich, "Critical Directions."

20. See Azzi, *zawāj al madanī*.

21. The department of execution (*da'irat al tanfītdh*) has jurisdiction over decisions to enforce foreign legal judgements in Lebanon.

22. Surkis, *Sex, Law, and Sovereignty.*

23. Human Rights Watch, *Women's Rights.*

24. For more on the struggle between lawyers, judicial authorities, and church authorities in Lebanon over the 1951 law, see Shehadeh, "Gender-Relevant Legal Change," 211.

25. The process of religious conversion in Lebanon was first articulated in French Mandate–era directives outlining the procedures governing the census and its employees in 1924. Muslim religious authorities were incensed by the matter-of-fact nature of religious conversion and continued to be upon the passage of 60LR, which repeated the procedures for conversion and insisted each religious community submit its family law to Parliament for ratification. The political response to 60LR was so strong that the French Mandate ultimately declared it inapplicable to Muslims. However, the procedures mentioned in this directive were subsequently repeated and amended in post-independence laws that regulate the census registry in 1951, and reformed the process of conversion. While the French Mandate required signatures from religious authorities of both the religion being left and the religion being joined, the independent Lebanese state did away with the stipulation that the convert interface with authorities from the religion being left. Religious conversion may occur officially (receiving a certificate from the faith being joined) or personally (converting without the recognition of religious authorities), the state considers religious conversion legal only when two conditions are satisfied: (1) the individual must obtain a certificate of conversion from the religious authorities of the religion or sect that they want to join and (2) that certificate must be registered with the census authorities in front of two witnesses. For a detailed and incisive historical and practical overview of the rules and procedures governing conversion see Rahhāl, *al qawa'id al 'āmma lil al- aḥwāl al-shakhsīyya. al jizi' al thani, ahkām al zawāj al dīnī wa al madanī*, 59–84.

26. Assembly decision 10/93.

27. Assembly decision 10/93. Also in I. Traboulsi, *al 'anzima al ahwāl al shakhsīyya fī lubnān.* The case is also discussed Mansour and Daoud, *Independence and Impartiality.* It's a famous case and is regularly cited as jurisprudence.

28. Mansour and Daoud, *Independence and Impartiality.*

29. See Kahn, "Geographies of Discretion"; Asad, *Formations of the Secular.*

30. Joseph, "Gender and citizenship."

31. Simpson, *Mohawk Interruptus.*

32. Povinelli, *Economies of Abandonment.*

33. Assembly decision 41/2008.

34. In 2012 the Assembly heard a case in which a person actually stated that he converted only to get married. Even then the Assembly refused, as they put it, to "interrogate" his conversion.

35. Joseph, "Public/Private."

36. The *ikhrāj al-qayd* (census document), the *hawiyya* (the national identification card), and the passport are interchangeable for many bureaucratic procedures. However, to receive or renew a *hawiyya* or a passport a new *ikhrāj al-qayd* must be produced and submitted with the application. The *ikhrāj al-qayd* lists a citizen's age, sex, marital/kinship status, municipality, and personal status.

37. Mamdani, *Citizen and Subject.*

38. In discussion with the author, January 2010.

39. Chatterjee, *Nation and Its Fragments*; Spivak, "Can the Subaltern Speak?"; Mamdani, *Citizen and Subject.*

40. Stoler, *Imperial Debris*; Khalili, *Time in the Shadows.*

41. For more on the relationship between assemblage and biopolitical rule, see Puar, *Terrorist Assemblages.*

42. Harm reduction is a public health strategy that recognizes that while addiction itself has no cure, the multifaceted harm that addiction itself engenders may be mitigated. I thank my sister Nadya Mikdashi for the many conversations where she has explained the practice and logic to me.

43. Chatterjee, *Nation and Its Fragments*; Thompson, *Colonial Citizens*; Weiss, *Shadow of Sectarianism*; White, *Emergence of Minorities.*

44. I. Feldman, *Governing Gaza*; B. Kafka, *Demon of Writing*; Zacka, *State Meets the Street.*

45. F. Kafka, *Trial.*

46. Arendt, *Eichmann in Jerusalem*; Weber and Andreski, *Max Weber on Capitalism.*

47. Foucault, *Security, Territory, Population*; Hacking, *Taming of Chance.*

48. Hull, *Government of Paper.*

49. I. Feldman, *Governing Gaza*, 220.

50. Foucault, *Foucault Effect.*

51. Khalili, *Time in the Shadows.*

52. Steedman, *Dust.*

53. Foucault, *Security, Territory, Population*; J. C. Scott, *Seeing*; Amar, *Security Archipelago.*

54. Povinelli, *Cunning of Recognition*; Marx, "On the Jewish Question."

55. For the centrality of "public order" and what it mediates in French-derived legal systems, see Surkis, *Sex, Law, and Sovereignty.*

56. Another interpretation is that the Assembly "hides" behind bureaucracy to justify its conservative interpretation of public order—an understanding that does not challenge the substantive rules of religious law and courts and instead settles for procedural grounds. This interpretation could also defer to political sensitivities: In 1987 Muslim leaders protested against the amendment of article 95, which introduced paragraph 4, allowing the Plenary Assembly to hear objections against the decisions from Muslim courts.

57. She used a phrase that roughly translates into "I will make him wear a skirt."

58. Interview with Zahra, 2010.

59. The Shiʿi counterpart to *Dar al Fatwa*.

60. Interview, Husayn, in discussion with the author, 2010.

61. Keane, *Christian Moderns*.

62. Interview, Husayn, in discussion with the author, 2010.

63. Taylor, *Secular Age*.

64. Wynter, "Unsettling."

65. Glissant, *Poetics of Relation*. Glissant beautifully wrote that the oppressed have a right to not be understood. This refusal of transparency is an important way of resisting colonial power or other regimes of securitization based on the ability to know, to fix, and to make transparent individual or communal difference.

66. Fernando, *Republic Unsettled*.

67. Marx, "On the Jewish Question."

68. Duggan, *Twilight of Equality?*; Fraser, "Rethinking Recognition."

69. Mahmood, *Religious Difference*.

70. Sandoval, *Methodology of the Oppressed*. Sandoval writes "this is the activity of the trickster who practices subjectivity as masquerade, the oppositional agent who accesses differing identity, ideological, aesthetic, and political positions." Ibid., 29.

71. To put it in plain language, the "universalism" of religion, of secularism, or of the nation-state is always marked and defined by regimes of difference. Only some forms of difference, however, are allowed to lay claim on the universal.

Chapter 4: Are You Going to Pride?

1. Interview with feminist organizer, 2019. The 2019 uprising was a loosely organized series of actions and included different groups planning and calling for specific actions, marches, and protests.

2. For more on the history of secular personal status laws in Lebanon, see I. Traboulsi, *al ʾanzima al ahwāl al shakhsīyya fī lubnān*, 106.

3. The relationship between Syria and Lebanon has always been symbiotic but unequal. Syria's role in Lebanon was intensified during the civil war and through the Taif Accord peace deal that ended the Lebanese Civil War. There was Saudi-American agreement on Syria's continued role in Lebanon. Syria maintained a military, security, and intelligence apparatus in Lebanon until 2005, when they withdrew after national and international furor following the assassination of Rafik Hariri.

4. Arsan, *Lebanon*; Mikdashi, "Lebanon."

5. Abu-Rish, "Garbage Politics"; Geha, "Politics"; Mikdashi, "Lebanon, August 2015."

6. Bou Khater and Majed, "2019 October Revolution"; Chalcraft, Hanieh, Mikdashi, and Shwedler, "Thinking Critically."

7. Sinno, "Reclaimed Public Spaces."

8. Haugbolle, "Social Boundaries."

9. The archive of the anthropology of secularism is rich and diverse, and much of it to date is grounded in Muslim majority states and/or on Muslims living in Western, secular states. My own intellectual trajectory on the subject was influenced by Talal Asad's assertion that thinking and writing about secularism, as a hermeneutic, as an ideology, and as a practice, should be a historically specific, research-based endeavor. See Agrama, *Questioning Secularism*; Fernando, *Republic Unsettled*; Mahmood, *Politics of Piety; Religious Difference*; Tambar, *Reckoning of Pluralism*.

10. See Jakobsen and Pelligrini, *Love the Sin*; Jakobsen and Pelligrini, *Secularisms*; Farris, *Women's Rights*.

11. Scott, *Sex and Secularism*.

12. Under pressure from Sunni opposition, Decree 53 was issued by the mandate authorities specifying that Decree 60 did not apply to Muslims. This effectively meant that Muslim sects did not have to submit their personal status laws to Parliament for ratification, that Muslims could not join the community without a sect which the decree specifies, and that Lebanese sharia courts had jurisdiction over marriage contracts conducted by two Lebanese Muslims anywhere in the world. Later the Plenary Assembly ruled that if both members of a civil marriage conducted abroad were Druze, the jurisdiction of that civil law would hold. See Rahhāl, *al qawaʿid al ʿāmma lil al- aḥwāl al-shakhsīyya. al jiziʾ al thani, ahkām al zawāj al dīnī wa al madanī*; Bakkar, *ʿabed al Munʿim. qadāyā al al- aḥwāl al-shakhsīyya wa al jinsīyya fī lubnan*.

13. At the time of my research, there was a secular university-student activist group that called itself the Nineteenth Sect.

14. Marie Rose Zalzal is a prominent feminist lawyer and professor who has published extensively on women's rights struggles, law, and the state in Lebanon. See Zalzal, "Secularism"; Zalzal, "Mixed Marriage"; Zalzal, "Protection of Women."

15. Human Rights Watch, *Women's Rights*.

16. Zalzal, "Secularism."

17. Fuentes, *Dispossessed Lives*; Stoler, *Race*; Weheliye, *Habeas Viscus*.

18. Gordon, *Ghostly Matters*.

19. See Cooper, Brittney. "Intersectionality." In The Oxford handbook of feminist theory. Crenshaw, Kimberle. "Mapping the margins: Intersectionality, identity politics, and violence against women of color." Stan. L. Rev. 43 (1990): 1241. 2016, and Nash, Jennifer C. "Re-thinking intersectionality." Feminist review 89, no. 1 (2008): 1–15.

20. Mikdashi, *Sex and Sectarianism*.

21. Schuller, *Biopolitics of Feeling*.

22. Farris, *Women's Rights*; Stoler, *Race*.

23. Abu-Lughod, *Do Muslim Women Need Saving?*; Mahmood, "Secularism, Hermeneutics, and Empire"; Puar, *Terrorist Assemblages*.

24. Hirschkind, *Ethical Soundscape*; Mahmood, *Politics of Piety*.

25. Deeb, *Enchanted Modern*.

26. Hirschkind, *Ethical Soundscape*, 112.

27. Hirschkind, *Ethical Soundscape*, 112.

28. McAlister, *Kingdom of God*; Makdisi, "Reclaiming the Land"; Makdisi, *Artillery of Heaven*; Mahmood, "Religious Freedom"; Sharkey, *American Evangelicals*.

29. I. Traboulsi, *al 'anzima al ahwāl al shakhsīyya fī lubnān*, 105–6.

30. Abillama, "Contesting Secularism."

31. Human Rights Watch, *Women's Rights*. See also Talal Husseini's comments on the bill, published by the *Legal Agenda* in 2014. Husseini, "Clarification."

32. If both members of a married couple are Druze or have removed their sect, civil courts can also have jurisdiction. See Assembly decisions 13/1996 and 44/2008. See Sāder fī tamyīz, qarārāt al hay'at al ' āmma, 2008, 2009, 2011.

33. Interview, T. H., in discussion with the author, 2009.

34. Allouche, "Queering"; Deeb, "Beyond Sectarianism."

35. Allouche, "Love, Lebanese Style."

36. Asad, "Thinking about Secularism." In the context of Lebanon, I am including Israeli and Syrian state violence in Lebanon as "secular state violence."

37. In May 2008 the Hizballah-led 8 Alliance took over large areas of Beirut and the Lebanese mountains in response to the government's sacking of the Hizballah-allied chief of airport security.

38. While Cain and Abel are perhaps the original story of war between brothers, Sophocles' *Antigone* is perhaps the most persuasive account of how social meaning is made from devastation.

39. This emphasis was inverted during the 2019 uprising, when protestors insisted that it was corruption, negligence, and sectarianism at the level of the state, and not of the people, that was the problem. However, neither in 2011 nor 2019 was the nation-state *form* put under critical review. For a nation-state that has existed for less than 100 years, was carved and hobbled together under colonialism, and was fought against by many in my father's and grandparents' generations, it is significant that the idea of a Lebanese nation-state in its current borders is a fait accompli.

40. Interview, Leila, 2009.

41. Interview Issam, in discussion with the author, 2009.

42. Arendt, *Human Condition*; Arendt, *Origins of Totalitarianism*.

43. In Arabic, *shi bila 'i al nafs* and *shi muqaddas*.

44. Hermez, "'War Is Going to Ignite.'"

45. Connolly, *Neuropolitics*.

46. Hermez, *War Is Coming*.

47. Interview with Issam at Dar al Fatwa, 2010.

48. Department of Consultation and Legislation of the Ministry of Justice, opinion 2007/276.

49. Abillama, "Contesting Secularism."

50. He is the author of the book *al zawāj al madanī: al haq w al 'aqed 'ala al arādī al lubnāniyya*.

51. For an overview of Gregoire Haddad's thoughts on secularism, see his book *al 'ilmaniyyat al shamila*. For more on his life and activism, see Abdullah, *gregoire haddad: mutran lil zaman al-qādem*.

52. Interestingly, many of the activists for the passage of a civil marriage law and/or a secular personal status use the example of conversion as a "problem" that will be solved when citizens are given the option to marry under a secular personal status.

53. I am using the language of coercively assigned sect to signal—via the comparative metonym of coercively assigned sex—the depth of injury that many secular activists feel. They believe that their categorization as this or that sect is an act of misrecognition and that they must break free of this categorization to be who they believe they *really* are.

54. See Saghieh, "To Remember."

55. Personal interview, Dar al-Fatwa, in discussion with the author, March 2010.

56. Although an "out" atheist cannot legally be barred from accessing the personal status courts, he or she may be discriminated against in court proceedings by the sheikh or priest who is presiding over the case.

57. In addition to these troubling developments, opinions issued by Lebanese legal institutions concerning the campaign to remove personal status are contradictory and have caused much confusion.

58. Mikdashi, "Sex and Sectarianism."

59. For debates on civil marriage from the perspective of women's rights see Hyndman-Rizk, "Question of Personal Status." For a comprehensive and different take on gender, law, sect, and nation, see Hyndman-Rizk, *Lebanese Women*.

60. See Najar, "Shatb al Maddhab."

61. When I first heard this term, I thought immediately of Ussama Makdissi's book *The Culture of Sectarianism*. I then realized that activists meant the word "culture" in the anthropological sense, in that it is closely correlated to how one builds and expresses meaning through group and individual affiliations.

62. Picard, *Lebanon, a Shattered Country*; F. Traboulsi, *History of Modern Lebanon*; Pursley, *Familiar Futures*; Thompson, *Colonial Citizens*; Mikdashi, "Magic of Mutual Coexistence."

63. Taylor, *Secular Age*.

64. Asad, *Formations of the Secular*; Mahmood, *Religious Differences*; Keane, *Christian Moderns*.

65. He told me where he had gone to university in the first sentence he spoke: Harvard

66. Interview, Khaled (*da'wa* secularist and corporate lawyer practicing in Beirut), in discussion with the author, 2009.

67. Interview, Khaled, in discussion with the author, 2009.

68. This image perhaps changed in the You Stink movement, but it was back in the 2019 protests, the difference between "peaceful" protestors and violent

ones. Paul Amar's work on securitization through discourses on masculinities, race and class is informative. Amar, *Security Archipelago.*

69. Interview, Jean, 2010.

70. See Moussawi, *Disruptive Situations,* for an elaboration of how "queer strategies," as he calls them, are deployed in nonqueer contexts. Of course, Laique Pride was a queer context. But it was a queer context expressly oriented toward expanding the structural possibilities for heterosexual marriage.

71. It is important to note here that 2009 was only three years after the Israel-Lebanon war and one year after the 2008 events. It was also before the wars in Syria and Yemen and before Hizballah's military and strategic involvement in both. Hizballah's popular support in Lebanon has shrunk dramatically since I began my research.

72. On Turkey, see Tambar, *Reckoning of Pluralism;* Navaro-Yashin, *Faces of the State.* On Egypt, see Agrama, *Questioning Secularism;* Asad, "Thinking about Secularism"; Mahmood, *Religious Differences.*

73. See Asad, *Formations of the Secular;* Asad, *Genealogies of Religion;* Asad, "Idea."

74. This reading of sectarian voting patterns ignores the ideological multiplicity among Lebanese Shi'a (and all sects) historically and in the present.

75. The founders of Laique Pride were largely disturbed by the discourse that surrounded them, including implicitly Islamophobic, anti-shia, homophobic, and sexist discourse.

76. Interview with Hala, 2010.

77. Deeb, *Enchanted Modern;* Deeb and Harb, *Leisurely Islam.*

78. Brown, *Regulating Aversion.*

79. This logic of deferral of explicit calls for women's rights is at least as old as the Algerian Revolution.

80. On the work of tolerance and its limits, see Brown, *Regulating Aversion;* Jakobsen and Pellegrini, *Love the Sin.*

81. Povinelli, *Cunning of Recognition.*

82. Brown, *Regulating Aversion;* Puar, *Terrorist Assemblages.*

83. Deeb, "Beyond Sectarianism." Deeb also suggests that we understand the deployment of anti-Muslim sentiment in Lebanon, including by Muslims, as circulating within and toward global whiteness.

84. Berlant, *Cruel Optimism.*

85. Berlant, *Cruel Optimism;* Povinelli, *Cunning of Recognition;* Trouillot, *Silencing the Past;* Seikaly, "Matter of Time."

Chapter 5: The Epidermal State

1. Mouawad and Baumann, "WAYN AL-DAWLA?" See also Mouawad, *Unpacking Lebanon's Resilience.* Baumann and Mouawad, *Arab Studies Journal* Special Issue.

2. Aretxaga, "Maddening States"; Das, *Life and Words*; Povinelli, *Cunning of Recognition*; Navaro-Yashin, *Faces of the State*; Trouillot, Hann, and Krti, "Anthropology of the State."

3. Mitchell, "Limits of the State"; Sharma and Gupta, *Anthropology of the State*; Povinelli, "State of Shame."

4. Bhattacharjee, "Public/Private Mirage"; Abu-Lughod, "Active Social Life"; Brown, *States of Injury*; Fraser, "From Redistribution to Recognition?"; Puar, *Terrorist Assemblages*; Shakhsari, "Killing Me Softly"; Hawkesworth, *Gender and Political Theory*; Joseph, "Public/Private"; Thompson, "Public and Private."

5. Amar, Paul. *Security Archipelago*; Grewal, *Saving the Security State*; Sehlikoglu and Zengin, "Introduction."

6. See Najmabadi, *Professing Selves*; Schuller, *Biopolitics of Feeling*; Puri, *Sexual States*.

7. For work on hymen exams, nationalism, and ideal citizenship, see Parla, "'Honor' of the State." For how "hymenal politics" articulates histories and practices of laicite, colonialism, and Islamophobia, see Surkis, "Hymenal Politics."

8. Zengin, "Violent Intimacies."

9. The term "epidermal state" is inspired by Fanon's concept of "epidermalization" and Povinelli's theorization of the "membrane of cultural difference." For both Fanon and Povinelli, subjectification ties the subject to, and within, a body that is a palimpsest of racial, economic, and colonial power. Sex and sexuality are key to the epidermalization of difference, hierarchy, and inferiority. My usage of the "epidermal state" foregrounds embodiment as a vector of state power that materializes the body and its racial, sexual, and classed stakes as sites for the performance of sovereignty. See Fanon, *Black Skin, White Masks*, Povinelli, *Cunning of Recognition*.

10. In Rosie Braidottis's words, the body is "an interface, a threshold, a field of intersecting material and symbolic forces, it is a surface where multiple codes (race, sex, class, age, etc.) are inscribed; it's a cultural construction that capitalizes on the energies of a heterogeneous, discontinuous and unconscious nature." Braidotti, "Becoming Woman."

11. LBCI News, "Closure."

12. Amar, *Security Archipelago*.

13. Moumneh, "Filth They Bring."

14. Moumneh, "Filth They Bring," 221.

15. Some local outlets and blogs called them "gay tests."

16. LBCI News, "31-7-2012."

17. Human Rights Watch, *Dignity Debased*.

18. Wansa, "Lebanon's Republic of Shame."

19. Human Rights Watch, *Dignity Debased*.

20. Interview with Karim Nammour, Sarde, 2021.

21. Karame, "Lebanese Article 534."

22. Eng, *Feeling of Kinship*, 11.

23. Legal decisions specifically use the language "homosexual." "Queer" is not a legal term, though many members of the LGBTQ community identify that way.

24. Frangieh, "Beirut Court of Appeals."

25. For the necessity of thinking queerness and intersectionality together in Beirut, see Moussawi, *Disruptive Situations*.

26. I differentiate between nationality and legal status because there is a racial hierarchy of foreign nationalities in Lebanon, one that works alongside and is informed by a multiplicity of legal statuses that include citizenship, refugee, displaced person, child of Lebanese mother, unregistered Lebanese, stateless person, migrant labor, trafficked woman, professional foreign worker (expatriate).

27. Intersectionality is key to understanding the LGBTQ community. For example, Lebanese gay men who are prominent in the LGBTQ community have been accused of trafficking and assaulting Syrian and Iraqi gay men who are refugees.

28. In Egypt, hymen exams were used to intimidate protestors during the uprising in Egypt. Samira Ibrahim sued the doctor who conducted the exam on her. I consider Ibrahim to be one of the most significant political actors of the Egyptian Revolution. For more, see Seikaly, "Meaning of Revolution." For the body as a site of politics in the uprisings, see Hasso, and Salime, *Freedom Without Permission*.

29. Interview with cassation judge, September 2011. Interviews with Druze court of appeals judge and with judge at Sunni Sharia Court of Beirut, 2009.

30. For example, see Decision 537/2000, Mount Lebanon Criminal Court; sāder fī al ahkām al jizāʾiyat. I have also interviewed lawyers and legal researchers who described cases where hymen exams were relevant. These included rape cases, cases regarding unlicensed sex work, divorce cases, and custody proceedings. In one case, a fourteen-year-old girl was subjected to a hymen exam to "prove" whether her mother was a good mother and should retain or be stripped of custody. The father had alleged that his ex-wife was not raising their daughter according to the communal and religious principles of their sect, a charge often used to strip custody from one or the other parent. Finally, I have interviewed anti-racism activists who said that migrant domestic workers were sometimes subjected to hymen exams by their employers to monitor their sexuality. In 2009 the Ministry of Labor published a guide for migrant domestic laborers that informed them that they would undergo pregnancy testing before arriving in Lebanon and shortly after. The guide also stated, in capital letters, that there is a "NO PREGNANCY POLICY" regarding migrant domestic workers in Lebanon. See *Information Guide*.

31. Karame, "Court Trends."

32. Halley, "Construction of Heterosexuality."

33. Salem and Shaaban, "Queers in Quarantine."

34. Rubin, "Traffic in Women"; Stevens, *Reproducing the State*.

35. Eng, *Feeling of Kinship*, 28.

36. Virginity exams—or the use of hymen tests to determine virginity—violate human rights according to the World Health Organization.

37. I am not identifying the name of the personal status court nor the years of its decisions so as to protect the identity of the plaintiffs. All personal status courts consider marriage a contract that can be annulled if one or the other party deceived the other into entering the contract under false pretenses.

38. Article 534 of the Lebanese penal code punishes "sex contrary to nature." It has been traditionally applied against members of LGBTQ communities with notable exceptions for heterosexual sodomy.

39. Decision 145/199 from the Mount Lebanon criminal court also featured the testimony of a forensic doctor testifying against a defendant who said that the woman he raped had not been a virgin at the time. He said there was trauma that could be dated to the rape. sāder fī al ahkām al jizā'iyat, 20.

40. Split into *mu'addam* and *mu'akkhar*.

41. Tucker, *House of the Law*, 47.

42. This "evidence" from a university dean points to the academy as a space of state adjacent power.

43. As Judith Surkis has shown, the idea that marriage can be annulled based on deception or lies related to the "essential characteristics" of a spouse is also intrinsic to secular marriage law in France, where it has colonial and Christian antecedents. Surkis, "Hymenal Politics."

44. Surkis, "Hymenal Politics."

45. These are all elements of Muslim personal status laws or fiqh when it comes to marriage; husbands are solely responsible for the household upkeep and are obligated to pay for their wives expenses as long as they are married. Husbands can demand that their wives return to their marital home, and wives can be found at fault for a divorce if they refuse.

46. Article 95 of the Lebanese code of organization of courts.

47. Article 95 of the Lebanese code of organization of courts.

48. For a more thorough explanation and analysis of these circumstances, see I. Traboulsi, *al 'anzima al ahwāl al shakhsīyya fī lubnān*.

49. The security branches are the Lebanese Armed Forces, Internal Security, Customs Police, and General Security.

50. Ali, *Sexual Ethics and Islam*, 43.

51. Women's sexuality, as Hana Kholoussy elucidated, threatens a wide range of actors, all of whom collude in its regulation. See Kholoussy, *For Better, for Worse*.

52. As a point of comparison, the Plenary Assembly decided to annul a decision from the Sunni Court of Appeals because of procedural violations that were

considered substantive. The case involved a custody ruling by the Sunni Court of Appeals involving a couple who had had a civil marriage in New York. The judges at the Plenary Assembly noted that had both members of the couple been Muslim, which they were not, the Sunni appeals court ruling would have not been annulled as its has jurisdiction over all Muslim marriages even if the marriage was conducted in a civil court in New York City. Assembly decision 12/2006. See sāder fī tamyīz, 2005, 2006, 2007.

53. In my interviews with judges at personal status courts and with their families, it was clear that cases involving violence, abuse, neglect, and deception weighed heavily on them. The son of one of these judges once asked me to imagine how difficult it is to live in a house where the phones ring twenty-four hours a day, full of horrible stories. To be a judge, he said, meant not being allowed to not respond, particularly for personal status judges who see "the worst situations."

54. The case occurred before Parliament passed the 2014 domestic violence law, though it is unclear if Hana would have been able to turn to that law for protection from Ramzi, particularly since husbands were exempted from punishment for sexual assault or rape as long as they were raping and assaulting their wives.

55. Sharia court trials and decisions, in theory, are public unless otherwise indicated by the judge or requested by one of the parties. However, in practice, access is limited due to logistical challenges, and efforts in publishing the decisions are limited to private initiatives. Volumes of personal status decisions from both Christian and Muslim personal status courts have been published by specialized presses. They are most often used in law school and in the arena of legal research. Despite this public record, there is a persistent myth that the decisions from personal status courts are clouded in secrecy. While it may be true that gaining access to personal status court archives is difficult for social scientists or humanities scholars, especially if they are based abroad or from the "wrong" sect, the good news is that law professors, lawyers, editors, and publishers have already done much of this work. See, for example, Hanna, *al ahwāl al shakhsīyya*, 2009; Hanna, *al ahwāl al shakhsīyya*, 1998.

56. The fact that an estimated 40 percent of women are born without hymens somehow did not come up.

57. There are invasive practices of hymen exams that involve inserting one or two fingers in an attempt to gage the looseness of the vagina. Like finger or object-involved anal tests, these are medicalized forms of rape. However, the evidence available on hymen exams in Lebanon come from legal cases, hospitals, and doctors—where the exam is stressed as visual.

58. Interview with Dr. Sami Kawas, a forensic medicine specialist in Beirut who has carried out anal examinations for years, as relayed in Human Rights Watch, *Dignity Debased*.

59. Interview with Dr. Hussein Chahrour, as relayed in Human Rights Watch, *Dignity Debased*.

60. In Ayse Parla's words, "virginity examinations [hymen exams] must be viewed as a particularly modern form of institutionalized violence." Parla, "'Honor' of the State," 66. For an account of virginity in Egyptian criminal law and its role in constructing normative sexuality, see Hammad, *Industrial Sexuality*.

61. Yasmine still does not understand what the officer meant by saying that he was with Hizballah, and she cut him off before he could complete his sentence. I assume he meant that he was a supporter of Hizballah and that he said this as escalation after Yasmine was unimpressed by his suggestion that because they were both Muslim they both "felt the same way" about gay people. This interaction illustrates the multiple ways Hizballah can and is rhetorically deployed in Lebanon, sometimes in ways that have nothing to do with the group itself.

62. Transcript of interview with Yasmine, 2010. Human Rights Watch later put out a statement linking hymen and anal exams both as examples of intimidation, interrogation, and torture. Human Rights Watch, *Lebanon: Stop "Tests of Shame."*

63. As Fanon writes, "the internalization—or, better, the epidermalization—of this inferiority." Fanon, *Black Skin, White Masks*, 4.

64. Mikdashi and Puar, "Queer Theory."

65. Similar to the "twinkie defense."

66. Mitra, *Indian Sex Life*.

67. Lebanese law states that there must be plausible evidence of a crime to investigate someone.

68. Hajjar, *Torture*.

69. Amnesty International, *Lebanon*.

70. Saghieh, "Torture in Roumieh Prisons."

71. McClintock, "Paranoid Empire"; Razack, *Casting Out*.

72. Puar, *Terrorist Assemblages*; Mikdashi, "Gay Rights"; Mikdashi and Puar, "Queer Theory."

73. Amnesty International, *Lebanon*.

74. Lebanese Ministry of Labor, *Information Guide*. Pregnancy tests are a formal requirement of artist (but not migrant) visas, under which many women have been sexually trafficked to Lebanon.

75. In one case, a woman filed a complaint against her adult son because she said he looked like a woman. The complaint was accepted by a prosecutor, and the man was investigated. The medical examiner determined that "no symptoms exist that prove the suspect's practice of such [same-sex] acts." Decision 746/2009, Ba'abda Judge, unpublished.

76. Many countries use and accept the expertise and evidence of hymen and anal exams in cases involving allegations of sexual assault and rape, where they are used to evidence trauma.

77. I have no doubt that hymen exams are more difficult to ban than anal exams, but this is partly due to the different ways these exams have been framed.

It is more difficult to frame hymen exams as "torture" because they implicate families. It is also more difficult to frame hymen exams as "shameful" precisely because women's premarital sexuality *is* more shameful than men's premarital sexuality, no matter the kind of sex being had.

78. Human Rights Watch, for example, is very clear on this: "No matter the circumstances or rationale, forced anal examinations in cases of consensual same-sex conduct are a human rights violation. They do not serve legitimate government interests, and they lack evidentiary value. As such, law enforcement officials should never order the examinations; doctors and medical personnel should not conduct them; and courts should not admit them into evidence. Human Rights Watch, *Dignity Debased*.

79. Benjamin, "Critique of Violence"; Aretxaga, "Maddening States."

80. Puri, *Sexual States*; Puar, Jasbir. "Rethinking Homonationalism"; Farris, *Women's Rights*.

81. Feldman, *Formations of Violence*; Scarry, *Body in Pain*; Bargu, *Starve and Immolate*; Zengin, Asli. "Violent Intimacies."

82. Nationalism, empire, and capitalism also traffic at the site of sexual difference.

83. Clarke and Newman, *Managerial State*; Gill-Peterson, *Histories*; Rajan, *Biocapital*; Navaro-Yashin, *Faces of the State*.

84. Bersani, "Is the Rectum a Grave?"; Edelman, *No Future*.

85. Schuller and Gill-Peterson, "Introduction."

86. I am grateful to Asli Zengin for this insight.

87. Schuller, *Biopolitics of Feeling*; Snorton, *Black on Both Sides*; Chen, *Animacies*; Povinelli, "Notes on Gridlock."

88. For example, in 2011 Egyptian security services conducted hymen exams on female revolutionaries to publicly and viscerally demonstrate the state's sovereignty over its citizens. The exams were also used to humiliate female protesters, to deter them from revolting, and, it was argued, to "protect" those same security services from allegation of rape. In effect, female protesters were forcibly given hymen exams by the state to prove that no violation by the state—represented by security services—had occurred.

89. Joseph, "Gender and Citizenship"; Mikdashi, "Sextarianism."

90. Million, "Felt Theory."

91. See Braidotti, "Embodiment"; Hird, "Feminist Matters."

92. Zengin, "Violent Intimacies."

93. For how law enables violence, see Esmeir, "Violence of Non-Violence"; Esmeir, *Juridical Humanity*.

94. Amar, *Security Archipelago*.

95. For an overview on how Syrian refugees and migrant laborers are racialized and securitized through sexual regulation and the heuristic of the "sex panic," see Moumneh, "Filth They Bring."

Epilogue

1. In 2021 the judiciary was closed, in effect due to a strike but also, more important, because public sector employees could not find or afford gas to put in their cars. Their salaries deflated to the extent that many stopped going to work because they could not afford to.

Acknowledgments

1. I am inspired by Matt Brim's call for a political economy of knowledge production. See *Poor Queer Studies*.

Bibliography

Abdullah, Bassel. *gregoire haddad: mutran lil zaman al-qādem*. Self-published, 2021.

Abillama, Raja. "Contesting Secularism: Civil Marriage and Those Who Do Not Belong to a Religious Community in Lebanon." *PoLAR: Political and Legal Anthropology Review* 41, no. S1 (2018): 148–62.

Abu-Lughod, Lila. "The Active Social Life of 'Muslim Women's Rights.'" In *Gender and Culture at the Limit of Rights*, edited by Dorothy L. Hodgson, 101–19. University of Pennsylvania Press, 2011.

———. *Do Muslim Women Need Saving?* Harvard University Press, 2013.

———. *Dramas of Nationhood: The Politics of Television in Egypt*. University of Chicago Press, 2008.

———. "The Romance of Resistance: Tracing Transformations of Power through Bedouin Women." *American Ethnologist* 17, no. 1 (1990): 41–55.

———. "Seductions of the 'Honor Crime.'" *Differences* 22, no. 1 (2011): 17–63.

Abu-Rish, Ziad. "Garbage Politics." *Middle East Report* 277 (2015): 35–40.

———. "Lebanon Beyond Exceptionalism." In *A Critical Political Economy of the Middle East and North Africa*, 179–95. Stanford University Press, 2020.

Agamben, Giorgio. *Homo Sacer: Sovereign Power and Bare Life*. Stanford University Press, 1998.

Agostinho, Daniela. "Archival Encounters: Rethinking Access and Care in Digital Colonial Archives." *Archival Science* 19, no. 2 (2019): 141–65.

Agrama, Hussein Ali. *Questioning Secularism: Islam, Sovereignty, and the Rule of Law in Modern Egypt*. University of Chicago Press, 2012.

———. "Secularism, Sovereignty, Indeterminacy: Is Egypt a Secular or a Religious State?" *Comparative Studies in Society and History* 52, no. 3 (2010): 495–523.

Ahmad, Attiya. *Everyday Conversions: Islam, Domestic Work, and South Asian Migrant Women in Kuwait*. Duke University Press, 2017.

Akar, Hiba Bou. *For the War Yet to Come: Planning Beirut's Frontiers*. Stanford University Press, 2018.

Al-Ali, Nadje. "Reflections on (Counter) Revolutionary Processes in Egypt." *Feminist Review* 106, no. 1 (2014): 122–28.

———. *Secularism, Gender and the State in the Middle East: The Egyptian Women's Movement.* No. 14. Cambridge University Press, 2000.

Alexander, M. Jacqui. "Not Just (Any)body Can Be a Citizen: The Politics of Law, Sexuality and Postcoloniality in Trinidad and Tobago and the Bahamas." *Feminist Review* 48, no. 1 (1994): 5–23.

———. *Pedagogies of Crossing: Meditations on Feminism, Sexual Politics, Memory, and the Sacred.* Duke University Press, 2006.

Alexander, M. Jacqui, and Chandra T. Mohanty. "Cartographies of Knowledge and Power." In *Critical Transnational Feminist Praxis*, edited by Richa Nagar and Amanda Swarr, 23–45. State University of New York Press, 2010.

Al-Hout, Bayan Nuwayhed. *Sabra and Shatila: September 1982.* Pluto Press, 2004.

Ali, Kecia. *Sexual Ethics and Islam: Feminist Reflections on Qur'an, Hadith, and Jurisprudence.* Simon and Schuster, 2016

Ali, Zahra. "Feminisms in Iraq: Beyond the Religious and Secular Divide." *Gender and Research* 20, no. 2 (2019): 47–66.

Allouche, Sabiha. "Love, Lebanese Style: Toward an Either/And Analytic Framework of Kinship." *Journal of Middle East Women's Studies* 15, no. 2 (2019): 157–78.

———. "Queering (Inter-sectarian) Heterosexual Love in Lebanon." *International Journal of Middle East Studies* (2018).

Amar, Paul, *The Security Archipelago: Human-Security States, Sexuality Politics, and the End of Neoliberalism.* Duke University Press, 2013.

Amnesty International. *Lebanon: Torture of Syrian Refugees Arbitrarily Detained on Counter-Terror Charges.* 2021.

"Angry Property Owners Accuse Solidere of Bribing Judges." *Daily Star*, October 15, 1999. https://www.dailystar.com.lb/News/Lebanon-News/1999/Oct-15/16469-angry-property-owners-accuse-solidere-of-bribing-7-judges.ashx.

Arendt, Hannah. *Eichmann in Jerusalem.* Penguin, 2006.

———. *The Human Condition.* University of Chicago Press, 2013.

———. *The Origins of Totalitarianism.* Duke University Press, 2007.

Aretxaga, Begoña. "Maddening States." *Annual Review of Anthropology* 32, no. 1 (2003): 393–410.

Arondekar, Anjali. *For the Record: On Sexuality and the Colonial Archive in India.* Duke University Press, 2009.

———. "In the Absence of Reliable Ghosts: Sexuality, Historiography, South Asia." *Differences* 25, no. 3 (2014): 98–122.

———. "The Sex of History, or Object/Matters." *History Workshop Journal* 89 (2020): 207–13.

Arsan, Andrew. *Lebanon: A Country in Fragments.* Hurst, 2018.

Asad, Talal, "Comments on Conversion." In *Conversion to Modernities: The Globalization of Christianity*, edited by Peter Van Der Veer, 263–74. Routledge, 1996.

————. *Formations of the Secular.* Stanford University Press, 2003.

————. *Genealogies of Religion: Discipline and Reasons of Power in Christianity and Islam.* JHU Press, 1993.

————. "The Idea of an Anthropology of Islam." *Qui parle* 17, no. 2 (2009): 1–30.

————. "Thinking about Secularism and Law in Egypt." *ISIM Paper* (2001): 1–24.

Austin, John Langshaw. *How to Do Things with Words.* Vol. 88. Oxford University Press, 1975.

Azoulay, Ariella. "Potential History: Thinking through Violence." *Critical Inquiry* 39, no. 3 (2013): 548–74.

Azzi, John. *zawāj al madanī: al qādi al lubnāni fi muwajahat qawānīn al ʾalam.* Sader, 2007.

Bakkar, Nada. *ʾabed al Munʾim. qadāyā al al- aḥwāl al-shakhsīyya wa al jinsīyya fī lubnan.* Sader, 2017.

Bargu, Banu. *Starve and Immolate: The Politics of Human Weapons.* Columbia University Press, 2014.

Barker, Joanne, ed. *Sovereignty Matters: Locations of Contestation and Possibility in Indigenous Struggles for Self-Determination.* University of Nebraska Press, 2005.

Baumann, Hannes, and Mouawad, Jamil. "The State in Lebanon." Special issue, *Arab Studies Journal* 25, no. 1 (Spring 2017).

Bell, David, and Jon Binnie. *The Sexual Citizen: Queer Politics and Beyond.* Cambridge: Polity Press, 2000.

Benjamin, Walter. "Critique of Violence." In *On Violence*, 268–85. Duke University Press, 2007.

Berlant, Lauren. *Cruel Optimism.* Duke University Press, 2011.

Bersani, Leo. "Is the Rectum a Grave?" *October* 43 (1987): 197–222.

Bessner, Daniel, "House of Cards: Can the American University Be Saved?" *Nation*, September 8, 2020. https://www.thenation.com/article/society/gig-academy-meritocracy-trap-universities-crisis/.

Bhattacharjee, Anannya. "The Public/Private Mirage: Mapping Homes and Undomesticating Violence Work in the South Asian Immigrant Community." In *The Anthropology of the State: A Reader*, edited by Aradhana Sharma and Akhil Gupta, 337–56. Wiley-Blackwell, 2006.

Bou Khater, Lea, and Rima Majed. "Lebanon's 2019 October Revolution: Who Mobilized and Why." Working paper, Asfari Institute for Civil Society and Citizenship, 2020.

Braidotti, Rosi. "Becoming Woman: Or Sexual Difference Revisited." *Theory, Culture & Society* 20, no. 3 (2003): 43–64.

————. "Embodiment, Sexual Difference, and the Nomadic Subject." *Hypatia* 8, no. 1 (1993): 1–13.

————. *Nomadic Subjects: Embodiment and Sexual Difference in Contemporary Feminist Theory.* Columbia University Press, 2011.

————. "Sexual Difference as a Nomadic Political Project." In *Klassikerinnen feministischer Theorie, Band III*, edited by Marianne Schmidbaur, Helma Lutz, and Ulla Wischermann, 146–72. Ulrike Helmer Verlag, 2013.

Briggs, Laura, Kathleen Brown, Nancy F. Cott, Gilbert M. Joseph, Catherine Hall, Damon Salesa, Emily S. Rosenberg, Martha Hodes, Gwenn Miller, and Laura Wexler. *Haunted by Empire: Geographies of Intimacy in North American History*. Duke University Press, 2006.

Brim, Matt. *Poor Queer Studies: Confronting Elitism in the University*. Duke University Press, 2020.

Brown, Wendy. "Finding the Man in the State." *Feminist Studies* 18, no. 1 (1992): 7–34.

————. *Regulating Aversion: Tolerance in the Age of Identity and Empire*. Princeton University Press, 2009.

————. *States of Injury: Power and Freedom in Late Modernity*. Princeton University Press, 1995.

Brubaker, Rogers. *Citizenship and Nationhood in France and Germany*. New ed. Harvard University Press, 1998.

————. "Myths and Misconceptions in the Study of Nationalism." In *The State of the Nation: Ernest Gellner and the Theory of Nationalism*, edited by John A. Hall, 272–306. Cambridge University Press, 1998.

————. *Nationalism Reframed: Nationhood and the National Question in the New Europe*. Cambridge University Press, 1996.

Buckser, Andrew, and Stephen D. Glazier, eds. *The Anthropology of Religious Conversion*. Rowman & Littlefield, 2003.

Butler, Judith. *Bodies that Matter: On the Discursive Limits of Sex*. Taylor & Francis, 2011.

————. *The Psychic Life of Power: Theories in Subjection*. Stanford University Press, 1997.

Cady, Linell E., and Tracy Fessenden, eds. *Religion, the Secular, and the Politics of Sexual Difference*. Columbia University Press, 2013.

Canaday, Margot. *The Straight State: Sexuality and Citizenship in Twentieth-Century America*. Vol. 64. Princeton University Press, 2009.

Chalcraft, John, Adam Hanieh, Maya Mikdashi, and Jillian Shwedler (convener). "Thinking Critically About Regional Uprisings." *MERIP* 292, no. 3 (Fall/Winter 2019).

Chanock, Martin. *Law, Custom, and Social Order: The Colonial Experience in Malawi and Zambia*. Cambridge University Press, 1985.

Chatterjee, Partha. "Anderson's Utopia." In *Grounds of Comparison*, 171–80. Routledge, 2013.

————. *The Nation and Its Fragments: Colonial and Postcolonial Histories*. Princeton University Press, 1993.

Cheah, Pheng, Elizabeth Grosz, Judith Butler, and Drucilla Cornell. "The Future of Sexual Difference: An Interview with Judith Butler and Drucilla Cornell." *Diacritics* 28, no. 1 (1998): 19–42.

Cheal, David. *The Gift Economy*. Routledge, 2015.

Chen, Mel Y. *Animacies: Biopolitics, Racial Mattering, and Queer Affect*. Duke University Press, 2012.

Clarke, John, and Janet Newman. *The Managerial State: Power, Politics and Ideology in the Remaking of Social Welfare*. Sage, 1997.

Clarke, Morgan. *Islam and Law in Lebanon: Sharia within and without the State*. Cambridge University Press, 2018.

———. *Islam and New Kinship: Reproductive Technology and the Shariah in Lebanon*. Vol. 16. Berghahn Books, 2009.

Committee on Academic Freedom, Middle East Studies Association. *Digitization of State Archives Could Affect Access to Archival Material*. 2016.

Connolly, William E. *Neuropolitics: Thinking, Culture, Speed*. Vol. 23. University of Minnesota Press, 2002.

———. *Why I Am Not a Secularist*. University of Minnesota Press, 1999.

Cooper, Brittney. "Intersectionality." In *The Oxford Handbook of Feminist Theory*, edited by Lisa Disch and Mary Hawkesworth, 385–406. Oxford University Press, 2016.

Cornell, Drucilla. *At the Heart of Freedom: Feminism, Sex, and Equality*. Princeton University Press, 1998.

———. *Beyond Accommodation: Ethical Feminism, Deconstruction, and the Law*. Rowman & Littlefield, 1999.

———. "Rethinking Legal Ideals after Deconstruction." In *Law's Madness*, edited by Austin Sarat, Lawrence Douglas, and Martha Merrill Umphrey, 147–68. University of Michigan Press, 2006.

Crenshaw, Kimberle. "Mapping the Margins: Intersectionality, Identity Politics, and Violence against Women of Color." *Stanford Law Review* 43 (1990): 1241.

Cvetkovich, Ann. *Archive of Feelings*. Duke University Press, 2003.

Das, Veena. *Life and Words: Violence and the Descent into the Ordinary*. University of California Press, 2006.

———. "Violence, Gender, and Subjectivity." *Annual Review of Anthropology* 37 (2008): 283–99.

Deeb, Lara. "Beyond Sectarianism: Intermarriage and Social Difference in Lebanon." *International Journal of Middle East Studies* 52, no. 2 (2020): 215–28.

———. *An Enchanted Modern: Gender and Public Piety in Shiʻi Lebanon*. Princeton University Press, 2011.

———. "Thinking Piety and the Everyday Together: A Response to Fadil and Fernando." *HAU: Journal of Ethnographic Theory* 5, no. 2 (2015): 93–96.

Deeb, Lara, and Mona Harb. *Leisurely Islam: Negotiating Geography and Morality in Shiʻite South Beirut*. Vol. 49. Princeton University Press, 2013.

Deleuze, Gilles, and Félix Guattari. *A Thousand Plateaus: Capitalism and Schizophrenia*. Bloomsbury, 1988.

Deringil, Selim. *Conversion and Apostasy in the Late Ottoman Empire*. Cambridge University Press, 2012.

Derrida, Jacques. *Archive Fever: A Freudian Impression*. University of Chicago Press, 1996.

———. "Force of Law: The Mystical Foundation of Authority." In *Deconstruction and the Possibility of Justice*, edited by Drucilla Cornell, Michael Rosenfield, and David G. Carlson, 3–67. Routledge, 1992.

Dirks, Nicholas B. *Castes of Mind: Colonialism and the Making of Modern India*. Princeton University Press, 2000.

Duggan, Lisa. *The Twilight of Equality? Neoliberalism, Cultural Politics, and the Attack on Democracy*. Beacon Press, 2012.

Doumani, Beshara B. *Family Life in the Ottoman Mediterranean: A Social History*. Cambridge University Press, 2017.

Edelman, Lee. *No Future: Queer Theory and the Death Drive*. Duke University Press, 2004.

El-Haj, Nadia Abu. *Facts on the Ground: Archaeological Practice and Territorial Self-Fashioning in Israeli Society*. University of Chicago Press, 2008.

———. *The Genealogical Science: The Search for Jewish Origins and the Politics of Epistemology*. University of Chicago Press, 2012.

El Khazen, Farid. *The Breakdown of the State in Lebanon, 1967–1976*. Bloomsbury, 2020.

El Shakry, Omnia. "'History without Documents': The Vexed Archives of Decolonization in the Middle East." *American Historical Review* 120, no. 3 (2015): 920–34.

Elyachar, Julia. "Before (and After) Neoliberalism: Tacit Knowledge, Secrets of the Trade, and the Public Sector in Egypt." *Cultural Anthropology* 27, no. 1 (2012): 76–96.

Eng, David L. *The Feeling of Kinship: Queer Liberalism and the Racialization of Intimacy*. Duke University Press, 2010.

Esmeir, Samera. *Juridical Humanity: A Colonial History*. Stanford University Press, 2012.

———. "The Violence of Non-Violence: Law and War in Iraq." *Journal of Law and Society* 34, no. 1 (2007): 99–115.

Fanon, Frantz. *Black Skin, White Masks*. Translated by Charles Lam Markmann. Pluto Press, 2008.

Farris, Sara R. *In the Name of Women's Rights: The Rise of Femonationalism*. Duke University Press, 2017.

Feldman, Allen. *Formations of Violence: The Narrative of the Body and Political Terror in Northern Ireland*. University of Chicago Press, 1991.

Feldman, Ilana. *Governing Gaza*. Duke University Press, 2007.

Ferguson, James. *The Anti-politics Machine: "Development," Depoliticization and Bureaucratic Power in Lesotho*. CUP Archive, 1990.

Fernando, Mayanthi L. *The Republic Unsettled: Muslim French and the Contradictions of Secularism*. Duke University Press, 2014.

Foucault, Michel. *The Birth of Biopolitics: Lectures at the Collège de France, 1978—1979*. Vol. 5. Picador, 2010.

———. *The Foucault Effect: Studies in Governmentality*. University of Chicago Press, 1991.

———. *The History of Sexuality: An Introduction*. Vintage, 1990.

———. *Security, Territory, Population: Lectures at the Collège de France, 1977–78*. Springer, 2007.

———. "The Subject and Power." *Critical Inquiry* 8, no. 4 (1982): 777–95.

Foucault, Michel, and François Ewald. *"Society Must Be Defended": Lectures at the Collège de France, 1975–1976*. Vol. 1. Macmillan, 2003.

Frangieh, Ghida. "Beirut Court of Appeals: Sexual Orientation is Not Punishable." *Legal Agenda*, May 28, 2019. https://english.legal-agenda.com/beirut-court-of-appeal-sexual-orientation-is-not-punishable/.

Fraser, Nancy. "From Redistribution to Recognition? Dilemmas of Justice in a 'Postsocialist' Age." In *The New Social Theory Reader*, edited by Steven Seidman and Jeffrey C. Alexander, 188–96. Routledge, 2020.

———. "Rethinking Recognition." *New Left Review* 3 (2000): 107–18.

Freeman, Elizabeth. *Time Binds: Queer Temporalities, Queer Histories*. Duke University Press, 2010.

Fuentes, Marisa J. *Dispossessed Lives: Enslaved Women, Violence, and the Archive*. University of Pennsylvania Press, 2016.

Gannagé, Pierre. *Le pluralisme des statuts personnels dans les États multicommunautaires: droit libanais et droits procheorientaux*. Bruylant, 2001.

Geha, C. "Politics of a Garbage Crisis: Social Networks, Narratives, and Frames of Lebanon's 2015 Protests and Their Aftermath." *Social Movement Studies* 18, no. 1 (2019): 78–92.

Gellner, Ernest. *Nations and Nationalism*. Cornell University Press, 2008.

Ghamroun, Samer. "Effets d'État. Les juges des enfants, les tribunaux de la charia et la lutte pour la famille libanaise." PhD diss., Université Paris Saclay (COmUE), 2016.

Gill-Peterson, Jules. *Histories of the Transgender Child*. University of Minnesota Press, 2018.

Glissant, Édouard. *Poetics of Relation*. University of Michigan Press, 1997.

Gordon, Avery F. *Ghostly Matters: Haunting and the Sociological Imagination*. University of Minnesota Press, 2008.

Grafton, David D. *The Christians of Lebanon: Political Rights in Islamic Law*. Tauris Academic Studies, 2003.

Gramsci, Antonio. *The Gramsci Reader: Selected Writings, 1916–1935*. New York University Press, 2000.

———. "State and Civil Society." In *The Anthropology of the State: A Reader*, edited by Aradhana Sharma and Akhil Gupta, 71–85. Wiley-Blackwell, 2006.

Grewal, Inderpal. *Saving the Security State: Exceptional Citizens in Twenty-first-Century America*. Duke University Press, 2017.

Griffiths, John. "What Is Legal Pluralism?" *Journal of Legal Pluralism and Unofficial Law* 18, no. 24 (1986): 1–55.

Hacking, Ian. *Rewriting the Soul: Multiple Personality and the Sciences of Memory*. Princeton University Press, 1998.

———. *The Taming of Chance*. Cambridge University Press, 1990.

Haddad, Gregoire. *al 'ilmaniyyat al shamila*. Dar Mukhtarat, 1996.

Hage, Ghassan. *Alter-politics: Critical Anthropology and the Radical Imagination*. Melbourne University Publishing, 2015.

Hajjar, Lisa. *Torture: A Sociology of Violence and Human Rights*. Routledge, 2013.

Hakim, Carol. *The Origins of the Lebanese National Idea: 1840–1920*. University of California Press, 2013.

Halley, Janet. "The Construction of Heterosexuality." In *Fear of a Queer Planet: Queer Politics and Social Theory*, edited by Michael Warner, 82–102. University of Minnesota Press, 1993.

Halley, Janet, and Kerry Rittich. "Critical Directions in Comparative Family Law: Genealogies and Contemporary Studies of Family Law Exceptionalism." *American Journal of Comparative Law* 58, no. 4 (2010): 753–75.

Hamill, Kathleen. *Trafficking of Migrant Domestic Workers in Lebanon: A Legal Analysis*. KAFA (enough) Violence & Exploitation, 2011.

Hammad, Hanan. *Industrial Sexuality: Gender, Urbanization, and Social Transformation in Egypt*. University of Texas Press, 2016.

Hanf, Theodor. *Coexistence in Wartime Lebanon: Decline of a State and Rise of a Nation*. IB Tauris, 2015.

Hanna, Badawi. *al ahwāl al shakhsīyya. ijtihādāt wa dirasāt qānunīyya, al jiz' al thālith*. Halabi, 2009.

———. *al ahwāl al shakhsīyya. ijtihādāt wa dirasāt qānunīyya, al jiz' al thāni*. Halabi, 1998.

Hardt, Michael, and Antonio Negri. *Empire*. Harvard University Press, 2000.

Harris, Cheryl I. "Whiteness as Property." *Harvard Law Review* 106, no. 8 (1993): 1707–91.

Hartman, Saidiya. *Lose Your Mother: A Journey Along the Atlantic Slave Route*. Macmillan, 2008.

———. "Venus in Two Acts." *Small Axe: A Caribbean Journal of Criticism* 12, no. 2 (2008): 1–14.

———. *Wayward Lives, Beautiful Experiments: Intimate Histories of Social Upheaval*. W. W. Norton, 2019.

Hasso, Frances S., and Zakia Salime, eds. *Freedom Without Permission: Bodies and Space in the Arab Revolutions*. Duke University Press, 2016.

Hatem, Mervat. "The Enduring Alliance of Nationalism and Patriarchy in Muslim Personal Status Laws: The Case of Modern Egypt." *Feminist Issues* 6, no. 1 (1986): 19–43.

Haugbolle, Sune. "Social Boundaries and Secularism in the Lebanese Left." *Mediterranean Politics* 18, no. 3 (2013): 427–43.

———. *War and Memory in Lebanon*. Vol. 34. Cambridge University Press, 2010.

Hawkesworth, Mary. *Gender and Political Theory: Feminist Reckonings.* John Wiley & Sons, 2019.

Hermez, Sami. *War Is Coming: Between Past and Future Violence in Lebanon.* University of Pennsylvania Press, 2017.

———. "'The War Is Going to Ignite': On the Anticipation of Violence in Lebanon." *PoLAR: Political and Legal Anthropology Review* 35, no. 2 (2012): 327–44.

Hird, Myra J. "Feminist Matters: New Materialist Considerations of Sexual Difference." *Feminist Theory* 5, no. 2 (2004): 223–32.

Hirschkind, Charles. *The Ethical Soundscape: Cassette Sermons and Islamic Counterpublics.* Columbia University Press, 2006.

Hudson, Michael C. *The Precarious Republic: Political Modernization in Lebanon.* Random House, 1968.

Hull, Matthew S. *Government of Paper: The Materiality of Bureaucracy in Urban Pakistan.* University of California Press, 2012.

Human Rights Watch. *Dignity Debased: Forced Anal Examinations in Homosexuality Prosecutions.* 2016.

———. *Human Rights Watch World Report.* 2009.

———. *Lebanon: Stop "Tests of Shame."* 2012.

———. *Why They Died: Civilian Casualties in Lebanon during the 2006 War.* 2007.

———. *Women's Rights under Lebanese Personal Status Laws.* 2015.

Husseini, Talal. *al zawāj al madanī: al haq w al ʿaqed ʿala al arādī al lubnāniyya.* Saqi, 2013.

———. "Clarification." *Legal Agenda,* 2014.

Hyndman-Rizk, Nelia. *Lebanese Women at the Crossroads: Caught Between Sect and Nation.* Lexington Books, 2020.

———. "A Question of Personal Status: The Lebanese Women's Movement and Civil Marriage Reform." *Journal of Middle East Women's Studies* 15, no. 2 (2019): 179–98.

Information Guide for Migrant Domestic Workers in Lebanon. Lebanese Ministry of Labor, 2012.

International Center for Transitional Justice. *Failing to Deal with the Past. What Cost to Lebanon.* 2014.

Irigaray, Luce, ed. *Luce Irigaray: Key Writings.* A&C Black, 2004.

Isin, Engin F. *Citizens without Frontiers.* Bloomsbury Publishing USA, 2012.

Isin, Engin F., and Greg M. Nielsen, eds. *Acts of Citizenship.* Zed Books, 2013.

Jakobsen, Janet R., and Ann Pellegrini. *Love the Sin: Sexual Regulation and the Limits of Religious Tolerance.* Beacon Press, 2004.

———, eds. *Secularisms.* Duke University Press, 2008.

"January Start Slated for Huge Project to Rebuild Ravaged Downtown Beirut." *Journal of Commerce Online,* October 20, 1993. https://www.joc.com/

maritime-news/january-start-slated-huge-project-rebuild-ravaged-downtown
-beirut_19931020.html.

Joseph, Suad. "Descent of the Nation: Kinship and Citizenship in Lebanon." *Citizenship Studies* 3, no. 3 (1999): 295–318.

———. *Gender and Citizenship in the Middle East.* Syracuse University Press, 2000.

———. "Gender and Citizenship in Middle Eastern States." *Middle East Report* 198 (1996): 4–10.

———. "The Public/Private—The Imagined Boundary in the Imagined Nation/State/Community: The Lebanese Case." *Feminist Review* 57, no. 1 (1997): 73–92.

Kafka, Ben. *The Demon of Writing: Powers and Failures of Paperwork.* MIT Press, 2020.

Kafka, Franz, *The Trial.* Xist, 2015.

Kahn, Jeffrey S. "Geographies of Discretion and the Jurisdictional Imagination." *PoLAR: Political and Legal Anthropology Review* 40, no. 1 (2017): 5–27.

Karame, Lama. "Court Trends in Rape Cases in Beirut and Mount Lebanon." *Legal Agenda*, January 16, 2021. https://english.legal-agenda.com/court-trends-in-rape-cases-in-beirut-and-mount-lebanon/.

———. "Lebanese Article 534 Struck Down: Homosexuality No Longer 'Contrary to Nature.'" *Legal Agenda*, July 11, 2016. https://english.legal-agenda.com/lebanese-article-534-struck-down-homosexuality-no-longer-contrary-to-nature/.

Kassamali, Sumayya. "Migrant Worker Lifeworlds of Beirut." PhD diss., Columbia University, 2017.

Kauanui, J. Kehaulani. *Hawaiian Blood: Colonialism and the Politics of Sovereignty and Indigeneity.* Duke University Press, 2008.

Keane, Webb. *Christian Moderns: Freedom and Fetish in the Mission Encounter.* University of California Press, 2007.

Kechichian, Joseph A. "Lebanon Contemplates a New Citizenship Law." *Gulf News*, 2015.

Khalaf, Samir. *Civil and Uncivil Violence in Lebanon: A History of the Internationalization of Communal Conflict.* Columbia University Press, 2002.

Khalidi, Rashid. *Under Siege.* Columbia University Press, 2014.

Khalili, Laleh. *Time in the Shadows: Confinement in Counterinsurgencies.* Stanford University Press, 2012.

Kholoussy, Hanan. *For Better, for Worse: The Marriage Crisis that Made Modern Egypt.* Stanford University Press, 2010.

Kobaissy, Farah. "Organizing the Unorganized: Migrant Domestic Workers Labor Union Organizing in Lebanon." Master's thesis, American University of Cairo, 2015.

Koselleck, Reinhart. *Futures Past: On the Semantics of Historical Time.* Columbia University Press, 2004.

Latour, Bruno. *The Making of Law: An Ethnography of the Conseil d'État*. Polity Press, 2010.

LBCI News. "Closure of a Gay Bar in Dekwaneh." YouTube, posted by "lbcgroup," April 23, 2013. http://www.youtube.com/watch?v=AVcTrkZ4W2Y.

———. "31-7-2012." YouTube, posted by "lbcgroup," July 31, 2012. http://www.youtube.com/watch?v=iOqMhTfutjY.

Leenders, Reinoud. *Spoils of Truce: Corruption and State-Building in Postwar Lebanon*. Cornell University Press, 2012.

Lowe, Lisa. "History Hesitant." *Social Text* 33, no. 4 (125) (2015): 85–107.

Maginn, Paul J., and Graham Ellison. "'Ulster Says No': Regulating the Consumption of Commercial Sex Spaces and Services in Northern Ireland." *Urban Studies* 54, no. 3 (2017): 806–21.

Mahmood, Saba. *Politics of Piety: The Islamic Revival and the Feminist Subject*. Princeton University Press, 2011.

———. *Religious Difference in a Secular Age: A Minority Report*. Princeton University Press, 2015.

———. "Religious Freedom, the Minority Question, and Geopolitics in the Middle East." *Comparative Studies in Society and History* 54, no. 2 (2012): 418–46.

———. "Secularism, Hermeneutics, and Empire: The Politics of Islamic Reformation." *Public Culture* 18, no. 2 (2006): 323–47.

Makdisi, Ussama. *Age of Coexistence: The Ecumenical Frame and the Making of the Modern Arab World*. University of California Press, 2019.

———. *Artillery of Heaven: American Missionaries and the Failed Conversion of the Middle East*. Cornell University Press, 2011.

———. *The Culture of Sectarianism: Community, History, and Violence in Nineteenth-Century Ottoman Lebanon*. University of California Press, 2000.

———. "Reclaiming the Land of the Bible: Missionaries, Secularism, and Evangelical Modernity." *American Historical Review* 102, no. 3 (1997): 680–713.

Maktabi, Rania. "The Lebanese Census of 1932 Revisited. Who Are the Lebanese?" *British Journal of Middle Eastern Studies* 26, no. 2 (1999): 219–41.

Mallat, Chibli. "The Lebanese Legal System." *Lebanon Report* 2 (1997): 29–45.

Mamdani, Mahmood. *Citizen and Subject: Contemporary Africa and the Legacy of Late Colonialism*. Princeton University Press, 2018.

Mansour, Maya, and Sarah Abou-Aad. "Women's Citizenship Rights in Lebanon." Working Paper Series #8, Research, Advocacy and Policy-making in the Arab World, American University of Beirut, Beirut, Lebanon, May 2012.

Mansour, Maya, Carlos Daoud, and Euro-Mediterranean Human Rights Network (EMHRN). "The Independence and Impartiality of the Judiciary-Lebanon." *Euro-Mediterranean Human Rights Network (EMHRN)* 70 (2009).

Markell, Patchen. *Bound by Recognition*. Princeton University Press, 2009.

Marx, Karl. *On the Jewish Question*. Routledge, 2014.

Mauss, Marcel. *The Gift: The Form and Reason for Exchange in Archaic Societies*. Routledge, 2002.

Mawani, Renisa. "Law's Archive." *Annual Review of Law and Social Science* 8 (2012): 337–65.

Mbembe, Achille. *Necropolitics*. Duke University Press, 2019.

———. "The Power of the Archive and its Limits." In *Refiguring the Archive*, edited by Carolyn Hamilton et al., 19–27. Springer, Dordrecht, 2002.

McAlister, Melani. *The Kingdom of God Has No Borders: A Global History of American Evangelicals*. Oxford University Press, 2018.

McClintock, Anne. *Imperial Leather: Race, Gender, and Sexuality in the Colonial Contest*. Routledge, 2013.

———. "Paranoid Empire: Specters from Guantánamo and Abu Ghraib." *Small Axe: A Caribbean Journal of Criticism* 13, no. 1 (2009): 50–74.

Merabet, Sofian. *Queer Beirut*. University of Texas Press, 2014.

Merry, Sally Engle. "From Law and Colonialism to Law and Globalization." *Law & Social Inquiry* 28, no. 2 (2003): 569–90.

———. "Legal Pluralism." *Law & Society Review* 22 (1988): 869.

Messick, Brinkley. *Shari'a Scripts: A Historical Anthropology*. Columbia University Press, 2018.

Mikdashi, Maya. "Gay Rights as Human Rights: "Pinkwashing Homonationalism." *Jadaliyya*, December 16, 2011. https://www.jadaliyya.com/Details/24855/Gay-Rights-as-Human-Rights-Pinkwashing-Homonationalism.

———. "Lebanon." In *Dispatches from the Arab Spring: Understanding the New Middle East*, edited by Paul Amar and Vijay Prashad, 266–81. University of Minnesota Press, 2013.

———. "Lebanon, August 2015: Notes on Paralysis, Protests, and Hope." *Jadaliyya*, August 26, 2015. http://www.jadaliyya.com/pages/index/22491/lebanon-august-2015 notes-on-paralysis-protests-an (2015).

———. "The Magic of Mutual Coexistence: The Taif Accord at Thirty." *Jadaliyya*, October 23, 2019. https://www.jadaliyya.com/Details/40134/The-Magic-of-Mutual-Coexistence-in-Lebanon-The-Taif-Accord-at-Thirty.

———. "Religious Conversion and Dawa Secularism: Two Practices of Citizenship in Lebanon." PhD diss., Columbia University, 2014.

———. "Sex and Sectarianism: The Legal Architecture of Lebanese Citizenship." *Comparative Studies of South Asia, Africa and the Middle East* 34, no. 2 (2014): 279–93.

———. "Sextarianism: A Way of Studying the Lebanese State." In *The Oxford Handbook of Contemporary Middle Eastern and North African History*, edited by Jens Hanssen and Amal N. Ghazal, 444–73. Oxford University Press, 2020.

Mikdashi, Maya, and Jasbir K. Puar. "Queer Theory and Permanent War." *GLQ: A Journal of Lesbian and Gay Studies* 22, no. 2 (2016): 215–22.

Million, Dian. "Felt Theory: An Indigenous Feminist Approach to Affect and History." *Wicazo Sa Review* 24, no. 2 (2009): 53–76.

Mitchell, Timothy. *Colonizing Egypt*. University of California Press, 1991.

———. "The Limits of the State: Beyond Statist Approaches and Their Critics." *American Political Science Review* 85, no. 1 (1991): 77–96.

———. "Society, Economy, and the State Effect." In *State/Culture: State-Formation after the Cultural Turn*, edited by George Steinmetz, 76–97. Cornell University Press, 2018.

Mitra, Durba. *Indian Sex Life: Sexuality and the Colonial Origins of Modern Social Thought*. Princeton University Press, 2020.

Moghnieh, Lamia. "'The Violence We Live In': Reading and Experiencing Violence in the Field." *Contemporary Levant* 2, no. 1 (2017): 24–36.

Mohanty, Chandra Talpade. *Feminism without Borders: Decolonizing Theory, Practicing Solidarity*. Duke University Press, 2003.

Moore, Sally Falk. "Law and Social Change: The Semi-Autonomous Social Field as an Appropriate Subject of Study." *Law & Society Review* 7 (1973): 719.

Mouawad, Jamil. *Unpacking Lebanon's Resilience: Undermining State Institutions and Consolidating the System?* Istituto Affari Internazionali (IAI), 2017.

Mouawad, Jamil, and Hannes Baumann. "WAYN AL-DAWLA?." *Arab Studies Journal* 25, no. 1 (2017): 66–91.

Mouawad, Nadine. "The Bigger Struggle for Women in Municipalities." *Sawt al Niswa*, 2018.

Moumneh, Rasha. "The Filth They Bring: Sex Panics and Racial Others in Lebanon." In *Beyond Virtue and Vice: Rethinking Human Rights and Criminal Law*, edited by Alice M. Miller and Mindy Jane Roseman, 220–32. University of Pennsylvania Press, 2019.

Moumtaz, Nada. *God's Property: Islam, Charity, and the Modern State*. University of California Press, 2020.

Mounzer, Lina. "Going Beyond the Veil; Against the Regime of 'Aib.'" *Baffler Magazine* no. 56, March 2021.

Moussawi, Ghassan. *Disruptive Situations: Fractal Orientalism and Queer Strategies in Beirut*. Temple University Press, 2020.

Najar, Hala. "Shatb al Maddhab." *Legal Agenda*, 2017.

Najm, Marie-Claude, Myriam Mehanna, and Lama Karamé, eds. "Lebanon." In *Filiation and the Protection of Parentless Children*, 165–203. TMC Asser Press, 2019.

Najmabadi, Afsaneh. *Professing Selves: Transsexuality and Same-Sex Desire in Contemporary Iran*. Duke University Press, 2013.

Nash, Jennifer C. "Re-thinking Intersectionality." *Feminist Review* 89, no. 1 (2008): 1–15.

Navaro-Yashin, Yael. *Faces of the State: Secularism and Public Life in Turkey*. Princeton University Press, 2020.

Nucho, Joanne Randa. *Everyday Sectarianism in Urban Lebanon: Infrastructures, Public Services, and Power*. Vol. 10. Princeton University Press, 2016.

Office of the Inspector General. *Audit of USAID/Lebanon's Rule of Law Program*. 2018. https://oig.usaid.gov/sites/default/files/2018-06/6-268-10-006-p.pdf.

Pande, Amrita. "'The Paper that You Have in Your Hand Is My Freedom': Migrant Domestic Work and the Sponsorship (kafala) System in Lebanon." *International Migration Review* 47, no. 2 (2013): 414–41.

Parla, Ayse. "The 'Honor' of the State: Virginity Examinations in Turkey." *Feminist Studies* 27, no. 1 (2001): 65–88.

Pateman, Carole. *The Disorder of Women: Democracy, Feminism, and Political Theory*. Stanford University Press, 1989.

———. *The Sexual Contract*. Polity Press, 1988.

Pateman, Carole, Charles Wade Mills, and Charles Wright Mills. *Contract and Domination*. Polity Press, 2007.

Peirce, Leslie. "Writing Histories of Sexuality in the Middle East." *American Historical Review* 114, no. 5 (2009): 1325–39.

Peteet, Julie. *Landscape of Hope and Despair*. University of Pennsylvania Press, 2011.

Picard, Elizabeth. *Lebanon, a Shattered Country: Myths and Realities of the Wars in Lebanon*. Holmes & Meier, 2002.

Povinelli, Elizabeth A. *The Cunning of Recognition: Indigenous Alterities and the Making of Australian Multiculturalism*. Duke University Press, 2002.

———. *Economies of Abandonment: Social Belonging and Endurance in Late Liberalism*. Duke University Press, 2011.

———. *Geontologies: A Requiem to Late Liberalism*. Duke University Press, 2016.

———. "Notes on Gridlock: Genealogy, Intimacy, Sexuality." *Public Culture* 14, no. 1 (2002): 215–38.

———. "The State of Shame: Australian Multiculturalism and the Crisis of Indigenous Citizenship." *Critical Inquiry* 24, no. 2 (1998): 575–610.

Pratt, Nicola. *Embodying Geopolitics: Generations of Women's Activism in Egypt, Jordan, and Lebanon*. University of California Press, 2020.

Puar, Jasbir. "Rethinking Homonationalism." *International Journal of Middle East Studies* 45, no. 2 (2013): 336–39.

———. *The Right to Maim*. Duke University Press, 2017.

———. *Terrorist Assemblages: Homonationalism in Queer Times*. Duke University Press, 2018.

Puri, Jyoti. *Sexual States: Governance and the Struggle over the Antisodomy Law in India*. Duke University Press, 2016.

Pursley, Sara. *Familiar Futures: Time, Selfhood, and Sovereignty in Iraq*. Stanford University Press, 2019.

qanūn ʾusūl al-muḥākamāt al- madaniyya, al-sāder bimūjab al-marsūm al-ʾishtirāʾī raqm 90/83 tārīkh 16/9/1983 wataʾdīlātihi.

qanūn al-ʾuqūbāt, al-sāder bimūjab al-marsūm al-ʾishtiraʾī raqm 340, tārīkh 1/3/1943 wataʾdīlātihi.

qanūn ʾusūl al-muḥākamāt al-jazāʾiyya, al-sāder bimūjab al-qanūn raqm 328, tārīkh 7/8/2001 wataʾdīlātihi.

qanūn al-qadāʾ al-ʾadlī waltanẓīm al-qadaʾī, al- sāder bimūjab al-marsūm al-ʾishtiraʾī raqm 150, tārīkh 16/9/1983 wataʾdīlātihi.

Qato, Mezna. "Forms of Retrieval: Social Scale, Citation, and the Archive on the Palestinian Left." *International Journal of Middle East Studies* 51, no. 2 (2019): 312–15.

Rahhāl, Wadīʾ. *al qawaʾid al ʾāmma lil al- aḥwāl al-shakhsīyya. al jiziʾ al thani, ahkām al zawāj al dīnī wa al madanī*. 1996.

Rajan, Kaushik Sunder. *Biocapital: The Constitution of Postgenomic Life*. Duke University Press, 2006.

Razack, Sherene. *Casting Out: The Eviction of Muslims from Western Law and Politics*. University of Toronto Press, 2008.

Rich, Adrienne. "Compulsory Heterosexuality and Lesbian Existence." *Signs: Journal of Women in Culture and Society* 5, no. 4 (1980): 631–60.

Rubin, Gayle S. "Postscript to 'Thinking Sex: Notes for a Radical Theory of the Politics of Sexuality.'" In *Deviations: A Gayle Rubin Reader*, 190–93. Duke University Press, 2011.

———. "Thinking Sex." In *Sexualities II: Some Elements for an Account of the Social Organisation of Sexualities*, 188–202. Routledge, 2002.

———. "The Traffic in Women: Notes on the 'Political Economy' of Sex." In *Toward an Anthropology of Women*, edited by Rayna R. Reiter, 157–210. Monthly Review Press, 2013.

Sāder fī al ahkām al jizāʾiyat. al jāraʾim al makhallat bil alkhlāq al ʾammat. Sader, 2003.

Sāder fī tamyīz, qarārāt al hayʾat al ʾ āmma, 1983–1992. Sader, 2000.

Sāder fī tamyīz, qarārāt al hayʾat al ʾ āmma, 1993. Sader, 2000.

Sāder fī tamyīz, qarārāt al hayʾat al ʾ āmma, 1994, 1995. Sader, 2005.

Sāder fī tamyīz, qarārāt al hayʾat al ʾ āmma, 1996, 1997, 1998. Sader, 2000.

Sāder fī tamyīz, qarārāt al hayʾat al ʾ āmma, 1999, 2000, 2001. Sader, 2002.

Sāder fī tamyīz, qarārāt al hayʾat al ʾ āmma, 2002, 2003, 2004. Sader, 2005.

Sāder fī tamyīz, qarārāt al hayʾat al ʾ āmma, 2005, 2006, 2007. Sader, 2010.

Sāder fī tamyīz, qarārāt al hayʾat al ʾ āmma, 2008, 2009, 2011. Sader, 2012.

Sāder fī tamyīz, qarārāt al hayʾat al ʾ āmma, 2011, 2012, 2013, Sader, 2015.

Safieddine, Hicham. *Banking on the State: The Financial Foundations of Lebanon*. Stanford University Press, 2019.

Saghieh, Nizar. "Lebanon's Law to Protect Women: Redefining Domestic Violence." *Legal Agenda*, December 23, 2013. https://english.legal-agenda.com/lebanons-law-to-protect-women-redefining-domestic-violence/.

_____. "A Principled Decision in the Case of Manal Assi: The Demise of the Macho?" *Legal Agenda*, January 1, 2018. https://english.legal-agenda .com/a-principled-decision-in-the-case-of-manal-assi-the-demise-of-the -macho/.

———. "To Remember: When the President of State Shura Council Contradicted His Own Decision 100%." *Legal Agenda*, 2012.

———. "Torture in Roumieh Prisons: How the State Deals with its Scandals." *Legal Agenda*, September 7, 2015. https://english.legal-agenda.com/torture-in -roumieh-how-the-state-deals-with-its-scandals-ii/.

Salem, Mona, and Zeina Shaaban. "Queers in Quarantine: Between Pandem-ics and Social Violence in Lebanon." FES Lebanon, 2020. https://lebanon .fes.de/fileadmin/user_upload/documents/covid-19/Queers_in_Quarantine_ __Between_Pandemics_and_Social_Violence_in_Lebanon.pdf

Salibi, Kamal. *A House of Many Mansions: The History of Lebanon Reconsid-ered*. University of California Press, 1990.

Salime, Zakia. *Between Feminism and Islam: Human Rights and Sharia Law in Morocco*. University of Minnesota Press, 2011.

Salloukh, Bassel, and Rabie Barakat. *The Politics of Sectarianism in Postwar Leb-anon*. Pluto Press, 2015.

Sandoval, Chela. *Methodology of the Oppressed*. Vol. 18. University of Minne-sota Press, 2013.

Sawalha, Aseel. *Reconstructing Beirut: Memory and Space in a Postwar Arab City*. University of Texas Press, 2010.

Sayigh, Rosemary. *Too Many Enemies: The Palestinian Experience in Lebanon*. Al Mashriq, 2015.

Sayigh, Rosemary, and Julie Peteet. "Between Two Fires: Palestinian Women in Lebanon." In *Caught Up in Conflict: Women's Responses to Political Strife*, by Rosemary Ridd and Helen Callaway, 106–37. Palgrave, Macmillan, 1986.

Scarry, Elaine. *The Body in Pain: The Making and Unmaking of the World*. Ox-ford University Press, 1987.

Schmitt, Carl. *Political Theology: Four Chapters on the Concept of Sovereignty*. University of Chicago Press, 2005.

Schuller, Kyla. *The Biopolitics of Feeling: Race, Sex, and Science in the Nine-teenth Century*. Duke University Press, 2018.

Schuller, Kyla, and Jules Gill-Peterson. "Introduction: Race, the State, and the Malleable Body." *Social Text* 38, no. 2 (143) (2020): 1–17.

Scott, James C. *Seeing Like a State*. Yale University Press, 2008.

Scott, Joan W. *Sex and Secularism*. Princeton University Press, 2017.

———. "Sexularism. On Secularism and Gender Equality." In *The Fantasy of Feminist History*, 91–116. Duke University Press, 2011.

Sehlikoglu, Sertaç, and Aslı Zengin. "Introduction: Why Revisit Intimacy?" *Cam-bridge Journal of Anthropology* 33, no. 2 (2015): 20–25.

Seikaly, Sherene. "How I Met My Great-Grandfather: Archives and the Writing of History." *Comparative Studies of South Asia, Africa and the Middle East* 38, no. 1 (2018): 6–20.

———. "The Matter of Time." *American Historical Review* 124, no. 5 (2019): 1681.

———. "The Meaning of Revolution: On Samira Ibrahim." *Jadaliyya*, January 28, 2013. https://www.jadaliyya.com/Details/27915/The-Meaning-of-Revolution-On-Samira-Ibrahim.

———. *Men of Capital: Scarcity and Economy in Mandate Palestine.* Stanford University Press, 2015.

Sertaç Sehlikoglu, and Frank G. Karioris, eds. *The Everyday Makings of Heteronormativity: Cross-Cultural Explorations of Sex, Gender, and Sexuality.* Lexington, 2019.

Shakhsari, Sima. "Killing Me Softly with Your Rights." In *Queer Necropolitics*, edited by Jin Haritaworn, Adi Kuntsman, and Silvia Posocco, 93. Routledge, 2014.

———. *Politics of Rightful Killing: Civil Society, Gender, and Sexuality in Weblogistan.* Duke University Press, 2020.

———. "The Queer Time of Death: Temporality, Geopolitics, and Refugee Rights." *Sexualities* 17, no. 8 (2014): 998–1015.

Sharkey, Heather J. *American Evangelicals in Egypt: Missionary Encounters in an Age of Empire.* Princeton University Press, 2013.

Sharma, Aradhana, and Akhil Gupta, eds. *The Anthropology of the State: A Reader.* John Wiley & Sons, 2009.

Shehadeh, Lamia Rustum. "Gender-Relevant Legal Change in Lebanon." *Feminist Formations* 22, no. 3 (2010): 210–28.

———. "The Legal Status of Married Women in Lebanon." *International Journal of Middle East Studies* 30, no. 4 (1998): 501–19.

Shepard, Todd. "'Of Sovereignty': Disputed Archives, 'Wholly Modern' Archives, and the Post-decolonization French and Algerian Republics, 1962–2012." *American Historical Review* 120, no. 3 (2015): 869–83.

Simpson, Audra. *Mohawk Interruptus: Political Life across the Borders of Settler States.* Duke University Press, 2014.

Sinno, W. "How People Reclaimed Public Spaces in Beirut during the 2019 Lebanese Uprising." *Journal of Public Space* 5, no. 1 (2020): 193–218.

Sleiman, Hana. "The Paper Trail of a Liberation Movement." *Arab Studies Journal* 24, no. 1 (2016): 42–67.

Snorton, C. Riley. *Black on Both Sides: A Racial History of Trans Identity.* University of Minnesota Press, 2017.

Spillers, Hortense J. "Mama's Baby, Papa's Maybe: An American Grammar Book." *Diacritics* 17, no. 2 (1987): 65–81.

Spivak, Gayatri Chakravorty. "Can the Subaltern Speak?" In *Can the Subaltern Speak? Reflections on the History of an Idea*, edited by Rosalind Morris, 21–78. Columbia University Press, 2010.

Steedman, Carolyn. *Dust: The Archive and Cultural History*. Rutgers University Press, 2002.

Stevens, Jacqueline. *Reproducing the State*. Princeton University Press, 1999.

Stoler, Ann Laura. *Along the Archival Grain: Epistemic Anxieties and Colonial Common Sense*. Princeton University Press, 2010.

———. "Colonial Archives and the Arts of Governance." *Archival Science* 2, no. 1–2 (2002): 87–109.

———. *Duress: Imperial Durabilities in Our Times*. Duke University Press, 2016.

———, ed. *Imperial Debris: On Ruins and Ruination*. Duke University Press, 2013.

———. *Race and the Education of Desire: Foucault's History of Sexuality and the Colonial Order of Things*. Duke University Press, 1995.

Stone, Alison. "Sexual Difference." In *The Oxford Handbook of Feminist Theory*, edited by Lisa Disch and Mary Hawkesworth, 874–93. Oxford University Press, 2016.

Surkis, Judith. "Hymenal Politics: Marriage, Secularism, and French Sovereignty." *Public Culture* 22, no. 3 (2010): 531–56.

———. *Sexing the Citizen*. Cornell University Press, 2018.

———. *Sex, Law, and Sovereignty in French Algeria, 1830–1930*. Cornell University Press, 2019.

Tabbāra, Wael. *muṭalaʿāt al niyāba al ʿamma al īstiʾnāfiyya ladā al mahkama al sharʿīyyat al sinyyat al ʿlyā*. Zein Legal, 2008.

Talhouk, Joumana. "Parliamentary Elections, Civil Society, and Barriers to Political Change." *Kohl Journal* 4, no. 1 (2018): 24–29.

Tambar, Kabir. *The Reckoning of Pluralism: Political Belonging and the Demands of History in Turkey*. Stanford University Press, 2014.

Taylor, Charles. *A Secular Age*. Harvard University Press, 2009.

Thompson, Elizabeth. *Colonial Citizens: Republican Rights, Paternal Privilege, and Gender in French Syria and Lebanon*. Columbia University Press, 2000.

———. "Public and Private in Middle Eastern Women's History." *Journal of Women's History* 15, no. 1 (2003): 52–69.

Traboulsi, Fawwaz. *A History of Modern Lebanon*. Pluto Press, 2012.

Traboulsi, Ibrahim. *al ʿanzima al ahwāl al shakhsīyya fī lubnān*. Sader, 2011.

———. *al zawāj wa mafāʿīlihi ladā al tawāʾif al mashmūla fī qanūn 6 nisān 1951*. Sader, 2000.

Trouillot, Michel-Rolph. *Silencing the Past: Power and the Production of History*. Beacon Press, 1995.

Trouillot, Michel-Rolph, Chris Hann, and Lszl Krti. "The Anthropology of the State in the Age of Globalization: Close Encounters of the Deceptive Kind." *Current Anthropology* 42, no. 1 (2001): 125–38.

Tsing, Anna Lowenhaupt. *Friction: An Ethnography of Global Connection*. Princeton University Press, 2011.

Tucker, Judith E. *In the House of the Law: Gender and Islamic Law in Ottoman Syria and Palestine*. University of California Press, 1998.

United Press International. "Rocket Strikes Beirut Justice Palace, Destroys Files." *Los Angeles Times*, 1985.

Van der Veer, Peter, ed. *Conversion to Modernities: The Globalization of Christianity*. Routledge, 1996.

Viswanathan, Gauri. *Outside the Fold: Conversion, Modernity, and Belief*. Princeton University Press, 1998.

———. "Religious Conversion and the Politics of Dissent." In *Conversion to Modernities: The Globalization of Christianity*, edited by Peter Van Der Veer, 89–114. Routledge, 1996.

Vokes, Richard. "Rethinking the Anthropology of Religious Change: New Perspectives on Revitalization and Conversion Movements." *Reviews in Anthropology* 36, no. 4 (2007): 311–33.

Volpp, Leti. "The Citizen and the Terrorist." In *September 11 in History: A Watershed Moment?*, edited by Mary L. Dudziak, 147–62. Duke University Press, 2003.

Wansa, Sara, "Lebanon's Republic of Shame: Law and Medicine as Means to Humiliate and Frighten." *Legal Agenda*, July 29, 2014. https://english.legal-agenda.com/lebanons-republic-of-shame-law-and-medicine-as-means-to-humiliate-and-frighten/.

Weber, Max, and Stanislav Andreski. *Max Weber on Capitalism, Bureaucracy, and Religion: A Selection of Texts*. Allen & Unwin, 1983.

Wedeen, Lisa. *Ambiguities of Domination: Politics, Rhetoric, and Symbols in Contemporary Syria*. University of Chicago Press, 2015.

———. *Peripheral Visions: Publics, Power, and Performance in Yemen*. University of Chicago Press, 2009.

Weheliye, Alexander G. *Habeas Viscus: Racializing Assemblages, Biopolitics, and Black Feminist Theories of the Human*. Duke University Press, 2014.

Weiss, Max. *In the Shadow of Sectarianism: Law, Shiism, and the Making of Modern Lebanon*. Harvard University Press, 2010.

Weld, Kirsten. *Paper Cadavers: The Archives of Dictatorship in Guatemala*. Duke University Press, 2014.

White, Benjamin Thomas. *Emergence of Minorities in the Middle East*. Edinburgh University Press, 2012.

White, Hayden. *The Content of the Form: Narrative Discourse and Historical Representation*. JHU Press, 1990.

Wittgenstein, Ludwig. *The Blue and Brown Books*. Vol. 958. Blackwell, 1969.

Wynter, Sylvia. "Unsettling the Coloniality of Being/Power/Truth/Freedom: Towards the Human, after Man, Its Overrepresentation—An Argument." *CR: The New Centennial Review* 3, no. 3 (2003): 257–337.

Zacka, Bernardo. *When the State Meets the Street*. Harvard University Press, 2017.

Zalzal, Marie-Rose. "Mixed Marriage in the Lebanese Law." *Al-Raida Journal* 23, nos. 111–112 (2005): 35–43.

———. "Protection of Women from Domestic Violence Under 'The Bill for the Protection of Women and Family Members Against Domestic Violence.'" *Al-Raida Journal* 1 (2014): 59–73.

———. "Secularism and Personal Status Codes in Lebanon: Interview with Marie Rose Zalzal, Esquire." *Middle East Report* no. 203 (1997): 37–39.

Zengin, Aslı. "The Afterlife of Gender: Sovereignty, Intimacy and Muslim Funerals of Transgender People in Turkey." *Cultural Anthropology* 34, no. 1 (2019): 78–102.

———. "Violent Intimacies: Tactile State Power, Sex/Gender Transgression, and the Politics of Touch in Contemporary Turkey." *Journal of Middle East Women's Studies* 12, no. 2 (2016): 225–45.

Index

Page numbers in *italics* indicate illustrations.

abortion law, 42
About Baghdad (film, 2003), vii
Abu-Lughod, Lila, 57, 205n5
activists and activism, 3, 11, 17,
    122–27
adultery, as crime, 43
Agrama, Hussein Ali, 16
Ahmad, Attiya, 84, 87, 215n6
Akar, Hiba Bou, 77
Alawites, 101
Alexander, M. Jacqui, 4
Amal (militia), 62, 145
Amar, Paul, 44, 222n68
anal/hymen exams, 23, 153–82;
    custody cases, hymen exams
    in, 224n30; in Egypt, 224n28,
    228n88; epidermal state and,
    23, 154–55, 171, 173, 180–82;
    evidentiary value, lack of, 169–71,
    177; Hana/Ramzi case, 161–69,
    176, 178, 179, 180, 226n55; HIV
    testing coupled with, 156; hymen
    reconstruction, 170; migrant
    laborers and, 23, 156, 157, 158,
    224n30; purposes and conduct
    of, 154; rape, allegations of, 160,
    177, 225n39, 227n76; refugees
    and, 23, 156, 157, 158; sexual dif-
    ference and, 159–61, 170, 177–78,
    228n77; social/political context
    and campaigns against, 155–61;
sovereignty of state and, 178–80;
    state power, violent exercise of,
    153–55, 177–78, 227n61; torture,
    as form of, 156, 157, 159, 172,
    175, 176, 181, 227n63, 228n77;
    "unnatural" sexual acts, as test
    for, 155–58, 171, 177; visual
    versus physically invasive, 170–71,
    173, 226n58; Yasmine, Basel, and
    Rula, interrogations of, 171–77,
    178–79, 180, 227n62
annulment, 88–90, 91, 94, 165,
    225n37, 225n44
anonymizing, banal, and reiterative
    nature of bureaucracy, 103–4,
    113, 114
Anti-Racism Movement (ARM),
    208n70
Aoun, Michel, 121–22, 206n44
archival research, 21, 22, 52, 58, 80,
    204n72
archives at Court of Cassation, 22,
    48–82; access to court trials and
    decisions, 226n56; description of,
    54–61, 60, 184, 185–87, 186, 188,
    189; digitization and moderniza-
    tion at, 70–72, 183–87, 213n53;
    ethnographic and archival re-
    search, approach to, 52–53; fire
    (1985), 22, 61–68, 72–73, 185–
    87, 189, 212n35; Samir Geagea

archives at Court (*continued*)
case, 53–54, 77–82; interlocutors
of author at, 48–53, 210n6; Lebanese Civil War and, 55, 56–57,
61–68, 72–75; life world of, 54–
58, 67–68, 80–82, 211n16; staff
and administration, 68–70, 210n6,
210n9; uprising of 2019 and,
183–87. *See also* Samera case
Armenian Orthodox, 24
Arondekar, Anjali, 19, 57, 67, 77
artist visas, 35, 207n48, 209n71
Asad, Talal, 16, 86, 144, 219n9
Assi, Manal, 207n57
atheists and atheism, 101, 105, 110–
11, 132, 137, 139, 221n56
Atlas Group, 56, 57
Azzi, John, *A Trip of a Lifetime to
Nationality*, 207n47

banality: bureaucracy, anonymizing,
banal, and reiterative nature of,
103–4, 113, 114; of religion as
category of secular governmentality, 17; of religious conversion, in
Lebanese context, xiii, 55, 87–88,
113–16
Barbir Bridge checkpoint, 64
Basel (Syrian detainee), 171–72, 174
Bashir, Emir, 101
Bass;amıl, Gibr;aman, 36, 207n54
Beirut Port, explosion at (2020), xi,
212n38
Berri, Nabih, 62, 145–46
biopolitical power: census as technology of, 5, 18, 114; citizenship
and, 27, 32, 115; defined, 33–34;
religion and, 16, 115; secularism and, 115, 129; sex and sect,
as biopolitical categories, 27–29,
36, 101, 137, 151, 154, 160, 179,
180; sexual difference and, 154,
179, 198n7

Braidotti, Rosie, 223n10
bureaucracy: anonymizing, banal, and
reiterative nature of, 103–4, 113,
114; of public order, 102–5

Catholics, 14, 72, 84, 88–95, 91, 99,
100, 126, 134, 142
census: patriarchal system perpetuated
by, 30–32; personal status laws
and census registries, 29–32; public order bureaucracy and, 102–5;
religious conversion, registration
of/failure to register, 84, 85, 88–
92, 99, 107; Samera case and manipulation of, 5–6, 12–13, 15, 17,
18, 19; sextarianism/state power
in Lebanon and, 5–6, 12
Chahrour, Hussein, 227n60
Chaldean Christians, 100
Chaml organization, 128
Christians in Lebanon: Chaldeans,
100; Melkites, 88, 89, 91, 134;
Muslim and Christian personal
status courts compared, 39; protestantism, evangelical, 126; religious conversion to Christianity
versus Islam, 83–116, 214n222;
sectarian balance, anxieties over,
146–48, 150; Syriac Orthodox,
95. *See also* Catholics; Greek
Orthodox; Maronite Christians
citizenship: acts of, 73, 213n58; as
assemblage, 32–34; census regime
and, 26, 32; evangelical secularism and, 131–34, 144; as kinship
regime, 26; noncitizen-to-citizen
ratio in Lebanon, 33, 205n12; personal status laws and, 26–27, 30,
32–38; Plenary Assembly and, 13,
60; sectarian balance and anxiety
over naturalization of refugees,
35–37; as sincere, 112, 133, 144;
stateless persons born in Lebanon,

207n50; women's inability to pass on, 30, 34–38, 111, 120, 146

civil marriage law and/or secular personal status law, optional, campaign for, 39–40, 120, 124–25, 127, 128–34, 139, 146, 151

civil marriage law proposals, compulsory, 40, 120–21, 124, 129

civil personal status law and court system, 25–26, 39–40, 95–96, 124–25, 205n6, 208n62

civil unrest in Lebanon: cycles of crisis in, vii–xii; evangelical secularism and concerns about political sectarianism, 129–34, 137–39; "mini" civil war (2008), xi, 20, 131, 222n71; national fears of prospects of, 55, 70, 131. *See also* Lebanese Civil War

class. *See* socioeconomic class

coexistence, 41, 46, 55, 61, 63, 88, 129, 158

coherence, 19, 56, 68, 114, 116, 133, 153, 154, 178–80, 204n2

colonialism: afterlife of, in postcolonial bureaucracy and politics, 102; French Mandate, vii, 1, 4, 5, 9, 18, 27, 40, 129, 155, 200n44, 216n25; nested/settler sovereignty and, 8–9, 200–201n44; Ottoman empire, vii, 1, 4, 7, 9, 87; personal status laws in Lebanon and, 27; religious conversion, legal procedures for, 216n25; sectarianism across imperial, colonial, and postcolonial eras, 4–6, 9

Columbia University, NYC, 48, 50, 81

Constitution of Lebanon, 34, 36, 94, 95, 97, 98, 138, 146, 167, 191, 206n44, 207n50, 212n44

contingency, viii, xii, 18–20, 22, 66

conversion, religious. *See* religious conversion

corruption in "failed" states, 70, 210n6

courts: *adliyya* courts, 202n62; administrative courts, 208n59; Cassation Courts, 13, 22, 54, 58–59, 96–97, 159, 187, 201n44, 202–3n62, 207n57, 224n29; civil courts, 13, 20, 25–26, 35, 40, 53, 59–60, 72, 92–94, 157, 160, 180, 198, 199n12, 205n6, 207n48, 208n62, 220n32; criminal courts, 23, 54, 157, 158, 207n57, 224n30, 225n39; Druze courts, 207n59, 214n2, 224n29; foreign marriage/family/civil courts, 93, 226n53; Greek Orthodox courts, 1, 13–15; Judicial Council, 53, 54, 58, 60, 61, 77, 79, 80, 208n59; judicial courts, 13, 208n59; Maronite courts, 94–97; misdemeanor courts, 157; personal status courts, 13, 18, 25–26, 35, 40, 41, 53, 54, 72, 90, 92–94, 95, 98, 102–3, 105, 107, 113–14, 124, 129, 135, 137, 139, 155, 159, 161, 163–70, 180, 198, 199n12, 202n62, 203n64, 204n74, 207n48, 221n56, 224–25n37, 225n43, 226n54, 226n56; religious courts, 13, 25, 93, 95, 97, 109, 120, 129, 139, 160, 161, 165, 202n62, 203n64, 205n6, 217n56; Roman Catholic courts, 14, 72, 88–94, 91; sharia courts, 91, 166, 207–8n59, 215n14, 219n12, 224n29, 226n56; Shi'i (Ja'fari) courts, 93, 101, 106, 107, 200n44, 207n59, 215n18; Sunni courts, 85, 89–92, 91, 101, 137, 200n44, 207n59, 224n29, 225–26n53; Syriac Orthodox court, 95, 97. *See also* Plenary Assembly, Court of Cassation

COVID-19, x, xi
criminal law: domestic violence and,
    42; personal status laws and, 38,
    41–45; prostitution, 43–44; sexual
    difference in, 43–44; "unnatural"
    sexual acts, 43, 155–58, 171, 177,
    225n38
crisis as recursive temporality, vii–xiii,
    197n7
culture of sectarianism, 17, 138, 149
The Culture of Sectarianism
    (Makdisi), 221n61
culture of secularism, 3, 17, 120, 123,
    124, 126, 128, 143, 144, 149
custody issues, 40, 51, 67, 88–89, 92,
    109, 120, 124, 167, 168, 187,
    190, 205n6, 208n63, 224n30,
    226n53

dabke, 120
Dar al-Fatwa, 83–85, 88–89, 91, 108–9
da'wa secularism. See evangelical
    secularism
Decree 60 LR, 27, 40, 124, 129,
    200n44, 216n25, 219n12
Deeb, Lara, 150, 222n83
deferral, politics of, 151–52
Deleuze, Gilles, 210n10
demography, 5, 10, 21, 27, 30, 34–37,
    46, 114, 146, 149, 199n14
Derengil, Selim, 86–87
digitization, 58, 70–72, 183–87,
    212n51, 213n53
Dignity Debased (Human Rights
    Watch report and video), 157,
    226–27nn59–60
diversity, 27, 30, 34, 41, 59, 61, 68,
    117, 147, 155
divorce: adultery as grounds for, 43;
    hymen exams and, 23, 161–69,
    176, 178, 179, 180, 224; Mona
    the archivist on, 51, 92; personal
    status laws/census registries and,

25, 29, 31, 39–41, 43, 93–94; reli-
    gious conversion and, 15, 83, 86,
    88–95, 91, 101, 103, 105–6, 108–
    11; in Samera case, 2, 5, 18, 19;
    sexual difference and reasons for,
    225n46. See also custody issues
domestic migrant laborers, 33, 35,
    42, 44–45, 176, 177, 208n70,
    209n79, 224n30
domestic violence, 42, 106, 108, 162–
    69, 226n55
Druze, 93, 101, 207n59, 208n62,
    214n2, 215n13, 219n12, 220n32

Egypt, hymen exams in, 224n28,
    228n88
El-Haj, Nadia Abu, 104n72
eminent domain, seizure of downtown
    Beirut by, 48–50, 78
epidermal state, 3, 19–21, 23, 154–55,
    171, 173, 180–82
epistemology, xiii, 7, 12, 19, 21, 29,
    56, 67, 71, 74, 160, 204n72,
    212n51
equality/inequality: anal/hymen
    exams and, 158, 167; archive
    ethnology and, 53, 55, 61, 81,
    214n76; evangelical secularism
    and, 120–22, 124, 129, 147, 152;
    personal status laws and, 27, 29,
    34, 36–37; religious conversion
    and, 88, 92, 99, 103–5, 113–15;
    sextarianism/state power and, ix,
    6, 8, 10, 11, 14, 16, 196, 199n12,
    201n49, 203n64; between Syria
    and Lebanon, 218n3
ethnography of archives. See archives
    at Court of Cassation
evangelical Protestantism, 126
evangelical secularism, 3, 23, 117–52;
    anti-/non-sectarianism and, 123–
    24, 143; citizenship and, 131–34,
    144; compulsory civil marriage

law proposals, 40, 120–21, 124, 129; culture and political associations of, 120, 124–25, 143–44, 149–50, 221n61; deferral, politics of, 151–52; defined and described, 16–17, 126–28; development of secular activism in Lebanon and, 122–26; epidermal state and, 21; feminism/women's rights and, 120, 124–25, 129, 146–49; inheritance law and, 129, 149; Kafa draft proposal, 120–22, 124, 129; Laique Pride march (2010–2013), 17, 23, 117–20, *118*, *121*, 122, 126–28, 142–50, 152, 222n70, 222n75; LGBTQ community and, 120, 127, 142–43, 147, 148–50; march for secularism (2019), *119*, 120; optional civil marriage law and/or secular personal status law, campaign for, 39–40, 120, 124–25, 127, 128–34, 139, 146, 151; political sectarianism and, 129–34, 137–39, 143, 145–48; problems faced by sectless individuals, 130–42; religious activism, drawing on practices and models of, 126–27; removal of religious and sectarian personal status from records, 110–12, 127, 132–37; sexual difference and, 128; state secularism versus, 16–18; uprising of 2019 in Lebanon and, *119*, 120–22, 137, 146, 147, 218n1, 220n39, 221–22n68

Evelyn (head archivist at Plenary Court), 52, 58, 59, 68, 71, 183–85

Facebook, 142
Fadlallah, Ayatollah Mohammed Hussein, 215n18
"failed" states, 20, 70
family law, 9, 26, 139, 216n25
Fath Al Islam, 76

Feldman, Ilana, 103, 213n53
feminism and women's rights: binaries, moving beyond, 200n31; census regime perpetuating patriarchal norms, 30–32; citizenship/personal status, women's inability to pass on, 30, 34–38, 111, 120, 146; criminal law and, 38, 42; domestic violence and, 42, 106, 108, 162–69, 226n55; evangelical secularism and, 120, 124–25, 129, 146–49; on intersection of sexual and sectarian difference, 28; Lebanese uprising (2019) and, 29; liberal political theory, revisions of, 6, 7; under National Social Security Fund law, 38; on private/public distinction, 6, 7; relationship to other research, knowledge production, and theory, xiii; rethinking of political theory and practice by, 46; sexual difference in personal status law and, 38–41; state power, theories of, 153–54; uprising of 2019 and, 155; vulnerable population, feminists as, 155. *See also* anal/hymen exams; sexual difference
Fernando, Mayanthi, 115
financial collapse in Lebanon (2019–2022), xi, 35, 69
fire at Plenary Assembly archive. *See* archive of Plenary Assembly, Court of Cassation
Forensic Medicine Society of Lebanon, 170
forum shopping, 204n2
Foucault, Michel, 213n68
freedom of religion, 16, 41, 94, 95, 97, 99, 100, 105, 123, 129, 134–36, 139
French Mandate, vii, 1, 4, 5, 9, 18, 27, 40, 129, 155, 200n44, 216n25
Fuentes, Marisa, 57

gays/gay rights. *See* LGBTQ community and queer theory in sextarian
state
Samir Geagea case, 53–54, 77–82,
214n74
gender versus sex, 10–11
General Security, 35, 206n34, 209n79,
225n50
Ghamroun, Samer, 199n18
Glissant, Édouard, 203n66, 218n65
global whiteness, 43, 125, 222n83
Gordon, Avery, 125
governmentality, 17, 33, 87, 104, 110,
112–14, 125
Greek Orthodox, 1, 4, 5, 7, 12–14, 18,
39, 41, 95, 101, 107, 109, 111,
126, 128, 203n63
green line, 20, 48, 64, 65, 78, 106
Griffiths, John, 199n18
Guattari, Félix, 210n10

Haddad, Gregoire, 134–35, 221n51
Hage, Ghassan, 197n1
Hana/Ramzi hymen exam case, 161–
69, 176, 178, 179, 180, 226n55
al Hariri, Rafik, 48, 69, 122, 128, 131,
198n2, 218n3
al Hariri, Saad, 79
harm reduction, 102, 217n42
Hartman, Saidiya, 57
hawiyya (the national identification
card), 216–17n36
heteropatriarchal family, 6, 9, 20, 25,
29, 30, 38, 44–45, 125, 127
heterosexuality/homosexuality and
straight/queer, as regulatory categories, 9, 11, 16, 17, 160, 201n52
hirak (2011), 122
Hirschkind, Charles, 126
HIV testing coupled with anal/hymen
exams, 156
Hizballah, 130, 140, 143, 172,
220n37, 222n71, 227n62

homophobia, 149–50, 154, 174–75,
178, 180, 222n75
homosexuality. *See* LGBTQ community and queer theory in sextarian
state
"honor" crimes, 42, 207n57
al Hrawi, Elias, 128
Human Rights Watch, 157, 170, 226–
27n59, 228n78
Husayn (religious convert), 105,
110–13
hymen exams. *See* anal/hymen exams
hymen reconstruction, 170

Ibrahim, Samira, 224n28
ikhrāj al-qayd (census document),
216–17n36
"illegitimate" children, 1, 2, 32,
199n12, 206n34
inequality. *See* equality/inequality
inheritance law: evangelical secularism and, 129, 149; personal status
and, 39, 41, 204n1, 208n64;
religious conversion and, 24, 41,
54–55, 83, 85, 86, 99–100, 129;
"selling" property to preferred
heirs during lifetime, 210–11n15;
Tripoli *waqf* religious conversion
case, 99–100
Internal Security Forces (ISF), 141,
155, 173
intersectionality: LGBTQ community
and, 224n27; of sectarian and
sexual difference (*See* sextarianism and state power in Lebanon);
state efforts to disambiguate,
125
intolerance. *See* tolerance/intolerance
Iraq/Iraqis, vii–ix, ix, 33, 57, 75, 77,
148, 205n12, 212n49, 224n27
ISF (Internal Security Forces), 141,
155, 173
ISIS/ISIL, xi, 76

Islam: Christians and Muslim personal status courts compared, 39; religious conversion to Christianity versus Islam, 83–116, 214n222; sectarian balance, Christian anxieties over, 146–48, 150; sharia courts, 207–8n59, 236n56; Shiʿi, 54, 86, 93, 101, 109, 136, 208n63, 222n74; *waqf* (Islamic charitable trust), 99–100. *See also* Sunni Islam

Islamophobia, 150, 222n75

Israel: evangelical secularism and, 131–33; Samir Geagea and, 77, 78; "Grapes of Wrath" campaign (1996), x, 76; legal system compared to Lebanon, 26, 203n65; occupation of parts of Lebanon by, x–xi, 20, 53, 72, 76, 130; Palestinians and, ix, 57, 72 (*See also* Palestinians); removal of PLO archives to Tel Aviv, 57

Israel-Lebanon War (2006), xi, 67, 76, 131, 222n71

Issam (evangelical secularist), 132–34

Jean (Laique Pride leader), 142, 143, 144, 148

Jean (son of Samera), 1–2, 4–5, 12–15, 18–20, 22

Jews and Judaism, 95, 100, 105, 149, 201n44

Joseph, Suad, 44, 100

Judicial Council, 53, 54, 58, 60, 61, 77, 79, 80, 208n59

judiciary. *See* courts

Kafa (NGO), 120–22, 124, 129

Kafala system of labor, 42–43, 44–45, 176, 177

Kawas, Sami, 226–27n59

Keane, Webb, 86

Khaled (evangelical secularist), 117, 139–41

Khalidi, Rashid, 214n75

Kholoussy, Hana, 225n52

kinship, 5, 9, 10, 19, 25–30, 32, 38, 39, 45, 93, 98, 127, 136–37, 212n37, 217n36

knowledge production, xiii, 19, 52, 53, 56, 58, 71, 82, 114, 229n1

Kurds, vii, ix, 29, 77, 205n12

Laique Pride march (2010–2013), 17, 23, 117–20, *118*, 121, 122, 126–28, 142–50, 152, 222n70, 222n75

Lebanese Bar Association, 1951 strike by, 95, 128

Lebanese Civil War (1975–90), 211n31; adjudication during, 72–75; archives at Court of Cassation and, 55, 56–57, 61–68, 72–75; author's experience of, x–xi; Barbir Bridge checkpoint, 64; downtown Beirut, postwar development of, 48; Samir Geagea case, 53–54, 77–82; personal status laws and, 27; pluralized wars of, 75–76; secularism, articulation of, 18; Syria and, 203n63, 218n3; Taif peace accord, 74, 76–77, 145, 212n44, 218n3

Lebanese Order of Physicians, 157

Lebanon, state power in. *See* sectarianism and state power in Lebanon; state power

Leila (evangelical secularist), 131–33

LGBTQ community and queer theory in sextarian state, 11; census regime and transgender individuals, 32; criminalization of "unnatural" sexual acts, 43, 155–58, 171, 177, 225n38; evangelical secularism and Laique Pride, 120, 127, 142–43, 147, 148–50, 222n70;

LGBTQ community (*continued*)
heterosexuality/homosexuality
and straight/queer, as regulatory
categories, 9, 11, 16, 17, 160,
201n52; homophobia, 149–50,
154, 174–75, 178, 180, 222n75;
intesectionality as key to understanding, 224n27; rethinking of
political theory and practice by,
46; trans individuals, 32, 155,
157, 158, 227n75; uprising of
2019 and, 155; as vulnerable
population, 155; Yasmine, Basel,
and Rula, interrogations of, 171–
77. *See also* anal/hymen exams
liberalism: evangelical secularism and,
124–28, 138, 144–46, 149, 151–
52; neoliberalism, 69, 81, 152,
211n30; personal status laws and,
26; religious conversion and, 87,
98, 99, 102, 104–5, 110, 112, 115;
sextarianism and, 3, 6–9, 17
"lines of flight," 53, 210n10

maddhab, 100
Mahmood, Saba, 26
Makdisi, Ussama, *The Culture of
Secularism*, 221n61
management/managerial state: archival files and, 71; evangelical secularism and, 123, 125, 139; Lebanese legal system and, 199n18;
personal status laws and, 25, 26,
28, 37, 41; public order and, 158;
religious conversion and, 87, 99,
102–4, 113, 115; sextarianism
and, xii–xiii, 3–5, 11, 16–18
Maronite Christians, 27, 38, 39, 41,
68, 77, 94–101, 128, 136, 137,
147
marriage: civil personal status law
and court system, 25–26, 39–40,
95–96, 124–25, 205n6, 208n62;

compulsory civil marriage law
proposals, 40, 120–21, 124,
129; consequences, researching/
thinking about, 85–86, 215n4;
evangelical secularism and, 17,
23; Hana/Ramzi hymen exam
case, 161–69, 176, 178, 179, 180,
226n55; Mona the archivist on,
51; optional civil marriage law
and/or secular personal status
law, campaign for, 39–40, 120,
124–25, 127, 128–34, 139, 146,
151; personal status laws/census
registries and, 25–26, 29, 31–
32, 34–38, 40–41, 44, 46, 51;
personal status versus marriage
laws, 39–40; religious conversion
and, 15, 24, 55, 83–86, 88–93,
91, 95–96, 99, 103, 105–8, 111;
in Samera case, 1, 4–5, 13, 15, 18;
sexual difference and responsibilities in, 225n46; state authority
over, 214–15n3. *See also* annulment; divorce
materiality/materialization, 20, 24,
154, 160, 170–71, 173, 174, 177,
179, 180–82, 185, 187, 201n47
Melkite Christians, 88, 89, 91, 134
meritocracy, 70, 81, 104, 122, 147
Middle East and North Africa
(MENA): cycles of crisis in, vii–
xii; as term, 197n1
migrant laborers: anal/hymen exams
and, 23, 156, 157, 158, 224n30;
on artist visas, 35, 207n48,
209n71; citizenship status of, 33;
domestic violence against, 42;
domestic workers, 33, 35, 42, 44–
45, 176, 177, 208n70, 209n79,
224n30; under Kafala system of
labor, 42–43, 44–45; number of,
in Lebanon, 205n12; patriarchal
employer control over, 44–45,

209n79; as trash collectors, 59; uprising of 2019 and, 155; as vulnerable populations, 20, 155

Mikdashi, Nadya, 217n42

"mini" civil war (2008), xi, 20, 131, 222n71

Ministry of Interior, 88, 89, 91, 110, 134, 135, 137

Ministry of Justice/Beirut Courthouse: Great Hall, 2; Roman statue outside of, 49. *See also* archives at Court of Cassation

misrecognition, 23, 32, 111, 112, 221n53

modernity/modern state: anal/hymen exams and, 176; evangelical secularism and, 126–27, 141–42, 147, 150, 152; personal status laws and, 33, 39; religious conversion and, 86–87, 104, 215n6; sectarianism and, 8, 16, 17, 22

Mona (Plenary Court's chief archivist and clerk): as archivist, 54, 59–61, 64–66, 68, 71, 73, 80–82; cases brought to author's attention by, 51, 52–53, 72, 77–82; during Civil War, 64–67; conversion from Sunni to Shiʻi, plans for, 54–55; on fire at archives (1985), 63, 185; Samir Geagea file and, 77–82; on marriage/divorce, 51, 92; relationship with author, 50–52, 66–67, 79; US control, concerns about, 71, 212n49

Mona el-Solḥ, 206n43

Moumneh, Rasha, 156

Moussa, Nadine, 34

Moussawi, Ghassan, 222n70

multiplicity, 12, 22, 54, 76, 77, 197n1, 199n18, 222n74

Nadim (evangelical secularist), 140

Nahr el Bared, shelling of, 76, 198n2

Nassar, Amin, 61

National Museum, 211n27

National Social Security Fund law, 38

nationalism, xii, 20, 37, 70, 112, 124, 131–33, 135, 138, 205n10, 228n82

neoliberalism, 69, 81, 152, 211n30

nested sovereignty, 8–9, 98–100, 200–201n44

al Nhaily, Mohammad, 207n57

Northern Ireland, sectarianism in, 198n4

Nucho, Joanne, 205n18

Nusra, xi, 76

opacity, right to, 16, 113, 203n66, 218n65

oppositional consciousness, 116

oriental/belly dancing, 90

origin stories and the nation-state, xii, 1, 5, 6, 7, 15, 18, 46, 57

Ottoman empire, vii, 1, 4, 7, 9, 87

Palestinian Liberation Organization (PLO), 57, 211n31, 213–14n73

Palestinians: demographic anxieties regarding, 36; evangelical secularism and, 131–33; Israeli state and, ix, 57, 72; Lebanese married to, 35, 51; as migrant workers, 35; as refugees, xi, 20, 33, 35, 36, 45, 61–62, 72, 76, 80, 205n12; violence/war experienced by, 75, 77

parastatal actors, 20, 44, 45, 160, 176, 177

Parla, Ayse, 227n61

parliamentary seats, sectarian allocation of, 27

passion, crimes of, 42

passports, Lebanese, 216–17n36

Pateman, Carole, 4

personal status laws, 21–22, 24–47; adjudication of, 198n1; as basis of law and politics in Lebanon, 26–29; census registries and, 29–32; citizenship and, 26–27, 30, 32–38; civil personal status law and court system, 25–26, 39–40, 95–96, 124–25, 205n6, 208n62; criminal law and, 38, 41–45; defined, 25; defined and described, 9–10; [hetero]sexuality, as key to production and management of, 25; inheritance law and, 39, 41, 204n1, 208n64; intersectionality of sexual difference and sectarian difference in, 24–26, 45–47; legal recognition of separate sectarian groups via, 27; marriage law versus, 39–40; for minor children, 215n11; nested sovereignty and, 8–9, 200–201n44; optional civil marriage law and/or secular personal status law, campaign for, 25–26, 39–40, 120, 124–25, 127, 128–34, 139, 146, 151, 208n63; parliamentary seats, allocation of, 27; political difference, importance to production of, 25; public order bureaucracy and, 102–3; religious conversion and, 40–41, 101; religious personal status laws, 25, 205n6; removal of religious and sectarian personal status from records, 110–12, 127, 132–37; Samera, legal case involving estate and marital status of, 13–15; sect, religion, and personal status, parsing differences between, 99, 100–102; secular system of law in Lebanon, as critical component of, 25; secular versus civil, 124–25; sexual difference in, 38–41; women's inability to pass

on citizenship/personal status, 30, 34–38, 111, 120, 146
Plenary Assembly, Court of Cassation: decisions of, 202n60; defined and described, 13; Hana/Ramzi case and hymen exams, 166–69; intersectionality, state efforts to manage and control, 125; jurisdiction of, 202–3n62, 203n64; Maronite personal status courts, conflicts with, 94–98; public order bureaucracy and, 105, 217n56; Samera's case appealed to, 13–15, 19–20; secularism narrative of, 16–17; sovereignty, performance of, 92–94. See also archives at Court of Cassation
pluralism: evangelical secularism and, 146, 147, 150, 151; Lebanese commitment to, 9, 129, 138, 142, 146, 147, 150, 151, 199n18; legal, 9, 199n18; political, 87; religious, 16–18, 37, 87, 100, 114, 121, 151; sexual, 151; sovereignty and secularism, relationship to, 87
political sectarianism and evangelical secularism, 129–34, 137–39, 143, 145–48
politics of deferral, 151–52, 191
postcolonialism, 1–2, 4–5, 7, 9, 18–19, 40, 46, 87, 102, 114, 198n10. See also colonialism, afterlife of
Povinelli, Elizabeth, 8
pregnancy tests on migrant domestic laborers, 45, 176, 224n30, 227n74
private/public distinction in sextarian state, 6, 7, 9–10, 25, 153–54, 160
Protestantism, evangelical, 126
Puar, Jasbir, 102
public morality, 41, 99, 156, 158, 171
public order: anal/hymen exams and, 166; bureaucracy of, 102–5, 203n64; courts/judiciary and,

208n59, 217n55; in French-derived legal systems, 217n55; personal status laws and, 14, 41; Plenary Assembly and, 13, 208n59; religious conversion and, 92, 97–99, 102–5, 113–14; sectarianism and, 17–18, 198n10, 202n

public/private distinction in sextarian state, 6, 7, 9–10, 25, 153–54, 160

Qortbawi, Shakib, 129
queer community/theory. See LGBTQ community and queer theory in sextarian state

Raad, Walid, 56
race/racism, 59; anal/hymen exams and, 154–56, 158, 159, 174, 178, 180, 223n10, 224n30; blackness/anti-blackness and, 42; evangelical secularism and, 125–26, 132; Kafala system of labor, 42–43, 44–45, 176, 177; personal status laws and, 33–36, 42, 208n70; religious conversion and, 108, 113; sectarianism, intersectionality with, ix, 3, 6, 8, 21, 125–26. See also migrant laborers; refugees

Ramzi. See Hana/Ramzi hymen exam case
rape: anal/hymen exams used in allegations of, 160, 177, 225n39, 227n76; in Hana/Ramzi case, 162, 166; hymen exams as, 172, 175; legal distinction between stranger/wife rapes, 38, 44, 176, 209n75

recognition, 9, 13, 27, 85, 100, 101, 112–13, 124, 129, 132, 134, 135, 141, 151, 200n44, 201n47, 216n25. See also misrecognition

refugees: anal/hymen exams and, 23, 156, 157, 158; citizen-to-refugee ratio in Lebanon, 33, 205n12;

under Kafala system of labor, 42–43; naturalization anxieties, 35–36; sexual difference and management of, 125–26; as vulnerable populations, 20

religious conversion, 22, 83–116; action versus intention in, 100; anthropological approaches to, 86–88; banality of, in Lebanese context, 87–88, 113–16; to Christianity versus Islam, 83–116, 214n222; consequences, researching/thinking about, 85–86; freedom of religion and, 94, 95, 97, 99, 100, 105; inheritance law and, 24, 41, 54–55, 83, 85, 86, 99–100, 129; Laique Pride march and, 144; legal procedures for, 216n25; lying, adjudication of, 15–16; Maronite conflicts with Plenary Assembly over, 1993 case illustrating, 94–98; mixed-multiple-marriage case involving, 88–92, 91; mother of author, conversion of, 83–85; nested sovereignty and, 98–100; opacity, right to, 16, 113, 203n66; patriarchy and, 31–32; personal status laws and, 40–41, 101; political economy of, in sextarian regime, 24, 84–88, 204n2; public order bureaucracy and, 102–5; registration/failure to register, 84, 85, 88–92, 99, 107; removal of personal status from government records versus, 110–12; sect, personal status, and religion, parsing differences between, 99, 100–102; sense of self and religious sensibility, case studies of, 105–13; sexual differences in experience of, 111–15; sovereignty, Plenary Assembly's performance of, 92–94; Tripoli *waqf* case, 99–100

religious difference, xii, 3, 9, 11, 16, 46, 61, 87–88, 99, 114–15, 139, 158
removal of sect (*shatb*), 110–12, 127, 132–37
Riad el-Solḥ, 206n43
Rich, Adrienne, 201n46
Rima (Laique Pride leader), 143, 149
Rula (human rights worker), 171–72, 176

Sabra and Shatila massacre, 62, 72, 78, 214n74, 214n76
Sahrawis, ix
Salibi, Kamal, 138–39
Samera case, 1–2; census, manipulation of, 5–6, 12–13, 15, 17, 18, 19; fire at archives and reconstruction of, 52, 53, 72–75; imperial, colonial, and post-colonial ramifications of, 4–6, 7, 18; legal steps and court decisions on, 12–15
Sandoval, Chela, 115–16, 204n73, 218n70
Saudi Arabia, ix, 26, 77, 197n2
Scott, James, 5, 199n13, 205n23
Scott, Joan, 3, 124
sects/sectarianism: anxieties over sectarian balance in Lebanon, 35–37, 146–48; as biopolitical category, 27–29, 36, 101, 137, 151, 154, 160, 179, 180; culture of sectarianism, 17, 138, 149; defined, 101; intersection of sectarian and sexual difference (*See* sextarianism and state power in Lebanon); parliamentary seats, sectarian allocation of, 27; personal status laws, legal recognition of separate sectarian groups via, 27; political sectarianism and evangelical secularism, 129–34, 137–39,

143, 145–48; problems faced by sectless individuals, 130–42; religion, sect, and personal status, parsing differences between, 99, 100–102; removal of religious and sectarian personal status from records, 110–12, 127, 132–37; secularism as anti-/non-sectarianism, 123–24, 143; sexual difference as sectarian/political difference, 24–25
secularism, 15–18; assignment of regulation of sexual difference to personal status law in Lebanon, 26; civil versus secular personal status law, 124–25; culture of, 3, 17, 120, 123, 124, 126, 128, 143, 144, 149; development of secular activism in Lebanon, 122–26; Lebanon and Israel compared, 203n65; opacity, right to, 16, 203n66; personal status law, secularized proposals for, 25–26, 39–40, 208n63; sexual difference as means of ordering, 125–26; state versus evangelical secularism, 16–18. *See also* evangelical secularism
securitization: anal/hymen exams and, 154, 156, 157, 160, 181; evangelical secularism and, 130, 152; personal status laws and, 29, 33–34, 37, 46; religious conversion and, 104, 218n65; sextarianism and, ix, 5, 12, 21, 23, 198n7; uprising of 2019 and, 79
Seikaly, Sherene, 57
settler sovereignty, 8–9
sex work: artist visas and, 35, 207n48, 209n71; single women suspected of, 43–44, 171–77
sexism, 30, 35, 37, 146, 149, 154, 168, 175, 222n75

sextarianism and state power in Lebanon, 1–23; analytic and governmental categories, dangers of collapsing, 198n9; census, role of, 5–6, 12; crisis as recursive temporality and, vii–xiii, 197n7; definition/description of sextarianism, 2–4; epidermal state and, 3, 19–21, 23, 154–55, 171, 173, 180–82; "failed" states and, 20; gender versus sex, 10–11; history and contingency affecting, 18–20; imperial, colonial, and postcolonial eras crossed by, 4–6, 9; Israeli legal system compared to Lebanon, 26, 203n65; Samera, legal case involving estate and marital status of, 1–2, 4–6, 7, 12–15, 18, 19; secularism as framework of, 15–18 (See also evangelical secularism; secularism and sectarianism); sovereignty and, 3, 6–12, 18. See also anal/hymen exams; archive of Plenary Assembly, Court of Cassation; personal status laws; religious conversion

sexual difference: anal/hymen exams and, 159–61, 170, 177–78, 228n77; biopolitical power and, 154, 179, 198n7; consent and force, as gendered, raced, and classed practices, 178; evangelical secularism and, 128; gender versus sex, 10–11; intersection with sectarian difference (See sextarianism and state power in Lebanon); marriage/divorce, responsibilities in, 225n46; in religious conversion experience, 111–15; as sectarian/political difference, 24–25; state power, as grounds for, 125–26; state power, violent exercise of, 153

sexuality: anal/hymen exams and, 154, 156, 160, 161, 164, 170, 174, 175, 177–80, 225n52, 227n61, 228n77; evangelical secularism and, 146, 148; personal status laws and, 25, 26, 28, 41, 44, 46; religious conversion and, 99; sect and sex, intersectionality of, xii, 2, 3, 5, 10–12, 21, 23, 187, 198n9

shahada, 84, 214n2

El Shakry, Omnia, 57

sharia courts, 207–8n59, 236n56

shatb (removal of sect), 110–12, 127, 132–37

Shehadeh, Lamia Rustum, 26

Shi'i Islam, 54, 86, 93, 101, 109, 136, 208n63, 222n74

Simpson, Audra, 8

single women in Lebanese law/bureaucracy/society, 43–44, 170, 171–77, 178

Sleiman, Hana, 213–14n73

social contract theory in sextarian state, 6–7, 46

socioeconomic class: anal/hymen exams and, 154–59, 172, 174, 178, 180, 223n10; archives ethnology and, 48, 50, 51, 59, 66, 68–71, 81, 210n7; personal status laws and, 28, 33, 36, 43; religious conversion and, 85, 105, 113, 140, 142, 147; sectarianism, intersectionality with, x, 8, 21

Solidere, 48, 209nn1–2

Sophocles, Antigone, 220n38

sovereignty, 3, 6–12, 18; anal/hymen exams and national sovereignty, 178–80; nested/settler sovereignty, 8–9, 98–100, 200–201n44; Plenary Assembly's performance of, 92–94; structures performing sovereignty of state, 13; violence and, 20, 21 state apparatus, 21, 52, 100, 152, 168, 175

state power: "failed" states, 20, 70; sexual difference as grounds for, 125–26; strong/stronger state, 21, 128, 130–33, 140; theories about, xii–xiii, 153–55; violent exercise of, 153–55, 177–78, 227n61; weak states, 153. *See also* sectarianism and state power in Lebanon; sovereignty

State Shura Council, 48, 81, 135–36

state versus evangelical secularism, 16–18

Steedman, Carolyn, 213n62

Stevens, Jacqueline, 214–15n3

Stoler, Ann, 211n16, 212n40

straight/queer and heterosexuality/homosexuality, as regulatory categories, 9, 11, 16, 17, 160, 201n52

strong/stronger state, 21, 128, 130–33, 140

structural difference, 28, 33, 114

Sunni Islam: evangelical secularism and, 131, 132, 136, 137, 146, 219n12; French colonial demotion of status of, 9; Iraqi Governing Council and, vii; Mona the archivist and author, as Sunnis, 50, 51, 54, 55; personal status laws and, 24, 25, 27, 36, 38, 39, 41, 45, 204n3, 207n59, 208n63; political leadership in Lebanon and, 68, 79; religious conversion and, 54–55, 83–86, 88–92, 91, 99–101, 105–7, 109–13

Surkis, Judith, 225n44

Syria: civil war in, xi, 76, 80, 130, 222n71; Lebanon and Syria, relationship between, 67, 75, 76, 78, 80, 203n63, 218n3

Syriac Orthodox, 95

Syrians: demographic anxieties regarding, 36; married to Lebanese, 35; as migrant laborers, 23, 35, 42–43, 45; as refugees, viii–ix, 23, 33, 35, 36, 42–43, 79, 130, 156, 205n12; violence/war experienced by, viii–ix, xi, 67, 75–77

Taif peace accord, 74, 76–77, 145, 212n44, 218n3

tarīq al jadīda (new street) neighborhood, Beirut, 50, 51, 62, 210n7

tolerance/intolerance, 9, 117, 123, 143–44, 149–50, 152, 172

torture, anal/hymen exams as form of, 156, 157, 159, 172, 175, 176, 181, 227n63, 228n77

transnationality: of anal exam protests, 177; biopolitical, 34; of Lebanese families, 42; of legal/political systems and sovereignties, 9, 93–94, 161, 176, 178, 181; of LGBTQ identity, 150, 156; mobility and, 51, 161; of networks of class and privilege, 81; race and, 42, 43; religious, 7, 14–15, 93–94, 126, 127, 140, 147; secularism and, 3; of war, 80

Tripoli *waqf* religious conversion case, 99–100

Trouillot, Michel-Rolph, 57

Tunisia, Arab uprisings in, 79

UN Convention Against Torture, 157

UN Convention on the Rights of the Child, 199n12

universal categories, 102

universal narrative, 7

universal subjects/citizens, 12, 32, 46, 113

universalism and regimes of difference, 6, 113, 116, 218n71

universalization, 3, 6, 46–47

uprising of 2019 in Lebanon, ix, xi, *190*, 190–91, 197n3; anal/hymen exams and, 153, 155, 182; archives at Court of Cassation and, 183–87; evangelical secularism and, *119*, 120–22, 137, 146, 147, 218n1, 220n39, 221–22n68; nation-state form, lack of critique of, 220n39; peaceful versus violent protesters in, 221–22n68; personal status laws and, 29, 35, 36; state power, violent exercise of, 153, 155

USAID, 70

violence: consent and force, as gendered, raced, and classed practices, 178; domestic, 42, 106, 108, 162–69, 226n55; post-Lebanese Civil War, 76–77; sovereignty and sectarianism in, 20, 21, 44–45, 199n15; state power and exercise of, 153–55, 177–78, 227n61. *See also* anal/hymen exams; *specific conflicts*

virginity tests. *See* anal/hymen exams

Viswanathan, Gauri, 87

vulnerable populations/communities, 20, 23, 39, 141, 148, 153, 155, 156, 158, 173, 174, 176, 181, 182

Al-Walīd bin Talāl (Saudi prince), 206n43

waqf (Islamic charitable trust), 99–100

"war on terror," 79, 125

weak states, 153

WhatsApp, ix, 197n4

whiteness, global, 43, 125, 222n83

women/women's rights. *See* feminism and women's rights; sexual difference

Yasmine (human rights worker), 171–76, 178–79, 180, 227n62

Yazidis, viii

Yemen, viii–ix, 33, 77, 222n71

You Stink protests (2015), 122, 221n68

Youssef (president of State Shura Council), 48–52, 68, 81–82, 135–36, 209n1

Zahra (religious convert), 83, 105–10, 111–13, 115

Zalzal, Marie Rose, 124–25, 219n14

Zengin, Asli, 178

CPSIA information can be obtained
at www.ICGtesting.com
Printed in the USA
JSHW041646230422
25071JS00005B/4